Thomas Pope

St. Peter's Day in the Vatican

Thomas Pope

St. Peter's Day in the Vatican

ISBN/EAN: 9783742814739

Manufactured in Europe, USA, Canada, Australia, Japa

Cover: Foto ©Thomas Meinert / pixelio.de

Manufactured and distributed by brebook publishing software (www.brebook.com)

Thomas Pope

St. Peter's Day in the Vatican

#
IN
THE VATICAN.

BY

THOMAS CANON POPE,
PRIEST OF THE ARCHDIOCESE OF DUBLIN.

IN CRUCE SALUS.

"*Thou wast the guide of the journey.*"—PSALM lxxix. 10.

DUBLIN:
JAMES DUFFY, 15, WELLINGTON-QUAY;
LONDON: 22, PATERNOSTER-ROW.
1868.

TO

THE ARCHDEACON OF DUBLIN,

VERY REVEREND

Laurence Dunne, P.P., V.F.

 DEDICATE to you this Volume. It is a feeble attempt to record an august event.

Pardon my ambition, thus publicly to associate your name, with my literary production. Your venerated character will reflect credit on its pages—will illuminate its merits, if it have any—and will eclipse its defects, of which it has many.

Retirement is the region, and the atmosphere, most congenial to true integrity, and exalted virtue.

The printed page—the carved steel—or the sculptured marble, are but the bribes offered by the ostentatious to fame, to perpetuate their memories. Your memory will be perpetuated on the interior tablets of thousands of grateful hearts, where your name is inscribed by a lengthened series of beneficent deeds; and on no heart more indelibly than that of

Your gratefully affectionate friend,

Thomas Canon Pope.

St. Peter's Day in the Vatican.

A NARRATIVE
OF
THE EIGHTEENTH CENTENARY
Of the Martyrdom of the Princes of the Apostles,
SS. PETER AND PAUL;
AND OF
The Canonization of the Twenty-five Saints,
AS CELEBRATED UNDER POPE PIUS IX.,
IN THE VATICAN BASILICA, ON JUNE 29, A.D. 1867.

CONTENTS.

Preface.

PAGE

THE great event of the Centenary—Its connexion with the Œcumenical Council—The conditions required to render a council œcumenical—The constitution, convocation, and infallibility of Œcumenical Councils—The Church dispersed always infallible—Proclamation of the approaching Œcumenical Council—The number of former Œcumenical Councils, and the objects for which they were convoked—What necessity for this Œcumenical Council—Authority of Œcumenical Councils, and their relations to the world, and to the temporal power of secular sovereigns—Their right to govern in every state, in all matters relating to morals, or in the order of grace—Union of Church and State, and reciprocity of services—Infallibility the only security for social integrity and stability—August character of the Centenary—Contrasted with the Council of Trent, . . xiii

To Rome!

Rome, an epitome of the history of men and ages—The Centenary—The ceremonies—Their grandeur and significance—The Vatican, a bulwark against anarchists—The functions illustrative of the rights of the Church—Our connexion with Rome, our security, ... 1

Doctrine and History of Canonizations.

Doctrine and history of canonizations—In what formal canonization consists—History of canonizations—Earliest records of formal canonizations—Notices of particular canonizations—The Japanese Martyrs—Antiquity of the Papal dynasty—Intervention of France in support of the Pope—Napoleon and Pius IX.—Numbers and places of canonizations—Irish and English saints canonized, . 5

The Invitation and Contention.

The Pope's invitation to the Bishops—Their journey from the most distant regions—The Spanish bishops leaving the Cathedral of Barcelona for Rome—How consolatory to our Holy Father, ... 12

The Pilgrimage.

Narrative of the pilgrimage to the shrines of the Apostles—Passing through Paris—The Czar shot at—Mass in the chapel of the Tuileries—Royal personages, visitors to the Great Exhibition—Marseilles—Sailing in company with two hundred and forty-nine priests from foreign countries, many ladies, and lay gentlemen, a Spanish marquis, and the Bishops of Philadelphia, Monte Video, and Porto Rico—Notre Dame de la Garde—Religious fervor, ecclesiastical spirit, and edifying character of the French clergy—The Irish Earls O'Neill and O'Donel—Sympathies of the French and Spanish priests with Ireland—Coasting along the south of France, passing Toulon, Hyéres, Cannes, Antibes, Nice, Genoa, Leghorn—Vespers at sea—Falling in with the ship *Buda*—Pilgrim salutations—The evening

CONTENTS.

	PAGE
gun—Arrival at Civita Vecchia—All the edifying incidents on the voyage—Coincidence on the 19th June, the morning on which the Emperor Maximilian was shot at Queretaro—Historical reminiscences of the political relations between France and Austria—The last moments of Maximilian—A brief biographical memoir of his Majesty—Arrival at Rome—Enthusiasm of the French clergy—Credo,	17

Private Life of the Pope.

Biographical memoir of Pope Pius IX.—Twofold character of the Pope—Personal appearance of the Pope—The Pope's rule of life—His daily avocations—His devotional exercises—His audiences—His recreations—His ministers of state—Etiquette at audiences—His civil list—Monsignor de Merode—Anecdote—Observations on the pontificate of our Most Holy Father Pope Pius IX., ... 32

Events during the Festivities.

Regulations of the municipality—Numbers of priests arrived—Anniversary of the Pope's election, ... 40

ARRIVALS.

Irish bishops at the Centenary—Bishops of France and other countries—Arrival of the Spanish bishops—Irish College of St. Agatha—Irish convents of the religious orders, ... 43

PETER PENCE OFFERINGS.

Presentations from individual bishops—Aggregate amount presented—Evidences of Catholicity and unity—Feast of Corpus Christi—Anniversary of the Pope's coronation—Feast of St. Aloysius, ... 44

REVIEW OF THE PAPAL TROOPS.

Brigades in the Pope's army—Their numbers—The names of the commanding officers—Manœuvres, . . . 48
Cardinal Archbishop of Seville, ... 50
Consecration of the Church of Santa Maria delli Angeli, . 51

CONTENTS.

PAGE

St. John Lateran's.

"Capella Papale"—The functions, ... 51
Biographical memoir of Cardinal Altieri, ... 51
Audience given to all the foreign priests, ... 52
Arrivals of his Grace of Westminster—The Bishops of Birmingham and of Beverley, of Monsignor Dupanloup, Monsignor Matah, and of Monsignor Languillot, Bishop of Nankin, ... 53

The College of the Propaganda.

His Eminence Cardinal Barnabo—Foundation of the College of the Propaganda—Objects of the institution—Endowments—Number of students—Library—Villa—Rectors, 54

The Cardinal Archbishop of Dublin, . 56

Padre Rillo, S.J.—Padre Bresciani, S.J., ... 57
Former students at the Centenary—Professors, . . 58
His Eminence Cardinal Reisach, ... 58
The red hat conferred on the Cardinal Archbishop of Seville, 58

The Pope's Allocution to the Assembled Bishops.

The Consistory—The number of bishops—The allocution, . 60

Illumination of the Coliseum.

Crowds of spectators—Change of coloured lights—Flights of birds—Reflections on bleeding martyrs, wild beasts, and dying gladiators, ... 68

Audiences to the Irish Bishops and Priests.

Obsequies for the Right Rev. Dr. Kilduff—The cardinal and bishops received by the Pope—His Grace of Cashel, his Eminence of Dublin, his Holiness—The Irish priests received by the Pope, ... 70

Cardinal Antonelli and the Irish Bishops.

The Cardinal's saloons—His personal appearance—Biographical sketch of his Eminence, ... 73

CONTENTS.

Address of the Bishops to the Pope.

The Altieri Palace—The representative bishops elected to draw up the address—The number of bishops who signed the address—Their number considered relatively to former assemblages of bishops, ... 74

Vigil of St. Peter and St. Paul's Day.

First Vespers—Grandeur of the ceremony—Splendour of the Basilica—Number of bishops, ... 77

The Pallium.

History of the pallium—Blessing of the lambs on the Feast of St. Agnes—Mystical significations typified by the pallium, ... 78

St. Peter's Chair.

Its removal—Its description—Its antiquity—Its identity, . 82

Illumination of St. Peter's.

Crowds in the piazza—The Egyptian obelisk—Education dark without religion—Reminiscences of the Crusaders—Instantaneous illumination—Change of lights—Number of lamps—Critical position of the men—Glories of the heavenly Jerusalem, ... 84

The Ceremonies of the Church.

External signs to create internal impressions—Convulsions of nature at the death of Christ, ... 90

Eighteenth Centenary of the Princes' Victory.

Description of the scenes the city presented on that glorious festival—The awakening—The congregating—Distinguished personages—Gorgeous equipages and pageantry—Bridge of San Angelo—Military saluting the cardinals—Scenes on the royal stairs—Costumes of the Swiss Guards—Decorations of the Basilica—The three choirs, 92

CONTENTS.

The Gregorian Chant.

Its origin and antiquity—Its simplicity, harmony, and devotional character adapted to choral exercises—Incompatibility of these qualities with operatic music—Palestrina—Incidents in the Basilica—Lighting the candles—Grandeur of the perspective—Stability of the Church, ... 105

The Procession.

The communities of religious orders, officials, officers of state, civil, military, and ecclesiastical—Mitred abbots, princes, bishops, and cardinals, who took a place in the procession, in their order of precedence, in the state costumes and vestments which they wore, observed as they pass on—The procession entering the Basilica—Catholic origin of England's constitution—Perpetuity of the Church—The homage, ... 113

The Canonization.

All the ceremonies, prayers, decrees, described and explained—The names of the saints—The days appointed for the celebration of their festivals, ... 132

The Solemn Papal Mass.

Vestments and ornaments peculiar to the Pope—The Papal procession to the altar, ... 138

The Presentation of the Offerings.

Their typical signification, ... 141

The Music at the Offertory.

The three choirs—*Tu es Petrus*—Ceremonies peculiar to the Papal Mass—Achilli Rossi—Royal personages present—Mr. Howard, of Corby Castle—His afflicting bereavement in the death of his daughter, Miss Howard—Numbers in the Basilica—Expenses of the functions, . 143

The Papal Benediction from the Loggia.

Description of the ceremony—The troops in attendance—The Zouaves, the number of the entire corps, and numbers from each country—The Benediction given—Sublimity of the scene, ... 154

The Girandola, or Grand Display of Fireworks.

Pyrotechnic wonders—Triumph of the cross—Glories of heaven, ... 159

St. Paul's Day.

Antiquity of the site—Burning of the old Basilica—Splendours of the present Basilica—The illuminations—The functions, ... 167

Address of the Patriarchs, Archbishops, and Bishops, to the Pope.

The commission appointed to draw up the address—The Hall of Consistories—The Pope reciting the *Angelus Domini*, and responded to by all the bishops—Mystery of the Incarnation—The address—The names, titles, and sees, of all the prelates who signed the address, .
The Pope's reply to the bishops' address, ... 192
Address to the Pope from the "Hundred Cities of Italy," —His Holiness' reply, ... 194

The Secular Fetes.

The Villa Borghese—The horse races—The chariot races—The balloon ascent, ... 196
The military officers entertained by the bishops, . . 200

Academy at the Roman College.

"Academia di poesia"—Church of St. Ignatius—Odes delivered in fourteen different languages—Charming music—The Senator—Number of cardinals, bishops, and priests present, ... 200

Illumination of the Roman Forum.

Ruins of Ancient Rome, circumscribed by one view—Illuminated by Bengal lights, ... 202
Illumination of the exterior of the Capitol, and of the statuary in the interior—The bishops entertained by the municipality, ... 203

SAN PIETRO IN MONTORIO.

The church—The Pope's visit—The temple—The Irish princes,	203
The Corso illuminated—The number of men in the pontifical army,	204
The chair of St. Peter replaced—The bronze cathedra—Its design and cost,	205
Return home—Fellow-travellers,	206
Journey from Rome to London,	207

ADIEU!

Utility of travel—Travel consecrated by religion—The end,	207

PREFACE.

THE CENTENARY—THE ŒCUMENICAL COUNCIL.

Respective Provinces of Church, and State—Relative Powers, and Rights of Church, and State—Union of Church, and State.

THE solemnity of the eighteenth centenary of the martyrdom of St. Peter, and St. Paul, was truly an important event—with the exception of a General Council, it was the most important assembly recorded in the pages of ecclesiastical history, since the institution of the Church. It was an event of the greatest moral significance—most illustrative of the great notes of Holy Church—it was a most expressive act of faith in Peter's supremacy, both in honour and jurisdiction—and was the most sublime interpretation ever rendered of the words of Christ, "Thou art Peter, and upon this rock I will build my Church." It was the most palpable, tangible, demonstration of the unity, universality, unanimity, and authority of the one, only Church of Christ on earth. It was the most eloquent, and conclusive, and incontrovertible argument ever urged, of the immutability of her identity, and the indefectibility of her vitality. It was a proof of the exalted superiority of the moral, over the material order of the world—and the external rite, or ceremonies, observed in celebrating it, were unprecedentedly magnificent—they were regal, sacerdotal, pontifical, and Papal—they were grand and sublime. The centenary derived additional importance, from the circumstance of its having been immediately connected, with the momentous event which is so proximate, the convocation of the Œcumenical Council—as it was to the august assembly of the bishops at the centenary, that the Holy Father first publicly announced his intention, on that important subject. The term "œcumenical," is derived from Greek words, which signify—"pertaining to the whole habited world." An Œcumenical Council is the solemn parliament of Catholicism—it is the general assembly of the teaching Church. It is the prerogative of the successors of Peter to say, when they regard the convocation of a General Council as expedient, or necessary—it is theirs to convoke a General Council—to direct it—to prorogue it—to translate it—to confirm it—and to dissolve an Œcumenical Council. It is infallible in its teachings. The infallibility of the Church, is the medium ordinarily employed by God, to convey the doctrine of faith to the world. No Council of the Church can be truly an Œcumenical Council separated from the Pope, or insubordinate to him. General assemblages of the bishops of the world, apart from the Pope, may teach what is consonant with truth, and may be guided by wisdom, and the Holy Spirit of God; but their doctrine does not necessarily enforce belief as an article of divine faith, established on infallibility. But when they are directed, and presided over by Peter's successor, and when their definitions are confirmed by his Papal sanction, then they cannot err—they are infallible—and belief in the dogma defined becomes obligatory, as an article of faith. The Pope convokes all the bishops of the Catholic world—they come, and with the Pope, who is their head, who presides over them, and confirms their acts, they represent all the Churches of the universe. The Holy Ghost is in the midst of them, and speaks through their lips the words of infallible truth; and here is their title-deed, their great charter, upon which is grounded their prerogative to doctrinal infallibility: "As My Father hath sent Me, so do I send you. Go, teach all nations; teaching them what I have taught you: and behold I am with you all days, to the consummation of the world."

A General Council creates no new article of faith; it merely affirms, and defines a dogma, which already existed, and was previously, and always contained in the deposit of faith. The infallibility of the Church dispersed, in defining, and enunciating her dogmas, or in her teachings, is not dependent on the infallibility of an Œcumenical Council, but the General Council is infallible in virtue of the infallibility of the Church, of which it is the representative, and the teaching assembly. The whole Church, uniting the Successor of Peter, and the episcopate diffused throughout the extent of Christendom, when she enunciates any doctrine of faith, as the "Ecclesia docens," is always infallible, even without the intervention of any Œcumenical Council.

The approaching Œcumenical, or General Council, announced by our Most Holy Father Pius IX., at the centenary, has since then, with the usual great formality and solemnity, been proclaimed, announced, convoked, and decreed on last St. Peter and St. Paul's day, to be holden in the year 1869, at Rome, in the Vatican Basilica, to be commenced on the 8th day of December, sacred to the memory of the Immaculate Conception of the Blessed Virgin Mary. The Papal Bull was signed on the 3rd of the kalends of July, in the twenty-third year of his Holiness' pontificate, by Pope Pius IX., and by M. Cardinal Mattei, Pro-Datarius, and N. Cardinal Paracciani Clarelli, and by all their Eminences the cardinals present in curia.

The elapsed centenaries and the confirmed General Councils coincide in number. We have had eighteen recurring centenaries, of the martyrdom of St. Peter and St. Paul, and we have had eighteen General Councils. After the first Council of Jerusalem, the model of all General Councils, for the first three hundred years of the Church's existence, we had no General Council—since the Council of Trent, for the last three hundred years of the Church's existence, we have had no General Council. The condemnation of various heresies, was the object of the convocation of the first six General Councils. The Iconoclasts were condemned in the seventh—the cause of Photius, was the object of the eighth. To promote energetic efforts for the deliverance of the Holy Land from the grasp of the Turks, was the cause of the convention of the ninth General Council. The tenth was to disclaim the pretensions of anti-Popes. The Waldenses were condemned in the eleventh. The twelfth was convoked to aid the Crusaders, and to condemn certain heretical doctrines then promulgated. The usurpations of Frederick II., were denounced in the thirteenth. The fourteenth was to condemn the errors of the unfortunate Greeks. Many heresiarchs, with their false doctrines, were condemned in the fifteenth Council. The sixteenth was convoked for the reunion of the Eastern Church. The seventeenth, for curing schisms, and regulating various laws. The eighteenth was the great Council of Trent, convoked to condemn the Lutheran heresy, and to correct many social evils. Thus each and all were convoked to condemn some particular heresy, or apply a remedy to some social disaster, or to promote some great good, or to attain some new triumph for holy religion.

It may be asked what necessity exists now for the convocation of a General Council? The days are evil—the Church is afflicted with many calamities—her doctrines are impugned—the supreme authority of the Sovereign Pontiff is disregarded—ecclesiastical property is invaded, and confiscated—the education of youth is usurped by unbelieving seculars—the laws which regulate matrimonial contracts violated—religion is outraged—and many social evils disseminated, to the danger, and injury of immortal souls. A General Council unites in one assembly, the deliberate wisdom of many prelates, where the united abilities of all, may prove more effective in probing the wounds, discovering the evils of the age, and applying the most efficacious cures. It elevates still higher the lamp of truth, to illuminate those who are wandering in darkness, and in the shadow of death. It concentrates in one formidable phalanx, the diffused forces of the Universal Church, and directs it, with irresistible power, to demolish the bulwarks of the enemy, and bear the standard of religion triumphantly over the debris of their strongholds, and dissipated forces, and thus winning another decisive victory for Christ. The Church has ever regarded it as a matter of importance, that the laws of those civil powers, to which her spiritual children are subjected, should be formed in perfect accordance with her own laws. The consciences of her children are then relieved from that violence, and those perplexing embarrassments to which they must ever be subjected, as long as the civil law is at variance with her own. Revolutions have convulsed civil society, to its very centre, since the last General Council of Trent. Hence the utility of a General Council at present, must appear most obvious to every reflecting mind. The Council will again proclaim to the entire world, the Church's laws, grounded on the immutable principles of justice. In those countries where the entire population profess the Catholic religion, as well as even under Protestant governments, where large proportions of their subjects profess that holy religion, political economy, good policy, and self-interest, irrespective even of more exalted motives, will urge the propriety and force of these views. The world can be presented with few occasions, or proofs, which more forcibly demonstrate the supreme authority of the Pope, than his prerogative of confirming, or condemning Councils, claiming to be œcumenical. The history of the Church records thirty-two such Councils, claiming the character of œcumenical—yet eighteen only are recognized as such—and that not from the number of congregated bishops being greater or less — but solely because the Successor of Peter, by his sole authority, partially condemned six, and absolutely condemned and annulled eight, and confirmed the eighteen. A General Council, then, in the present anti-Papal tone of the world, in these degenerate days, will be most salutary, as the most demonstrative, and conclusive proof, of the unchangeable supremacy of Peter's authority-- the same yesterday, to-day, and for ever!

Our Holy Father, then, guided by the Spirit of God, convokes a General Council, in order, to use the words of Pope Paul III., that he may apply "the greatest remedy in the greatest peril of Christianity."

The world may affect to disregard the authority, and infallibility of a General Council, and cry, What have ecclesiastical laws, or the definition of Church dogmas, to do with the world, or with our political or social relations? The Council will vindicate its authority over the world, and prove its right, founded on a divine commission, to enter most intimately into all the spiritual concerns of the world, to supervise the acts of the king, the diplomatist, the philosopher, and the general—to circumscribe the limits of their speculative inquiries—to hold up the lamp which is to light their only path to knowledge, and education—to subjugate human reason to the yoke of faith—to extinguish liberals, rationalists, and deists by one stroke of her infallibility. Infallible dogma is a brilliant light, which every intellect must recognize, whether willingly, or reluctantly. At first sight it may not clearly discern it, or be overwhelmed by it; for eyes long immured in darkness, are dazzled by a sudden powerful effulgence; but when the vision becomes accommodated to it, this infallible teaching illuminates all around it. The dogmas, and teachings of an infallible Council, will purify the morality, integrity, and religion of mankind—will impart vitality to the torpid action of society—will curb the downward, vicious tendency of man's will—and will insensibly impart a salutary tone, even to the political relations of secular governments. Peter will speak, and the world will be electrified, and feel the shock. It is futile to say, the Church has its own legitimate limits, and the world its boundaries, beyond which the Church must not intrude. The Church claims its right to enter the world's domain, and recognizes no limits but• the circumference of Christendom, to enforce her laws over her subjects, to control their reason, and judgment, to guide their morals, their thoughts, words, and actions, and to regard temporal sovereignties, though entitled to exercise power in secular affairs, as auxiliaries, and subordinates, to the attainment of the end of her institution, the glory of God, and the salvation of the immortal souls of men, and to secure for them their everlasting inheritances. And this order of things she regards, as true liberty—*Ubi Spiritus Domini ibi libertas !*

The Church recognizes the temporal sovereignty of temporal princes; she not only recognizes it as useful, and necessary for the public good, for social order, and the protection of property, but she supports it, she enforces it; nay, she professes that "there is no power but from God." The Church, by inculcating and enforcing principles of subordination, and loyalty, has ever proved herself the most powerful bulwark of the temporal power of temporal princes. The Church may not wish to interfere, in the purely secular concerns of other states, or in the enactments of purely secular laws, for the government of foreign subjects, but she claims a right, and a right divine, to prevent any secular law, or power being exercised for the injury of religion, the destruction of morals, and the spiritual ruin of her children. She claims a right, to supervise such laws, to support their use, if salutary, to control their abuse. In the domain of morals, it is the province of the Church to reign. Wherever there is moral responsibility, it is her prerogative, by divine commission, to guide and to govern, to sanction, to commend, or to condemn, to reward merit, and to punish moral delinquency.

It betrays an ignorance, or a denial of the Church's mission, to assert, that she may control the acts, and scrutinize the morality, and punish the faults of the religious in the cloister, or of the private individual in the world, but that she has no right to intrude into the social relations of the general community of worldlings. She has that right; she is the salt that is to insinuate itself into all their most intimate relations, to preserve them from the corruption of error, and to secure their soundness, and health. She has a right to supervise the lectures of the professor, the diplomacy of the statesman, the government of kings, and to scrutinize their morality, and punish their faults; and that duty becomes more necessary, and obligatory, in proportion as their acts more vitally affect the welfare of society, and the interests of religion ; and, consequently, on their greater influence, involve a greater amount of responsibility, than the acts in the cloister, or of the private individual. This the world may protest against, and pronounce as arrogance, and despotism. Ah! history teaches us, that despotism is on the other side. The Church has ever proved the sanctuary of the fugitive from tyranny—the formidable citadel to protect the persecuted—the staff that has raised the standard of liberty—the bond of society—the salutary spice of civilization— *Ubi Spiritus Domini ibi libertas!*

Nay, the Council will hold a great assize, before which it will read the indictment against the world, will arraign it for its errors, will confound and condemn them, and will prove the truth, on the most incontestable evidence. Christ came to bear testimony to the truth against the world: "For this was I born, for this came I into the world, that I should give testimony to the truth." (*St. John*, xviii. 37.) The Church is the representative of Christ. "As My Father hath sent Me, so do I send you." Thus the Council will be the great proof, of the opposition of the world to the truth, and the great testimony of the truth, against the world.

Political theorists, now-a-days, presume so far as to proclaim the right of secular states to be, what they call free, and independent of the Church's laws—that is, they profess to take their temporal governments, out of the Church, in which God intended to place, and to bless them—and to utilize them—and to consecrate them in, and through the Church. There are even those who have the temerity to advocate the deordination, of a church dependent in the legislative enactments of a secular state! Statesmen! know the object of your transitory existence—it is to enact secular laws, for secular jurisprudence, and for the secular common weal—and then to live in the Church—to co-operate with the Church—to be sanctified through the Church—and by this happy union, to enjoy the reciprocity of the Church's influence over the consciences of your subjects, which is the solid foundation of their loyalty, and your stability; and to assist the Church in promoting what is useful for saving their souls, which should be to you, also, an object of paramount solicitude. Is the world, then, come to this!—that social diplomatists should sever the State from the Church, or domineer over Christian society? Is nature to separate from grace, and set up a dynasty for itself? No, no! *Quis separabit?* The holy alliance of Church and State, constitutes the union of the soul and body—the life and vigour of Christian society! It is time that a General Council should teach statesmen, this salutary lesson—and that they must not put their foot on the step of Peter's throne—that it is their duty to co-operate with the Church—and that in all matters appertaining to the order of grace, their position is, to sit down, and listen respectfully before the Church's teaching chair.

Infallibility is the only security, of the stability of dynasties, and empires—the health of society, and the reign of integrity, and truth. Without an infallible authority, human reason would grope in darkness—the world would waft to destruction. Since those horrifying days of reeking revolution, when wicked men—creeping clods of clay—audaciously attempted to dethrone the Most High, and elevate iniquity, society is sick from the shock—a General Council will restore its health, and vigour. This infallible authority is the citadel of truth—the shield against error—the security of temporal governments—the immovable rock, to which society may cling in every wind of doctrine, in every torrent of revolutionary vicissitudes.

The centenary was a momentous event. The Council of Trent marked, indeed, a momentous era in the Church annals; it was a shield which has since protected her in formidable dangers; it was a power, which, for three hundred years, has guided her destinies in safety, and has prudently directed her discipline, and wisely governed her prelates and people. Yet, the centenary was an event which, in many respects, I might presume to contrast in importance with, even the great Council of Trent. The locality of Trent, was an undistinguished town in the Tyrol—the locality of the centenary, was the centre of Catholicity—the seat of Peter's chair, and of Catholic unity—the *limina apostolorum*—the very shrines of the Princes' relics. The Council of Trent, was presided over by legates—the centenary was presided over by the visible head of the Church, the representative, and vicar of Jesus Christ Himself. The faithful who journeyed to Trent, were comparatively few, and not far distant. The faithful pilgrims to the centenary, numbered one hundred thousand, and many of those from the utmost ends of the earth. The number of bishops congregated at any one time at Trent, was considerably under three hundred, the number of prelates at the centenary, amounted to more than five hundred. We must not, however, urge the contrast too extremely, for the Council of Trent was the august power, the *Ecclesia docens;* whereas the centenary was but a gorgeous rite, or commemorative ceremonial. The one was invested with substantial power, and majesty, and infallibility; the other was but an external ordeal, a visible demonstration—but I do believe that, during the eighteen years during which the Council of Trent continued its sessions, there was no function celebrated at all comparable, to the transcendently grand ceremonies of the centenary; and no external rite at Trent, so visibly exhibited the supremacy of Peter, the vitality, unity, and universality of Holy Church, as did the assemblage, and rites at the centenary of 1867.

I have undertaken to write the history of that memorable event of the centenary, and to describe the ceremonies with which it was solemnized: it was an important, and difficult undertaking, and the labour employed, was fully equal to both. If the narrative, or descriptive passages, prove imperfect, and deficient, I plead as an apology, and indulge as a consolation, that at least I have said something, of what the most erudite, and eloquent cannot say sufficient.

Errata.

Page 31,	For scitis, ... read	"sitia."	
" 68,	For Miss Corby, . . . "	"Miss *Howard of* Corby."	
" 68,	For Mr. Howard Corby, . "	"Mr. Howard *of* Corby."	
" 143,	For disoaraveram, . . "	"*desidera*veram."	
" 156,	For Infanta, ... "	"Infanta."	
" 183,	For Johannes Franciscus Wheland, . . "	"Johannes Franciscus Whelan."	

There are other inaccuracies in this volume, but as they involve no substantial error, I deem it unnecessary to correct them.

In counting the Popes by their order of succession from St. Peter, different modes are adopted. In this volume our present Holy Father is counted as the 253rd Pope—others, however, count Pius IX. as the 256th in succession, and perhaps this is the more accurate.

I am not aware of having fallen into any error against doctrine—if, however, in alluding to dogmatic subjects, I should unknowingly have fallen into any such errors—I now retract them—and I profess my disposition to subject my faith, my judgment, my will, and my pen, with the utmost humility and docility, to the faith and teachings of the Holy Catholic Church, in which, with God's grace, I resolve to live and die.

Invitation to the Bishops.

THE Letter of Invitation to the bishops of the Catholic world to repair to Rome, to celebrate the Eighteenth Centenary of the Martyrdom of St. Peter, and St. Paul, and to assist at the Canonization of the Twenty-five Saints, was dated the 8th of December, 1866, a day sacred to the Immaculate Conception of the Mother of God, and was signed by Prospero Catarini, Cardinal Prefect of the Sacred Congregation of the Council.

The names of the Blessed Martyrs, Confessors, and Virgins, who were to be canonized, are as follows:—

1. The Blessed Josaphat, Archbishop of Poloesk, of the Ruthenians, in White Russia, martyr.

2. The Blessed Peter D'Arbues, of the Order of Canons Regular of St. Augustine, Inquisitor of Spain, and Canon of the Metropolitan Church of Saragossa, martyr.

3. The nineteen blessed martyrs of Gorkhum, belonging to divers Regular Orders, or Secular Clergy.

4. The Blessed Paul of the Cross, Confessor, Founder of the Discalced Clerics of the Holy Cross, and of the Passion of our Lord Jesus Christ.

5. The Blessed Leonard of Port-Maurice, Confessor, Apostolic Missionary of the Minor Order of St. Francis, of the Strict Observance.

6. The Blessed Maria Francesca, of the Five Wounds, virgin, of the Third Order of St. Peter of Alcantara, in Naples.

7. The Blessed Germaine-Cousin, Secular Virgin of the Diocese of Toulouse.

INTRODUCTION.

To Rome!

Dux itineris fuisti.—Psalm lxxix. 10.
"*Thou wast the guide of the journey.*"

ROME!—all that word comprises!—an epitome of the story of all men and ages to remote antiquity! It throws a gleam on the historic page of classic times—it tells of the unfolding of undiscovered worlds—of the wreck of armadas —of crumbling dynasties—of the crash of tyrants' rods—of the foundation, perpetuity, and triumphs of religion! It records the swelling tide of progressive civilization, refinement, the fine arts, and tells thrilling stories of Christian chivalry! Rome! that name strikes a chord to which every fibre of our Irish hearts beats in harmony.

I invite you to accompany me, in idea, to Rome, to assist at the ceremonies commemorative of the eighteenth centenary of the martyrdom of St. Peter and St. Paul, and the canonization of the twenty-five saints. As an external rite or spectacle, these ceremonies have never been surpassed in grandeur, and impressiveness. For the momentous event they commemorated—for the number and the august character of the dignitaries who assisted—for the thronging multitudes who congregated from every country, clime, and people—for the display of all that was refined in art, in sculpture, and in painting—all that was charming in music, and exquisite in decorations—for military parade—regal magnificence—for pageantry, and splendour, and secular pomp—these ceremonies have been, and ever will be, unrivalled. But these ceremonies were but the external habiliments of an interior majesty—and when the external rite is contrasted with their interior moral significance, then the ceremonies dwindle into inconsiderable trifles. No matter how great their magnificence, when contrasted with the significance of the ceremonies, they seem but as little specks in a valley viewed from a lofty mountain,—and in that moral significance they can never be sufficiently appreciated. Wonderful must ever be regarded as their characteristic—mysterious their signification—no attempt at their description can ever be regarded as extravagant.

I invite you to accompany me to the festivities of the centenary—we shall celebrate them, in idea, over again. Come—and I shall tell you of the event they commemorate—I shall tell you of the solemn functions of the canonization, and beatification, and of the processions—shall explain the ceremonies—and unveil their mystic signification—and describe the transcendant scenes that astonished the eyes of the world. Come—and I shall tell you of my pilgrimage to the shrines of the Apostles, and all the incidents by the way. I shall tell you all about our Holy Father the Pope—of the cardinals and the foreign bishops, and of the people congregated from all parts of the world,—and of the interior and exterior illuminations of St. Peter's. I shall tell you of the audiences given by the Holy Father to the Irish bishops and Irish priests—of the Papal army, and of the Knights of Malta, the flourish of the silver trumpets, and the lady pilgrims to the shrines at vesper time. I shall tell you of my visit, in company with many dignitaries, to Cardinal Antonelli, and many other remarkable events.

Come to Rome, and I shall tell you of the wonders I have seen—wonders such as the world has never seen before, or ever shall see again—wonders astonishing, interesting, and edifying—this latter character will, I doubt not, render them most acceptable to you. To Rome, then!—whither kings, and bishops, and people have flocked in every age—Rome, the city of the Popes!—our Father's home—seat of religion—solace of the sorrowing—land of the truly free, where the well-disposed are protected from the tyranny of anarchists—land of the fine arts, and every social refinement!

This is the Rome, the rock that unbelieving anarchists and revolutionists would undermine—this is the Vatican, that modern social economists would pull down. If they could but succeed in removing it, those anarchists expect to discover beneath its foundations a river yielding copious floods of liberty, prosperity, and progress. Beware!—that Vatican is like the ponderous rock in the desert, to which Moses led the languishing people to slake their thirst! Pius IX., like another Moses, strikes this rock with his mysterious rod, and behold, copious streams of salutary waters flow, to invigorate the social economy, polity, and religion of the world! Beware!—if you undermine it, the ponderous weight may fall and crush the social fabric you attempt to erect, and, rolling down the hill, crush both the idol and the multitude; and in place of meeting with the more copious fountain you expect, you may find beneath the foundation nothing but desolation and arid sterility, and may discover too late that the water ceased to flow when the rod of Peter was removed.

No functions have ever been celebrated which elevate more conspicuously two of the great notes of the true Church, which, as two brilliant beacons, guide the distant and wandering to the fold of Christ. These two notes are those which were so triumphantly adduced by St. Augustine to confound the errors of the Donatists, and to guide them to the truth—these are its being "dispersed throughout the world" and "its possession of the chair of Peter"—*Diffusa per orbem et cathedra Petri.* There they are in the celebration of that centenary—you can not only read them, but you can feel them—you can lay your hands on them!—then put your finger into the holes of their hands, and into their side, and be no longer incredulous. I have seen and have believed—blessed are you that have not seen, and have believed!

Our connexion with Rome, too, is our security that we belong to the true Church. The true Church is Roman—"the place of the power and of the doctrine of the faith" is Rome—there is the "Cathedra Petri." Rome is the seat of the Primacy, both of honour and jurisdiction—it is the bond of unity, by communion with which all the other churches are connected with and cemented into "the one only;" and if that bond be removed, they all go to pieces, and fall into total dissolution. The Church of Rome is as it were the keystone of the vast arch that spans the world—in Rome, then, as in the centre, all the notes of the true Church should be concentrated, and again diverge, as from a focus, and appear more brilliantly there even than in other parts of the Church—and do they?—oh! come with me to the functions of the centenary, and I shall show them to you, and if you say you cannot see them, I shall say "you have eyes and see not!" Come, then, to Rome, the city of the "seven hills"—the seat of religion—the channel of every heavenly blessing—*Vadam ad montem myrhæ, et collem thuris* (Cant. iv. 6)—"I will go to the mountain of myrrh, and to the hill of frankincense."

Before commencing our journey, I shall present to your notice some preparatory observations, on the doctrine of the Church on the "canonization of saints," and some remarkable historical events associated with it.

Doctrine and History of Canonizations.

Ecce quomodo computati sunt inter filios Dei, et inter sanctos sors illorum est.—Sap. v. 5.

"*Behold, how they are numbered among the children of God, and their lot is among the saints.*"

THE strictly formal canonization of a saint, consists in a public decree of the Apostolic See, and an express declaration, that a certain servant of God has practised virtue in a heroic degree, has attained sanctity, and is now in glory, and associated with the saints in heaven, and that God wrought miracles at his intercession—and consequently authorizes that he be honoured as a saint, that his name be inscribed on the calendar, that his relics be exposed for the veneration of the faithful, that his intercession be supplicated, and that the holy sacrifice of the Mass be celebrated, and the divine office recited in his honour.

The process previous to canonization is very lengthened, and a most rigid juridical scrutiny is instituted, to test the sanctity of life, and the authenticity of the miracles attributed to the intercession of the servant of God.

The canonization of saints in the holy Catholic Church, as decreed by some ecclesiastical authority, under some form, rite, or ceremony, is coeval with the earliest ages of the Church's history. In the earliest Christian times, the honour and exalted dignity of canonization, was conferred almost exclusively on those heroic champions, who sacrificed their lives in testimony of the truth, and by shedding their blood on the fertile soil of religion, propagated the faith, and sowed the prolific seed, which produced an abundant harvest of fervent Christians. In those glorious ages of faith and Christian heroism, the Christians, sanctioned by ecclesiastical authority, erected altars over the spot that had been purpled by the martyr's blood ; or, in the labyrinths and recesses of the catacombs, over the shrines that inclosed their relics, celebrated the holy sacrifice in their honour, introduced their names in the Church's liturgy, and publicly invoked their intercession, and in this simply, consisted the act of canonization, exemplifications of which may be adduced in the instance of St. Ignatius, and St. Polycarp. In subsequent centuries, the bishops of the district within which the martyr shed his blood, carefully recorded, on undoubted testimony, the acts of his martyrdom; he then communicated them to the patriarch or primate, who summoned all his suffragans to a synod, wherein, after a rigid scrutiny, he pronounced his canonization, and declared his intercession might be lawfully invoked by the faithful. In still later years, the promulgation of all decrees of canonization, was reserved exclusively to the Sovereign Pontiffs themselves, in order that the titles to canonization might be more rigidly and juridically scrutinized, and that the examination, by being instituted in Rome, might be more entirely divested of local prejudices, as well as to provide that the function should be celebrated with greater solemnity, and that the edification of the exalted virtues of the saint, emanating from the fountain head, might be more generally diffused throughout the entire Christian Church. The records of ecclesiastical history, are believed by many to furnish evidence of several such solemn canonizations by the Popes, even before the year 1000 of the Christian era. One of the first of those functions, we are told, celebrated with much of the splendour and solemnity which now invest them, was solemnized by Leo III, who, with great magnificence and imposing ceremony, canonized St. Swidbert, who was an Englishman, and the first apostle of the Westphalians. What attaches still greater historical celebrity to this event, is the circumstance that the Emperor Charlemagne assisted at the canonization, surrounded by a brilliant array of courtiers, a vast army, and with great pomp and military display. At this time Charlemagne subdued, in several signal victories, the Lombards, the formidable and inveterate foes of Rome. He also confirmed the grants of temporal possessions made by his father, Pepin, to the Holy See, and was crowned Emperor by the Pope, Leo III. He was the first Emperor who had been so crowned, and with him originated the usage which so generally prevailed in after ages, of Christian Emperors receiving their crowns at the hands of the Vicars of Christ. The coronation took place in St. Peter's, on Christmas Day. Leo III. first bowed before Charlemagne, significant of his acknowledgment of his temporal power—then imparted the holy unctions—placed the diadem on his brow—and then celebrated a solemn Mass amidst dazzling magnificence and thrilling exultation. These memorable events occurred during the closing days of the year 799, and the opening ones of the year 800. The next canonization we notice—one which finds a sure place in history—is that of the holy Bishop, St. Ulric, whose name will be found inscribed in the Roman martyrology, on the 4th of July. It was celebrated in Rome, and is one to which there was attached great ceremony, and acquired great celebrity throughout the Christian world. It was solemnized by Pope John XV., in the year of our Lord 993. Not many years subsequently, Pope Benedict IX. canonized St. Simon, a monk of Treves, in the year 1042—it was the seventh recorded canonization. Leo IX. canonized St. Gerard, Bishop of Toul, in the year 1050, and St. Urius and his companions in the year 1053, and they were respectively the tenth and thirteenth recorded canonizations,—and St. Erlembaldus, who was martyred in defence of celibacy, was canonized by Urban II. in the year 1095, and it was the nineteenth recorded canonization. All canonizations invested with the strict and solemn formalities, celebrated since the tenth century, have been carefully registered, and are recorded in ecclesiastical history. Since that period the discipline of the Church, has been uninterruptedly preserved, of reserving exclusively to the Popes, the prerogative of the canonization of saints; and as years rolled on the ceremony increased in splendour, sublimity, and solemnity. But, perhaps, of all those that have preceded it, not one exceeded in grandeur and devotional effect that of the Japanese Martyrs, solemnized on Pentecost Sunday, 1862, by our present Most Holy Father, Pope Pius IX. There were present at it 44 cardinals, 243 bishops, and probably 50,000 people,—the church of St. Peter being gorgeously decorated, illuminated interiorly and exteriorly by myriads of wax lights and flickering lamps, surrounded by all the glittering pageantry of military display of the Pontifical and French armies, charming music, chiming of bells, and booming salvos of artillery.

The Japanese Martyrs were twenty-six in number, including three Jesuits, many Franciscans, and some natives. They were martyred near the city of Nangasasky, on the 5th of February, 1597, during the reign of the Emperor Taicosama, and their sanctity was attested by many wonderful miracles. The canonization, however, of the twenty-five saints, on the occasion of the centenary of 1867, exceeded even that of the Japanese Martyrs, in the number of dignitaries, clergy, and people, of whom there were present 45 cardinals, 503 bishops, 25,000 priests, and 100,000 strangers, in addition to the ordinary population of Rome—and exceeded it still more in the transcendently magnificent and sublime character of the ceremonial, and the general solemnization.

At the time of the first solemn canonization here alluded to, when St. Swidbert was canonized by Leo III., during his sojourn in Germany, in the year of our Lord 804, the temporal possessions of the Popes, were threatened by the audacious rapacity of the Lombards, and those possessions were defended by the Emperor of the West, Charlemagne, and his powerful army. Since then more than 1000 years have passed away, and the successor of Leo, Pius IX., is still in Rome, in St. Peter's, solemnizing a similar ceremony—the insatiable Lombards still yearn for his patrimony, and not content with that portion of the world's division which Providence assigned as their territory, seek to aggrandize "God's acre" also—attempt to erect their throne on the spot occupied by Peter's chair—and covet all the Sovereign Pontiff's possessions, which he acquired, not by conquest, but by pious and voluntary donations—possessions which he governed peaceably—which he retained without ambition to extend—and which are the inalienable right of our Holy Father, and the entire Christian family of the faithful throughout the world, by the sanction of more than a thousand years. These possessions are still defended by the successor of Charlemagne, and his powerful French army—let us hope that all diffidence in his continued protection is groundless, and that, with the noble magnanimity of his imperial predecessor, he will wield the mighty power with which Providence has invested him, in shielding our Holy Father from his enemies, who are panting for their unoffending victim. His Majesty will thus confer new glory on the arms of France, will erect a monument of gratitude in every Catholic heart, bring the benediction of heaven on his pious Empress, and youthful heir, and, perhaps, thereby merit the perpetuation of his temporal dynasty—for, let him remember, no matter what his prestige—no matter how extensive his empire, or how powerful his navy and army, " Unless the Lord keepeth the city, he watcheth in vain that keepeth it."

The canonization celebrated on this 29th of June, 1867, was the 191st solemn and formal canonization of which the archives of the Church can produce any authentic record. Though canonizations are almost invariably celebrated in St. Peter's in the Vatican, there are instances in which they have been celebrated in the Basilica of St. John Lateran—for instance, Benedict XIII. canonized St. John Nepomucen in St. John Lateran; Clement XII. canonized in that church St. Vincent de Paul, St. Francis Regis, St. Julianna Falconeri, and St. Catharine of Genoa; and in the year 993, Pope John XV. canonized St. Ulric, in the Hall of the Council of Lateran. Benedict XIV., the immediate successor of Clement XII., published a Bull, the Bull *"Ad Sepulchra Apostolorum,"* to establish and confirm that right to the Vatican Basilica. In the year 1390, on the night previous to the intended canonization of St. Brigid, Pope Boniface IX.

fell alarmingly ill, and the canonization was celebrated in the chapel in the Vatican Palace, and the solemn Mass of the newly canonized saint was celebrated next morning in the Vatican Basilica.

During the political revolutions which convulsed central Europe in the thirteenth and fourteenth centuries, the Popes were frequently obliged to leave Rome, and, during their exile, celebrated several canonizations in the various cities in which they sought refuge. St. Francis of Assisium, St. Elizabeth of Hungary, and St. Peter the Martyr, were canonized at Perugia, St. Edmund and St. William at Lyons, St. Anthony of Padua at Spoleto, St. Dominic at Rieti, St. Clare at Anagni, St. Stanislaus at Assisium, St. Richard and St. Hedwigis at Viterbo, and St. Louis, the King of France, was canonized at Orvieto.

This nineteenth century will probably stand pre-eminent in ecclesiastical history for the number of canonizations celebrated. Up to the present period, it can number thirty-seven canonizations, whereas thirty-eight is the largest number celebrated within the entire period, of any previous century, and that one was the twelfth century. In the tenth century, the authentically recorded canonizations are few; for there were at most but three—in the eleventh, nineteen—in the thirteenth, twenty-nine—in the fourteenth, eleven—in the fifteenth, fifteen—in the sixteenth, eleven—in the seventeenth, twenty-four—in the eighteenth, twenty-nine—and in this century, to the present date, thirty-seven.

The canonizations of the thirteenth, and seventeenth centuries, were particularly remarkable for the number of founders of religious orders who were included in the saints canonized. Amongst them were, in the thirteenth century, St. Francis of Assisium, St. Dominic, St. Clare—and, in the seventeenth, St. Charles Borromeo, St. Philip Neri, St. Ignatius of Loyola, St. Theresa, St. Francis of Sales, St. Cajetan. The first flower that heaven declared she culled from the southern garden of the American Church, was also canonized in that century, by Clement X.—St. Rose of Lima, being the 144th solemn canonization.

Amongst the many fervent disciples of Christ, whom Ireland has presented to holy Church, and whom she recognizes and honours as saints of God, some have also been honoured by the formal process, decree, and declaration of canonization. St. Malachy, Archbishop of Armagh, was canonized in the year 1190, by Pope Clement III.—it was the 52nd canonization, and occurred not long after that of St. Thomas of Canterbury, which was the 40th canonization, and was celebrated in the year 1173, by Pope Alexander III. St. Edward, King of England, was canonized in 1161, by the same Pope, and it was the 36th in order. St. Laurence O'Toole, Archbishop of Dublin, was canonized in the year 1226, by Pope Honorius III., and is the 69th in the order of canonizations. Those take us back to a period, not far removed from the earliest undisputed instance on record of the strict forms of canonization, that of St. Ulric, Bishop of Augsburg, who was canonized by Pope John XV., in the year 993, and, as I have before stated, in "*Aula Concilii Lateranensis.*"

The Invitation, and Convention.

SURGE, PROPERA, ET VENI.—CANT. ii. 10.
"*Arise, make haste, and come.*"

IN the early part of the year 1866, our august Sovereign Pontiff, Pope Pius IX., recollecting that on the 29th June of the following year, 1867, would be completed the eighteenth centenary of the martyrdom of St. Peter and St. Paul, and desiring to anticipate all that might be necessary to celebrate it with unusual splendour, and solemnity, and having invoked the guidance of the Spirit of God, his Holiness, in an audience given to the Cardinal Prefect, in one of the halls of the Vatican, breathed a wish, that the prelates who preside over the great Christian family dispersed throughout the entire world, might assemble round the shrines of the Apostles, to celebrate together that great anniversary. His Holiness also expressed a desire, that in order to add to the general exultation, and solemnity of the festival, the same day should be chosen for that important exercise of the Church's authority—the solemn declaration, that twenty-five other members of the family, having fought the "good fight," had won the palm of victory, had entered on the possession of their everlasting inheritances, and are numbered amongst the members of the Church triumphant. The Holy Father wished, moreover, to collect around him on that occasion, his dispersed children,

INVITATIONS ISSUED.

to communicate to them in person that his heart was pressed by a ponderous weight of trials—and that wicked men, had presumptuously attempted to erect their own thrones, on the very site which Christ selected for his Vicar Peter's chair—and to solicit their united prayers to heaven to avert every calamity from holy Church. It was the third time during the present Pontificate, that our Most Holy Father, Pope Pius IX., invited the bishops of the world to assemble round the shrines of the Apostles. The two former invitations were, that on the occasion of the definition of the Immaculate Conception, in the year 1854; and in 1862, that on the occasion of the canonization of the Japanese Martyrs. The letter inviting all the bishops of the Christian world to Rome on this occasion, was issued on the 8th of December, 1866, and was signed by Prospero Cardinal Catarini, Prefect of the Congregation of the Council of Trent.

The wish, though merely whispered in the gentle accents of an aged prelate, is instantly wafted to the utmost ends of the earth—for it was the Holy Ghost inspired it—and *Spiritus ubi vult spirat*—"the Spirit breatheth where it will." (John, iii. 8.) How was the message conveyed? Was it by the electric telegraph? Electric telegraph!—loitering laggard! resign the despatch to a courier who knows how to expedite it, and convey it to foreign regions over which you have never traversed, to deliver it on mountain ranges, gelid climes, impenetrable fastnesses, and distant island specks, in the midst of vast oceans, which you have never explored! Your domain, no matter how extended, is circumscribed by a needle's point, and is measured by the diameter of a wire—but the Church's extent is the length and width of the world, "*diffusa per orbem.*" Away it goes, that Papal invitation—"he walketh on the wings of wind!" See, it is delivered in the country beyond the Ganges and in India, and is echoed from the vales of the Hymalays, to the lofty peaks of Chimborazo, and the Andes, from Pekin to Valparaiso, from New Zealand to the Arctic regions—it traverses over Saba, and Arabia, to tropical climes, and back again from Tharsis, to the distant isles of the southern seas—"the Spirit of the Lord filled the whole earth!"

The Pope's wish is whispered to the dispersed prelates, and the "noise filled the whole house"—and see they are coming—coming in thronging multitudes—" devout men out of every nation under heaven. Parthians, and Medes, and Elamites, and inhabitants of Mesopotamia, Judea, and Cappadocia, Pontus and Asia, Phrygia and Pamphilia, Egypt, and the parts of Lybia about Cyrene, and strangers of Rome, Jews also, and proselytes, Cretes, and Arabians: we have heard them speak in our own language the wonderful works of God." (Acts ii.) They are coming!—the prelates not only of every country, but of every rite in communion with Rome—the Copt and the Greek, the Ruthenian and the Chaldean, the Syrian and the Armenian, the Roumanian, Melchite, Maronite, and Slavonic. Antioch, and Alexandria, and those Eastern Churches which attained such celebrity from the earliest ages of faith, now also in our own days, send their representatives to Rome. Patriarchs, primates, archbishops, and bishops, all start in obedience to the whispered wish of their common centre, head, and father! What unity, subordination, charity, and discipline!

Their Holy Father is afflicted, and he asks them to gather round him to alleviate his sorrows by their prayers and sympathies; and see, they are coming! The instant the wish is whispered, that instant they rise, gird themselves, and commence the journey—no difficulty is too formidable to be overcome—no distance too remote to be traversed—the whole earth over which they have to travel is, in their estimation, no bigger than an imperceptible speck—the circumference of the globe but as that of the rings that encircle their fingers—and the vast expanse of waters, the boisterous oceans over which they have to voyage, seem but as a drop of morning dew, pendant from the point of a reed! The number of prelates who left their homes for Rome, to assist at that memorable convention, amounted to more than 506. Some, however, fell sick on the journey, and some were destined, like Moses in the desert, never to reach that promised land. One bishop commences his journey from that little spot of land far away over the world of waters, Vancouver's Island, to visit the Vicar, but the distance was too great for his attenuated frame, he was stricken down by sickness, and never reached his happy destination! Another, more robust, hears the whispered invitation, and, in compliance, travels from San Francisco to Rome, a distance of 8000 miles! Now look into the Cathedral of Barcelona, and see there are congregated the bishops of Spain—they walk in procession through the streets of the city, to the port, where a Spanish frigate of war is placed at their command by the Admiralty, and all expenses of the pilgrimage are paid by the Treasury. They hoist the flag of the Madonna from the main, and sail away amidst the united voices of thousands singing *Ave Maris Stella!* See, some of them are coming up from the torrid zone—others issuing from icy fastnesses, amidst the towering glaciers of the Arctic regions—some are travelling over the table lands of those eastern countries, along the horizon which is first dyed by the crimson tinge of the rising sun—now turn round about, and see others traversing the prairie countries; see the figures of others relieved on the red sky as they come over the crests of those western hills, behind which the setting sun descends! Look, some of them are mounted on camels, for fourteen hours each day, for forty days, traversing over sandy deserts a distance of 400 miles, before they can reach a seaport to take shipping. Who are those who are following them? See, they are 25,000 priests from distant churches hurrying to the 'same destination—they are again followed by 100,000 "devout laymen, from every nation under heaven," with complexions some white, and some red, copper-coloured, bronzed, and black, proclaiming their native latitudes. "Before him the Ethiopians shall bow down, and his enemies shall lick the ground." (Ps. lxxi. 9.) Their hands are laden with the most valuable treasures which the bowels of the earth can yield, to be presented as tributes of their veneration, loyalty, and submission to the Vicar of Christ. "This is the sign of the great King." (Isaias, lx.) "The kings of Tharsis and the islands shall offer presents—the kings of the Arabians and of Saba shall bring gifts." (Ps. lxxi. 10.)

How consolatory to our Holy Father!—at home, in his own Italy, he reared up children, and they despised him: his own pulled down his walls : but—" Lift up thy eyes round about, and see : all these are gathered together, they are come to thee : thy sons shall come from afar, and thy daughters shall rise up by thy side. And the children of strangers shall build up thy walls, and their kings shall minister to thee. And the children of them that afflict thee, shall come bowing down to thee, and all that slandered thee shall worship the steps of thy feet, and shall call thee the city of the Lord, the Sion of the Holy One of Israel." (Isaias, lx.)

The Pilgrimage.

SUPER FLUMINA BABYLONIS, ILLIC SEDIMUS ET FLEVIMUS, CUM RECORDAREMUR TUI SION.—PSALM CXXXVI. 1.

"*Upon the rivers of Babylon, there we sat and wept, when we remembered Sion.*"

THE approaching celebration of the centenary, elicited the liveliest interest, and the most ardent devotion, throughout the entire Christian world, to visit the shrines of the Apostles—and as the multitudes of the faithful were congregating towards that centre of Catholicity, it might be said of Rome, *ad te conversio mea*—" to thee is my turning." I shared in the general fervour, and joined in the pilgrimage. On a balmy summer's evening, on the 4th June, I stepped on board the royal mail ship *Leinster*. She soon glided out of the harbour, over a smooth sea, and under a cloudless sky. I stood long, looking back at the varied outline, and picturesque scenery, which surround our bay, till the receding shores became dimmed in the distance, and in the evening shades, and gradually faded from my vision like the charming scenes of a dissolving view. I travelled rapidly through England, crossed the Straits of Dover, and arrived in Paris on the 6th of June, on the very evening that the entire city was in a state of feverish excitement, in consequence of his Imperial Majesty the Czar having been shot at, after the grand military review at Longchamp, by the Pole,

Berezowski. On Pentecost Sunday I obtained the privilege, of assisting at High Mass in the private chapel of the Tuileries, with their Imperial Majesties. The Prince Imperial was not present, as he had gone to Bagnères, in the south of France, to recruit in that salubrious clime. The solemn Mass was sung by a bishop, who formerly had been Curé of Ham, during the time Napoleon had been imprisoned in that fortress. Paris was filled to repletion with strangers, celebrities, and several of the royal personages of Europe, visitors to the Great Exhibition. In the gardens of the Tuileries, in the Champs Elysèes, and other public places, I met the Emperor Napoleon, and the Empress Eugenie, and several of the marshals of France, and Baron Haussman, Prefect of the Seine—also his Imperial Majesty Alexander, Emperor of Russia, King William of Prussia, the Princes, and Count Bismarck. Every day witnessed some distinguished arrival; amongst others came the Sublime Porte, his Majesty the Sultan of Turkey, Abdul Aziz Khan, accompanied by a brilliant suite—and by Youssouf Izzedin, the Sultan's son, a youth ten years of age—by his two nephews, Abdu Ahmed and Mohammed Meerat, son of the late Sultan, Abdul Medjid, and who was then twenty-seven years of age, and is heir apparent to the throne; by Fuad Pacha, the prime minister of Turkey, and by the Imaun, or Grand Almoner of the Sultan, Haironlah Effendi, who waited on the Papal Nuncio, and the Archbishop of Paris, who courteously returned his visits. Then came the Viceroy of Egypt—the Grand Duke, and Duchess of Baden—Prince Nicholas I. of Montenegro—the Grand Duke of Saxe Weimar—and Charles, the King of Wirtemburg. I visited the Great Exhibition several times—but I fancied I saw the fair figure of Religion beckoning to me with both her hands—come! come to Rome!—why loiter there gazing on mortal men, and on material toys!—come, and I shall show real glories, commemorative of a martyred fisherman, who, to win the crown of a blessed immortality, and everlasting inheritances, died to extend the kingdom of Christ, and triumphed over a Cæsar's power, and over a Roman Empire!

I travelled with rapidity to Marseilles, the Liverpool of France, containing 200,000 inhabitants, and which, after the

Ascension, was consecrated by the residence of Martha, who had once the honour of having our Blessed Lord for her guest. On Trinity Sunday I embarked for Civita Vecchia, on board the steamship *Prince Napoleon*. She was built by the Messrs. Scott of Glasgow ; her boilers and fittings were very superior. Her saloon was constructed to accommodate 40 cabin passengers, whereas we had 202, of whom it was announced 110 were priests ! After long chafing and puffing, our ship, at nine o'clock, slipped her moorings, and with her tapering spars pointing aloft, her yardarms stretched to their utmost capacity, her blanched canvas swollen into the most graceful curves by the favourable breeze, the French tricolour flying from the fore, the *Prince Napoleon* glided as gracefully as a seagull through the old port of Marseilles, and, like a thing of life, bounded over the undulating waters, with apparent delight at having escaped again into her native element. On the highest pinnacle of the rocky cliffs which surround the city, stands the votive chapel of the Blessed Virgin, called " Notre Dame de la Garde." As our ship rounded the lofty promontory, the craggy rocks were gradually screening from our view the environs and the city—but before we lost sight of " Notre Dame de la Garde," the French priests gave a signal, and all on board knelt on deck, and, with uncovered heads, sung several psalms to our Lord, and sweet hymns to our Lady, and amongst them the *Ave Maris Stella*. Those fervent priests seemed to have no other ambition than the grace to live holily—to obtain a safe journey to the shrines of the Apostles—the happiness of seeing the representative of Jesus Christ, which should prove to them ever afterwards an abundant source of joyous consolation, all of which petitions were included in the sweet verses :

> " Vitam præsta puram,
> Iter para tutum,
> Ut videntes Jesum,
> Semper collætemur."

The greater number of the priests were from various parts of France—very many were Spaniards from Andalusia, Granada, Castile, and the Basque provinces—some Portugese, Hollanders, Italians, and one Irish priest with myself.

We had on board a young gentleman connected with a
family of the grandees of Spain, who was travelling to
Rome under the protection of a Spanish ecclesiastic. There
was also a young gentleman, a member of one of the highest
families in England—he was one of the Oxford converts—
and was a true type of a young member of the English
aristocracy, highly educated, of refined and prepossessing
manners—elegant in dress, in deportment, and in phrase-
ology. He was going to Rome to confirm his faith, and
enliven his piety—he seemed to have been abundantly
blessed with both. We had a Protestant young gentleman
from New York, who was making the tour of Europe.
There was on board a Spanish marquis, Mariano Conrado
y Asprez de Heoburg, a commander in the Spanish navy,
a native of Palma in Majorca. He made many anxious
inquiries regarding the O'Neills, and O'Donnells, the Irish
Earls, as he said he had an intimate acquaintance in Palma,
who was son of a General O'Neill, who served with distinc-
tion in the Spanish army, and was a direct descendant
of the princely chieftain O'Neill. I told of their fidelity and
their trials, their having fled from Ireland, and their landing
in France in the year 1607—their journey to Rome, where
they were honorably received by Pope Paul V.—their residing in the Palazzo Salviati—of Tyrconnell's death in the year
1608—of the death of the great Earl of Tyrone eight years
later, and of their monuments in the church of San Pietro
in Montorio, where their ashes repose, with those of Eugene
Matthews, a former Archbishop of Dublin. There were
several ladies, both French and Italian. Amongst the second-
class passengers was an Irishman, who resided lately in
Scotland ; he told me he was going to Rome to take service
for a limited time in the Papal army—that he had led a life
of irregularity, that he regretted it, and that with God's
grace he hoped, by subjecting himself to military discipline,
especially in the Pope's army, he might acquire habits of
system and virtue, and become, on his return, a good citizen,
and an edifying Christian. Amongst our passengers we had
also Jacinto Vera, Bishop of Megara, and Vicar-Apostolic of
Monte Video. The French priests, by their prepossessing
politeness, their easy familiarity of manner, and versatility

of conversational powers, soon introduced themselves to every one on board, and each one to the other. No person asked another whither he was going—that was known to all—the only question asked was, whence he had come. Like purling streamlets issuing from unexplored fastnesses, all became tributary to the mountain torrent, which rushed on to the expansive lake at Rome, there to blend with the calm waters, and reflect on their glossy surface, the surrounding scenes of every exalted Christian virtue. The French and Spanish priests, on learning that I was an Irish priest, manifested the liveliest interest in me, and in my country, and seemed most anxious to fraternize with me—a disposition I most cordially reciprocated. Two in an especial manner, were pre-eminent in their manifestations of courtesy to me, and of attachment to Ireland—one a parish priest of Valladolid, the other Juan Marti y Canto Pbro, parish priest of St. Michael's, Barcelona. A sympathetic attachment has, for centuries, established a most affectionate alliance, in all the relations of the French, and Spaniards, with the people of Ireland. In dress, in deportment, in conversation, those good priests were in every particular ecclesiastical. They were most enthusiastic in their expressions of attachment to the Holy Father the Pope, seemed filled with the spirit of their holy ministry, with ardent zeal for the promotion of religion, and relished nothing but what savoured of Jesus, Mary, and Peter. Happy France and Spain, that merit such a priesthood! *Sancta gens beatus populus, cui Dominus dedit pastorem juxta cor suum.*—"Holy is the nation, and blessed the people, to whom the Lord has given a pastor according to his own heart!" The wind was off the land, and our vessel hugged the shore so closely, that we were within easy view of the passing landscape. At midday the heat became most oppressive—I retired to my berth, and reclined at full length. Beside my pillow, the ship's side was pierced with a circular bull's-eye window, on opening which, the circumference formed a circular frame to the picture which was continuously moving before my view, like one of those moving panoramas, which, in early youth, we loved to view through a magnifying lens, charming our minds with the captivating scenes of foreign climes, and the romance of future travel. Above me was the sky, so transparent that the eye seemed to penetrate the depths of ether into infinite space—beneath, the clear indigo blue of the Mediterranean waters, and the foreground presented towering promontories of serrated craggy rocks, chafed and fringed by the foam of the fretted sea. Occasional interstices in the rocks revealed pretty villas, verandas, parterres of flowers, the spires of village churches, lawns planted with vine-trees and fig-trees, embroidered with the beautiful flowering caper plants, which here flourish with great luxuriance—picturesque demesnes, studded with pine-trees, and bordered with myrtles, jessamines, rhododendrons, olives, mulberries, the pistachio, pomegranate, and orange trees. The air was redolent of their spicy fragrance. Occasionally my view was intercepted by the white sail of an Algerine felucca, like that of a "caique," flitting over the waters of the Bosphorus, under the Sultan's gardens of the "Valley of the Sweet Waters." See, now, in that land-locked bay, surrounded by moles of formidable fortresses, lies the city of Toulon, the Plymouth of France, and those many vessels are the "Gloire," and other iron-clad ships of the French navy, looking "all-ataut," and riding at anchor. On that frowning fortress to the left, called "Eguillette," a young captain of artillery, aged 23 years, first displayed his great military genius, when, in 1793, he showered 8,000 shot and shell in thirty-six hours on the doomed citadel, forcing the garrison of British, Spanish, and Neapolitan troops to abandon the fortifications, and their fleet to evacuate the port. Subsequently the world heard more of that young officer—his name was Buonaparte! This city is also memorable in our modern history for the remarkable event, of the destruction by fire of the French fleet, by Sir Sidney Smith, who was despatched in command of a squadron of the English fleet on that service, by Admiral Lord Hood, in November, 1793, during the reeking days of the Red Republic. We are now passing the rocky isles of the Hyéres, and on the mainland opposite is the city of Hyéres, which has attained celebrity as having been the birthplace of Massillon. The next beautiful town, imbosomed in the mountains, and washed by a picturesque bay, is Cannes. Here Napoleon landed in March, 1815, on his return from Elba—adjacent, also, stands the villa of Louise Elèonore, built by Lord Brougham, regarded as the most charming villa in France, and enjoying the most salubrious climate in the world. We have now arrived opposite the ancient and flourishing town of Antibes, situated on a projecting promontory, and which gives title to the French legion, at present in the Pontifical army. How fast we are sailing!—there is Nice, and the torrent of the Var, which formerly divided the frontiers of France, and Italy. After long enjoying the scenes of this charming moving panorama, my ears were captivated by a powerful harmonious burst of vocal music aloft, which at once I recognized as the Church's family song, of the Gregorian chant. I seized my Breviary, and got up on deck. What was my surprise!—all the priests were seated under a white awning, in two continuous lines, the entire length of the quarter-deck, forming a perfect choir, presided over by the Bishop of Monte Video, with deacons at either side, singing the vespers of the feast of the Holy Trinity—the ladies and gentlemen passengers, and the entire crew crowding around, and constituting a most pious, and edifying congregation. One of the French priests officiated as master of ceremonies, and another conducted the music, and vespers were chanted with as much precision, and solemnity, as they could be in the Cathedral of Notre Dame. The solemn tones wafted over the waters, were peculiarly devotional and plaintive, and appropriate for so many pilgrim priests, journeying from so many distant countries, to the happy land of their Holy Father. *Vox Domini super aquas.* (Psalm xxviii. 3.) "The voice of the Lord is upon the waters." After vespers the Bishop imparted his benediction, and his lordship announced, that all would assemble again at sunset, to recite night prayers, and sing the litanies, and the *Ave Maris Stella.* During the voyage, we breakfasted at 9 o'clock, "dejeuner à la Fourchette," we dined at 5 o'clock, and had coffee at night, the fare " Le menu de la jour," was varied and recherché, and quite "à la Française." We assembled again at sunset—the litanies were chanted, and night prayer recited, whilst the glories of the setting sun were sublime, and transcendently magnificent. We prepared our hammocks for the night as best we could —many slept on deck. I rose at 4 o'clock next morning, and found we were within view of the bay, and city of Genoa. Our ship was sailing in smooth water, and close to shore—high craggy cliffs, and receding hills rose abruptly from the sea—their sloping sides were covered with verdure, and groves of olives and vine trees, and dotted with pretty rural churches, and villas, and villages imbosomed in the glens. The glimpses of the cascades, and the white houses, seen through the foliage, seemed like the bloom of the summer's blossoms—and far in the distance above, the landscape terminated in faint views of the towering peaks of the maritime Alps. We entered and cast anchor in the harbour—the water was as smooth as a mirror. We were surrounded by an amphitheatre of hills, and on them rose "the city of palaces, Genoa the superb"—terrace above terrace, spires and cupolas, interspersed with gardens, marble balustrades, trees, statues, and playing fountains, and capped with churches, convents, palaces, and frowning fortifications. The sun was just now rising—glorious spectacle! The eastern sky was tinted with the most delicate tinge of crimson, as if modestly blushing at the approach of the great monarch of the day, and was gradually glowing into a deeper scarlet, till it attained so brilliant a vermilion, that the eye was pained by the intensity of the glare. Soon after the serrated outline of the hills, seemed bordered with a cornice of the most dazzling bullion—then the first rays commenced darting in scintillating pencils through the lowest interstices, as if from the tops of the fingers of the great luminary, who grasped the summits to raise his radiant orb above the range, and look down upon the beauteous bay in which we lay anchored, and salute our arrival. The sombre shades of azure, and blue, and neutral tint, all fled from the hills' sides, and trees, and flowers seemed to spring up spontaneously into light, and the charming landscape was developed in the most expressive touches of Nature's pencil, and in her highest artistic colouring. The water of the bay was as red and glowing as the molten iron of a fiery furnace. Genoa is a very flourishing city, possesses many manufactories—a fine harbour—beautiful environs—a most genial climate—very many sumptuous palaces—superb churches, decorated with the most gorgeous ornamentations in statuary, painting, and gilding, the splendours of the Annunziata, being astonishing, and transcendently grand and superb—and the city contains 110,000 inhabitants. It is memorable to Irishmen, as being the city in which O'Connell died, on his pilgrimage to the shrines of the Apostles. The passengers went ashore, and spent the day in making excursions through the city, and environs—in visiting the palaces, picture galleries, and churches. After our day's excursions, so replete with interest, we returned, fatigued by the oppressive heat, to our ship, where we found a general rendezvous of all the passengers for dinner. After dinner, whilst on deck, enjoying the evening air before sunset, another large steamship from a foreign port entered the harbour, and at half cable's length from us cast anchor. Her decks were thronged with passengers. She proved to be the *Buda*, bound also for Civita Vecchia; and amongst many lay gentlemen and ladies going to the festivities at Rome, she had also on board the Right Rev. Dr. Wood, the Bishop of Philadelphia, and Right Rev. Mgr. Paul Benigné Carrion, the Bishop of Porto Rico, and no less a number than 140 priests from different nations. Immediately after the *Buda* rode at her moorings, the French priests of our ship congregated on the poop, and sides of the vessel, and saluted the newly arrived, by singing the *Laudate Dominum omnes gentes*, which was fervently responded to by a powerful, harmonious volume from the 140 voices singing, *Quoniam confirmata est super nos misericordia ejus, et veritas Domini manet in æternum.* The priests of our ship, next intoned the *Sub tuum præsidium*, and the Litany of the Blessed Virgin, exercising their voices to the utmost capability of their strength, singing most enthusiastically, and waving their hands and hats, to mark the time of the music; and the responses were equally enthusiastically chanted by the multitudes on board the *Buda*. The soldiers collected on the bastions, and many crowds of the Genoese, on the parapets, and balustrades of the houses, and along the quays, manifested the deepest interest in these edifying demonstrations of religion. The young English gentleman, the Oxford convert, seized me by the arm, saying: "Oh! sir, I am exceedingly edified—I was not at all prepared for these enthusiastical manifestations of piety!" I secretly exulted at this triumph of religion, and at the sources of delight, and edification they afforded to our Oxford neophyte. An interval of quietude and silence intervened—at this moment the sun went down beneath the horizon—the evening gun was fired from the fortress that capped the hill—the booming report reverberated from side to side, and through the ravines, and all round the amphitheatre of hills, but finding egress impracticable on the land side, the report went off to sea and the rumbling echoes died away over the distant waters! Then followed the martial notes of a flourishing trumpet, summoning the soldiers of the garrison to quarters, from which the harmonizing echoes formed seemingly a full band; and before the last prolonged notes had died away on the stillness of the evening, the French priests again intoned the vesper hymn, *Ave Maris Stella*, which was most devotionally responded to by the bishops, priests, and all on board the *Buda*. The bishops at its termination gave their benediction, and then all the voyagers of this memorable pilgrimage retired to repose. The ship soon after got up steam, slipped her moorings, and proceeded on her voyage. The *Buda* sailed soon after, but as our ship sailed quicker, we parted company, and lost sight of her in the gloom of the evening. Early next morning we entered, and cast anchor in the bay of Leghorn. The *Buda* presented herself in two hours after. As in the ports we had previously visited, the little boats, brilliantly coloured and covered with white awnings, flitted round our vessel's side, the importunate boatmen, in every variety of oratorical gesture, inviting us to take a seat, and go ashore. Our ship's company formed many parties to visit the churches, palaces, and city of Leghorn—and others to make excursions to visit the Cathedral, Baptistery, "Campo Santo," and wonderful Leaning Tower of Pisa, which were distant only a short drive by rail. A band of Italian musicians came on board, and entertained us with some exquisite music. In the evening, Monsignor Paul Benigné Carrion, Bishop of Porto Rico, came alongside in the *Buda's* barge, accompanied by the captain and his secretary, a smart, dapper, vivacious, and intelligent-looking young priest, to pay us a visit in the *Prince Napoleon*. His lordship looked most benignant and venerable, his white beard flowing down to his breast, and forming a fine contrast with the colour of his episcopal costume. Our Bishop of Monte Video summoned all the priests, and, kneeling with them himself, solicited his lordship's benediction. "Oh! no, no," he cried, "ask me not to bless you. We are all brothers—children journeying to our Father—when we arrive at his house, our home, his Holiness will bless us all!" To repeated solicitations, however, he yielded, and blessed us all. The captain of the *Buda* examined our ship minutely, and was ardent in his expressions of admiration of her arrangements, engines, and general fittings. We parted our moorings early this evening, and after a smooth night's sailing, at 5 o'clock next morning, 19th of June, we cast anchor before Civita Vecchia. On gliding into the harbour, our Bishop, surrounded by all the French, Spanish, and foreign priests, entoned the *Te Deum*, which was most enthusiastically sung by all, in thanksgiving for our safe voyage to our Father's territory. A communication was made to the governor of the port on shore, that there was a Monsignor on board; and soon after a state barge of the Papal marine, of twelve oars, manned by twelve able seamen, was launched, and commanded by a coxswain and captain. The boat was painted purple outside, and white inside; the spaces for the oars were edged with brass mouldings, and the entire boat, and her appointments, looked extremely "ship-shape," trim, and exquisitely clean. The yellow Papal flag, on which were emblazoned a figure of St. Peter, and overhead the tiara and cross-keys, floated from a flag-staff at the stern. The men wore white-coloured trousers, white shirts with blue facings, white hats with blue silk bands. They seemed smart, cleanly fellows, and able seamen. The captain wore a uniform similar to that of a British naval officer, blue, with gilded buttons, and gold epaulettes, blue cap, and gold lace band and belt. He seemed every inch a seaman; and his bronzed wrinkled, and weather-beaten countenance, indicated that he had gone through many adventures in many climes, incident to his profession, and that he had ere now encountered the dangers of "the battle and the breeze." The boat soon hove alongside, the gangway was lowered—the Bishop of Monte Video descended, all the boat's company receiving his lordship with their oars erect, and the captain saluting—the painter was parted, and they rowed away, the priests and all on board our ship waving their hats, and the Bishop also waving his in parting adieu; and thus, after an agreeable voyage of three days, we parted, nevermore, perhaps, to enjoy his society. Some hours elapsed before the necessary arrangements could be completed with the police authorities on shore, to examine our passports, and the custom-house authorities, to examine our luggage, and thus enable us to land. Our ship lay side by side with an Austrian war frigate. It was the morning of the 19th of June—a memorable era for Austria! On that very morning, and at that very hour, a terrible and tragic event occurred at Quaretaro, when Mexico wrought a deed of blood, which must for ever stigmatize her history, by the foulest blot in the annals of time—a withering deed, which blanched the cheek, and chilled to gelidity the blood of Christendom—and shall ever elicit the horror, and indignation of future generations. The same brilliant ray which here, from an Italian sun, was reflected on the blanched canvas of that Austrian frigate, was the last with which a tropical sun lit up the picturesque scenery of Mexico, to the eye of the Emperor Maximilian, upon whom the sentence of court-martial was about to be executed, by order of Diaz, Escobedo, and Juarez. At that moment the Emperor Maximilian, stood with the intrepidity of a Christian prince, and military hero, before the file of soldiers from whom he was to receive the fatal fusilade. On either side stand his two faithful generals, Miramon and Mejia, who were sentenced to a similar death, and to whose families the generous Emperor bequeathed 100,000 dollars. After piously receiving the sacraments—administered by the Bishop, and by Abbé Fischer—he was recommending his soul to God—kissing the portrait of his beloved, and afflicted Empress Carlotta—soliciting the soldiers for the only favour he had now to expect in this world—to aim for his heart, in order that an eventful life, pregnant with crosses and sorrows, might not be protracted in the agonies of death. The Mexican soldiers promised to concede the request, on receiving an equivalent in gold—they load—present arms—the fatal tubes are levelled—the eye guides the sight with unerring precision—the order is given to fire !— a flash and volume of curling smoke—the deadly bullets sped their invisible flight, and opened sluices in the heart of Maximilian, through which gushes out the crimson tide of life—the quivering body of the Emperor falls, and rests for some time, upon the black cross which stood before his grave—two soldiers advance, and fire the "coup-de-grace" into his side— he expires ! May the merits purchased on a cross like that which in that trying hour supported his body, support his soul by grace, confidence in God, and the hopes of a blessed immortality ! The event electrified the world, and rudely struck a chord, to which every fibre of humanity vibrated. The coincidence of our French ship *Prince Napoleon* lying beside the Austrian frigate, at the time of this event, recalls to my recollection the remarkable fact, that since the days of Richelieu, France rarely approached towards Austria, either as a friend or foe, without bringing disasters to the house of Hapsburg. Very many instances may be adduced in exemplification. In the Thirty Years' War, France deluged Austria with a torrent of calamities. The relations of France with Austria, during the days of Napoleon, how disastrous ! Austerlitz, Lodi, and Marengo, have written the truth in streams of blood. The defeats at Magenta, and Solferino, covered the Austrian arms with bitter humiliation. The expulsion of Austrian rule from Lombardy—the loss of Venice, and the Quadrilateral, and their prestige in Germany—and their privation of the proud privilege of the protectorate of the temporal power of the Father of the Faithful, are all additional proofs of this historical fact. The loss of the kingdom of Naples to a royal family allied to the house of Austria, was caused by French intervention in Italy. The seven days' campaign against the Prussians, and the disasters of Sadowa, though not directly attributable to France, were rendered possible by the war in Venice and by the alliance of France with the enemies of Austria. Even in the sacred ties of matrimonial alliances,

France brought disaster to Austria. A Dauphin, afterwards King of France, Louis XVI., solicits in marriage the hand of an Austrian Archduchess, Marie Antoinette, and the alliance leads the royal lady to a death upon a scaffold, amidst the jeers of a Parisian canaille! Now, France after searching Europe, selects an Austrian Archduke to crown him Emperor of Mexico, and the crown on Maximilian's head directs to his heart the bullets of the military executioners, and deranges the brain of his amiable Empress Carlotta! How disastrous! The Emperor Ferdinand Maximilian was the second brother of Francis Joseph, Emperor of Austria, and was born at Shoenbrunn on the 6th of July, 1832, and married on the 27th of July, 1857, the Princess Charlotte, daughter of Leopold, King of Belgium ; she was then not quite seventeen years of age. On the 3rd of October, 1863, he accepted of the crown of Mexico, offered him by the Mexican Assembly of Notables, at the castle of Marimar. Immediately after, their Imperial Majesties went to Rome, to visit the shrines of the Apostles, and obtain the benediction of the Pope, Pius IX. He and the Empress, entered the capital of Mexico, on the 12th of July, 1864. The Empress returned to France, and thence went again to Rome, to visit the Pope, where she gave the first symptoms of the derangement with which she is since afflicted. She is now residing in Belgium.

After lying in the bay for some hours, it was announced that arrangements had been made for our landing, and that the custom-house officials were prepared to examine our luggage, and the officers to *viser* our passports. We got ashore—it was a busy scene. We ran up by rail in two hours to Rome. The French priests were anxiously on the look out for the dome of St. Peter's—the instant it came within view—in one thrilling, harmonious burst, they sang the *Credo in unum Deum*, dwelling again and again with increased fervour on the words, *et unam sanctam Catholicam et Apostolicam Ecclesiam*—" and one, holy, Catholic, and Apostolic Church "—of which Rome, where we had happily arrived, is the chief see, the mistress of churches, the centre of unity! Rome! towards which the weak have ever turned for support—the oppressed for redress—the afflicted for consolation! Rome! centre of all that is erudite in literature and science—all that is attractive in sculpture, painting, and the fine arts—and all that is enchanting and fascinating, even in fashionable life! Rome! it is a sanctuary which expands, ennobles, and exalts our minds—it enkindles our enthusiasm, delights our senses, enlivens our faith!—it is the tabernacle of God with men—the place where His glory dwelleth—it is the very threshold of the eternal Sion! *Ut Christiani, ita et Romani scitis*—" As you are the children of Christ, so be you children of Rome!"— *St. Patrick.*

Private Life of the Pope.

ORDINATIONE TUA PERSEVERAT DIES.—PSALM cxviii.
"*By thy ordinance the day goeth on.*"

OUR present Sovereign Pontiff, and Most Holy Father, Pope Pius IX., was formerly called John Mary Mastai Ferretti. He is the son of Count Mastai Ferretti, and was born on the 13th May, 1792, at Sinigaglia, a small town in the March of Ancona, and at the time of the centenary was 75 years of age. In early life he adopted the military profession, and enrolled himself in that distinguished corps the Noble Guard, an honour to which he was entitled by his birth. He served in the Noble Guard during the Pontificate of Pope Pius VII., who was much attached to the young officer. The discriminating eye of Pius VII. discovered under the gorgeous uniform, and glittering accoutrements of the Noble Guard, a heart devoted to God, animated with a spirit of piety, and stimulated with zeal for the promotion of religion. The aged Pontiff, advised the military youth, to resign his commission, at the foot of the altar of Santa Maria delli Angeli, and enter the ecclesiastical state. He assented—he resigned his sword-hilt for the crucifix—his sabre-dash for a beads—and took off his plumed helmet, and bent his head to receive the tonsure, saying: *Dominus pars hæreditatis meæ et calicis mei, tu es qui restitues hæreditatem meam mihi.* (Psalm xv.) " The

Lord is the portion of my inheritance, and of my cup : it is thou that wilt restore my inheritance to me." He made his early studies at Volterra—he was ordained, and was engaged on a special mission in Chili : on his return to Italy, he was, in the year 1832, consecrated Archbishop of Spoleto ; and was subsequently translated to Imola. He was reserved "in petto" on the 23rd of December, 1839 : published Cardinal Priest, under the title of SS. Peter and Marcellinus, on the 14th of December, 1840 : created Pope on the 16th of June, 1846 : and was crowned on the 21st of June in the same year.

The Pope is invested with a twofold character—that of a private personage—and that of his exalted august character of Sovereign Pontiff, Visible Head of the Church, and Vicar of Christ. In his character of a private individual, the Pope is most accessible, humble, gentle, prepossessing in his manners, highly refined in his deportment, evincing brilliant exemplifications of exalted rank, erudition, and the most perfect inspirations of religion. He is naturally most benevolent in his disposition, delicately sensitive to the wants of others, most munificent in his contributions on occasions of public calamities, of which even our own country, in the desolating days of famine, can afford ample testimony. The service of his table, is regulated by the strictest observance of simplicity, and frugality. Every hour of his day is husbanded with the utmost economy of time, and according to prescribed order. In his converse with his household, he is easy of address, familiar, enjoys an amusing anecdote, and is habitually cheerful. In a word, the private character of the Holy Father, may be said to be what is called "a constant and perennial softness of manner, easiness of approach, and suavity of disposition." In stature he is of the middle height. His features are decisively marked, but his countenance displays none of the usual wrinkles of age. His face is smooth, and his complexion fair, and transparent, and his eye is most vivacious, and penetrating. His lips are thin and compressed, and his whole visage is engaging, and beaming with goodness. His head is thickly covered with hair, but is blanched with age. His voice is clear and sonorous, and his musical capabilities as a church vocalist, are of a very high order. His family are very long lived, and his own constitution is robust, and he usually enjoys excellent health—although in the year 1860, and in the two subsequent years, having been oppressed with sorrow, and worn out with unceasing anxiety, his Holiness' health was in a very precarious condition, and excited serious alarms. He has, however, since then, happily rallied, and regained his usual vigour of constitution. When Pope Pius IX. appears in his character of Supreme Pontiff, he is invested with great dignity—can manifest great determination of purpose—and when required to repel the invasions of error, or revolution, like Moses when he appeared to the rebellious people, after his converse with God, the Pope has proved himself inflexible, nay, I may say, even terrible, to the enemies of religion! His countenance, at different times, is most expressive of these various phases of character.

His Holiness rises every morning at five o'clock. He spends a long time in mental prayer, before his crucifix— the Vicar and Christ, in intimate converse!—what momentous events are poised in those instants!—events affecting the Church suffering, militant, and triumphant, and the destinies of immortal souls! The conferences of sovereigns, the diplomacy of statesmen, the strategy of generals, may be regarded as matters of weighty importance; in comparison to those, they weigh not even as the weight of a grain of sand! After his religious exercises, he is waited on by his "valet-de-chambre," to adjust his person,—he then receives a visit from his physician. He celebrates Mass every morning at seven o'clock, and assists at another Mass of thanksgiving immediately after, celebrated by an ecclesiastic of his household. He then receives his letters, after which he gives audiences, to the Cardinal Secretary of State, and to the Major-Domo. He breakfasts at ten o'clock, when his refection consists of a cup of coffee or chocolate, a little bread, and a glass of water. After breakfast, he gives audiences to his ministers, in the various departments of the Church, State, and Household. At two o'clock he dines, and the expenses of his table are most moderate, not exceeding five francs a day. He dines usually alone, and always at a separate table. A gentleman, who was an "attaché" of one of the embassies, told me that on one occasion, when presenting an urgent dispatch to the Holy Father, he was present whilst he was at dinner—it was a day of abstinence, and his dinner consisted of a bowl of vegetable soup, a plate of maccaroni with olive oil and pomo-dore, two gurnets, which in Rome are little larger than sardines—some French beans, some bread and cheese, and three apples. After dinner he usually takes a drive. Even the Pope's ordinary drive is attended with considerable state—his carriage is drawn by four black horses, is preceded by a mounted officer, the "batta la strada"—is followed by the carriages of his suite—and surrounded by a troop of dragoons, and an escort of the Noble Guards, in undress uniform. When he reaches the Pincian Hill, or the Porta Angelica, or the suburbs of the city, he walks, and at so lively and brisk a gait, that his chamberlains find it difficult to keep within their prescribed distances. All carriages meeting his Holiness' cortege, draw up—the occupants descend, and kneel down to receive his blessing. As his carriages pass along, persons frequently present petitions, at the windows, which are graciously received by one of the assistant-cardinals, and within a few days are punctually replied to, no matter how humble the applicant. During those drives, His Holiness associates works of mercy with recreation—he visits the religious houses of recluses, to solicit their prayers, orphanages, to evince his interest for the children, and hospitals, to speak words of consolation, and urge motives of resignation, on the sick, and the dying. He every day makes a visit to the Blessed Sacrament—frequently visits the shrines of the Apostles; the other relics in St. Peter's, and those enshrined in other churches. On his return to the Vatican, or Quirinal, he again gives audiences to a late hour in the evening. Certain days in each week, and certain hours, are assigned to give audiences to the Cardinal Secretary of State, and to the Cardinal Prefects, and other state officers, who preside over the various ecclesiastical, civil, and military departments of the Church, and State—such as the Master of the Sacred Palace—the Prefect of the Propaganda—the Cardinal Prefect of the Congregation of the Council—of Briefs, of Public Works, the Minister of the Interior, of the Police, of the Finances, of Arms, Advocate of the Poor, Secretary of Latin Letters, of Rites, of Bishops and Regulars, of the Holy Office, the Cardinal Grand Penitentiary, and very, very many others. Add to these the audiences given to bishops, priests, strangers, and pilgrims, from all quarters of the world, and you will at once be convinced that every instant of the Pope's time is unceasingly occupied, and filled up with important business, to its utmost capacity.

The present Holy Father is a Pontiff of great erudition—he speaks the Latin language in quite a classic style,—and possesses great versatility in language. He can read, and speak with fluency, the French, German, and Spanish languages, and understands the English also tolerably well—he is an eminent antiquarian—is a good science scholar—and a zealous patron of the fine arts. He is gifted with an extraordinary memory, and after the lapse of years, will remember a person, who had a previous audience, of merely a few minutes' duration. All those who obtain the honour of an audience, appear in the Pope's presence in the full dress of the Roman court—the wearing of gloves on the occasion is prohibited. On entering the hall of audience, each visitor kneels three times before he approaches the person of His Holiness, and then bows down to kiss his foot, which he extends. In the instance of protestant, or non-catholic visitors, His Holiness usually waves his hand, to signify he then dispenses with that ceremony. The language spoken during the audience, is the Italian—and if the visitor do not understand that language, it is required that he should be accompanied by an approved interpreter, lest any expression might subsequently be misinterpreted. Each visitor remains until the Pope delicately signifies, that the audience has terminated—he then kneels, and retires, walking backwards, as it were a violation of etiquette, should the visitor turn his back on His Holiness.

He rarely attends the councils of ministers, but all the measures adopted by them, are submitted for his approval, by the Secretary of State, who is at present Cardinal Antonelli, in whose administration the Holy Father has un-

MONSIGNOR DE MERODE.

bounded confidence. The Pope's civil list amounts to about 3,500,000 frs., which is in our money £140,000. Out of this sum, the Pope supports the Nuncios at foreign courts—gives to some cardinals residing in Rome, annually, 22,000 frs.— £880—pays his "camerieri"—and pays the Palatine Guard, the Noble Guard—supports his household, his horses, and a large staff of domestics—and keeps up the Vatican Palace —a palace which contains 4,000 rooms, and occupies, with its gardens, the same area as the city of Turin.

The Pope is fond of enjoying agreeable conversation after dinner, and appreciates an amusing anecdote. Monsignor de Merode, to whom his Holiness is much attached, entertains him in that way sometimes. Monsignor Xavier de Merode, who is the son of Count Ghistain, Marquis of Westerloo, was born 1820. He is brother-in-law to Count Montalembert, who was married to his sister, Anne de Merode. He was a Belgian officer, attached to the staff of Marshal Bugeaud, and fought with the French army, during the campaigns in Africa, and for his distinguished services in the field, was decorated with the cross of the Legion of Honour. Subsequently he resigned his commission, and retired from the army, and entered the ecclesiastical state, and eventually was appointed by Pope Pius IX. Minister of War, in the Papal Government. One evening during the centenary, he amused the Pope with this anecdote. An ecclesiastic who came to Rome to the fêtes, and who professed to know more of antiquities than his colleagues, undertook to become "cicerone" to a party of priests, and other friends, who wished to visit the Coliseum. Whilst there, he pointed out the particular part of the Coliseum, upon which Nero usually stood, when he viewed and enjoyed the sufferings of the martyred Christians, and the dying gladiators! The Pope laughed heartily,—as everyone knows, that the Coliseum was not built till after the death of Nero—that it was erected on Nero's gardens —that the first stone was laid by Vespasian, in the year A.D. 72—and that it was advanced and dedicated by Titus A.D. 80, ten years after the destruction of Jerusalem—and was completed by Domitian.

He assigns certain hours, at which he punctually recites

the divine office, and employs his soul in other devotional exercises. His Holiness takes his evening refection at 7 o'clock. After a day, every hour of which is occupied in important, and anxious duties, and filled with good works, he retires to pray, and then retires to rest, at 10 o'clock. His chamber, and private study, and sitting-rooms, are furnished with the most monastic simplicity.

The pontificate of our Holy Father Pope Pius IX. will be a memorable one indeed—for the consummate wisdom and prudence displayed, in all the ecclesiastical, political, and diplomatic relations of the Holy See, with the great powers of the world—for the formidable bulwark he erected, in opposition to the assaults of error, and revolution—for his support of the true liberties of the great human family, under every government—for the heroic defence of the States of the Church, and the temporal power—for the diffusion of knowledge, and education, and the patronage of science, and the fine arts—for the definition of the dogma of the Immaculate Conception—for the number of saints canonized—for the triumphant progress of religion over the world, more especially over the vast regions of America—for the concentration of the sympathies of all Christendom, and the vast concourse of the faithful, and the number of priests, and prelates, who have converged on Rome, for the august celebration of this centenary—and for the announcement of his intention, to convene a General Council. The lengthened pontificate of Pope Pius IX., even already one of the longest since the days of Peter, will assuredly occupy the brightest page in ecclesiastical history—whilst for the sanctity of his life, the munificence with which his finances were devoted to the succour of suffering nations—the tender solicitude with which he visited the prisoner, alleviated the pangs of the suffering, and smoothed the pillow of the dying—charity, and religion, will present his Holiness the palm, and crown him as their most distinguished patron.

Thus "ordinatione tua perseverat dies," the Pope's day of life goeth on, till his day too decline, and another link be added to that continuous chain of succession, which unites the last Pope with Peter, and through him with Christ. Few pontificates have been more eventful, and experienced more bitter trials to the Church—but amidst all the fluctuating vicissitudes, and revolutionary convulsions, the Holy Father evinced magnanimous fortitude, and with imperturbable serenity, and equanimity of mind, watched with the same unceasing, uniform, solicitude, over the interests of the Church. Then faithful passengers in the ship of holy Church,—though the tempest rage, and the waves roll mountains high!—and the ship appear in danger!—be calm—under such a pilot you are secure—" Why are you fearful, O ye of little faith?" (Matt. viii. 26.)

Events during the Festivities.

Quæ? .... Tu solus peregrinus es in Jerusalem, et non cognovisti, quæ facta in illa his diebus?—St. Luke, xxviii. 18.

"What events? .... Art thou only a stranger in Jerusalem, and hast not known the things that have been done there in these days?"

THE celebration of the eighteenth centenary of the martyrdom of St. Peter, and St. Paul, has marked an era, and will ever be recorded, as the most memorable event in the ecclesiastical history of modern times. As the period for the celebration of the memorable event approached, multitudes from all quarters of the world poured into Rome, in one continuous torrent, and in continually increasing numbers. It was expected that a large number of visitors would arrive, but the numbers far exceeded the anticipations of the most sanguine. On my arrival at the terminus, whilst waiting for my luggage, trains from Florence arrived at the station, conveying no less a number than 1,700 passengers.

The most perfect organization, and police regulations, were established for the preservation of good order; and every precaution which prudence could suggest, was adopted by the military authorities, to repulse any hostile invasion of the Papal territories, during the festivities, by the Italian revolutionary party of action, which was at that time much apprehended. The Holy Father, with his usual paternal solicitude, anticipating that an extraordinary increase of military duty, would be imposed upon the soldiers during the fêtes, signified his wish, that during their continuance the soldiers should receive double pay. The officials of the Exchequer respectfully asked his Holiness where the finances were to be procured; and how such would be compatible with payments in other departments of the State. The Holy Father replied: "Even at a sacrifice to myself, let the soldiers receive double pay."

The municipality have evinced great munificence, in allocating large sums of money to impart brilliancy to the fêtes, both in the intended unusual splendour of the "Girandola," and the illuminations, as well as in the abundant distribution of alms to the poor of the city. The Roman princes have determined on giving public entertainments—horse-races, balloon ascents, and concerts for the amusement of the people. Directions were given that the museums, picture-galleries, libraries, palaces, and all places of public interest, whether devotional, artistic, literary, or antique, should be thrown open to all visitors. The churches of Rome, though four hundred in number, and many of them containing very many chapels, and altars, were found insufficient to afford facilities to the thousands of priests, who daily solicited accommodation, to celebrate the divine mysteries, and it became necessary to erect temporary altars in addition; and the Holy Father granted to all, the privilege of saying Mass, at any hour, from two o'clock in the morning till two in the afternoon. Even with all these provisions, many were obliged to wait for a considerable time, every morning. Books were laid on the vestry tables, and each priest on entering wrote his name, and said his Mass in that order of rotation. To ascertain the precise number of priests in the city, was difficult; but some days previously to St. Peter's day, the number of letters of permission to say Mass, issued by the vicariate, was 21,884—but many more were subsequently issued, and many priests obtained permission from the generals of religious orders, or from the superiors of religious houses, and colleges; so that it is very probable the entire number of priests in the city, on the memorable occasion, amounted to 25,000. The credentials, or letters presented at the vicariate, by all the priests who applied for permission to say Mass, were retained, and in exchange they received an official certificate. Many of the priests were very poor, and spent the little they possessed, on that journey to the shrines. Some time since, an inhabitant of Geneva, left to the Pope a bequest of 1,330 frs., as a yearly income for ever—this had accumulated, and the Holy Father now devoted it to the support of poor priests, coming to Rome during this month.

An American photographer applied for permission to collect, and publish, an album of portraits of the prelates who assisted at the centenary, with the Holy Father as a frontispiece. The permission was granted. Alessandri, the celebrated Roman photographer, previously obtained a similar permission, and the exquisite character of his artistic taste, and manipulation, can with difficulty be rivalled.

The number of applications for tickets to the reserved seats for the great functions in St. Peter's, became overwhelming, and although the "palchi" afforded accommodation to very many thousands, the applications exceeded four times the number of seats. Monsignor Talbot, Chamberlain to his Holiness, and brother of Lord Talbot of Malahide, with his usual urbanity, evinced the most courteous solicitude, in providing accommodation for all applicants from these countries.

June 17*th.*—The festivities of the centenary may be considered to have commenced on this day, on which was celebrated the 21st anniversary of the election and elevation of John Mary Mastai Ferretti, his Holiness Pope Pius IX., to the see of Peter, which occurred on the 17th June, 1846. At dawn of day a salvo of artillery was fired from the bastions of the Castle of San Angelo. A "capella Papale" was held at the Vatican, in the Sistine Chapel, and was attended by the cardinals, patriarchs, primates, archbishops, and bishops, superiors of colleges, and other distinguished personages. The solemn Mass was celebrated by his Eminence Cardinal Morichini, who was the second cardinal created by the present Pope.

Arrivals.

June 18th.—The number of prelates who have arrived is very great. There were fifteen bishops at the centenary from Ireland. His Grace the Cardinal Archbishop of Dublin; his Grace the Archbishop of Cashel, Dr. Leahy; Dr. Dorrian, Down and Connor; Dr. Conaty, Kilmore; Dr. Donnelly, Clogher; Dr. Nulty, Meath; Dr. Gillooly, Elphin; Dr. M'Evilly, Galway; Dr. Power, Killaloe; Dr. Butler, Limerick; Dr. O'Hea, Ross; Dr. O'Keane, Cloyne; Dr. Delany, Cork; Dr. Whelan, Bombay; Dr. Brady, Perth.

The cardinals, archbishops, and bishops of France, numbered sixty-three. Hungary was represented by ten bishops—distant Australia by two, Right Reverend Dr. Goold, and Dr. Shiel, Bishops of Melbourne and Adelaide; New Brunswick, North America, by Dr. Sweeney; New Chatham, by Dr. Rodgers—Canada by many prelates—the United States, by twenty-three Bishops—the Church of Madras, by Dr. Fennelly—Grahamstown, South Africa, by Dr. Moran; Glasgow, by Dr. Lynch; and Newfoundland, by Dr. Mullock; North and South America sent their Bishops; and China was represented at Rome by the Vicar-Apostolic of Nankin.

A few days since, the Spanish war frigate *St. Quintin* arrived at Civita Vecchia, conveying his Eminence the Cardinal Archbishop of Seville, and twenty-two bishops of Spain. They were received on landing by Monsignor Scapetta, who is the Apostolic Delegate of the province. He had carriages prepared for their conveyance, but they declined to enter them, saying they were pilgrims; and they walked to the church, where they heard Mass, celebrated by one of themselves; and thence they walked to the palace of the Delegate, who entertained them at breakfast. At a later period of the day, they were conveyed to Rome by a special train. The entire number of Spanish bishops arrived at Rome now amounts to thirty-five.

Very many of the cardinals, patriarchs, archbishops, and bishops, already arrived, occupied apartments prepared for them, either in the Papal palaces, or the palaces of some of the Italian princes, colleges, convents, and in the governmental establishments. The Holy Father has undertaken to extend his hospitalities, for the entire maintenance of two hundred bishops, which will probably cost his Holiness one million of francs. Ireland's only Cardinal, his Eminence Paul Cullen, Archbishop of Dublin, whose arrival in Rome is daily expected, will be accompanied by Monsignor Moran, a dignitary of great erudition, and author of several highly esteemed theological, and historical, works. His Eminence will reside at the Irish College, of which he had been president for very many years—a suite of rooms have been fitted up for his reception in princely style, through the solicitous attentions of the present Rector, Monsignor Kirby, D.D. The hospitalities of the Irish College of St. Agatha, always so generously dispensed to the Irish hierarchy, clergy, and other Irish residents in Rome, were, on this occasion, extended to the utmost limits of their capabilities, and accommodation. The Very Reverend Rector invited the Bishops of Meath, Dr. Nulty; of Down and Connor, Dr. Dorrian; of Cork, Dr. Delany; of Cloyne and of Ross, Dr. O'Keane, and Dr. O'Hea, to fix their residence in the Irish College, during their sojourn in Rome; and they availed themselves of the favour of the Monsignor's invitation. Dr. Fennelly, Vicar-Apostolic of Madras, and Dr. Moran, of Grahamstown, were favoured with similar invitations. St. Clement's exercised hospitality to Dr. Conaty of Kilmore, and to Dr. Brady. St. Isidore's entertained the Bishops of Newfoundland, and Adelaide, Dr. Mullock, and Dr. Shiel. Dr. Goold, of Melbourne, resided at St. Maria in Posterula. Dr. Butler, of Limerick, Dr. M'Evilly, of Galway, and Dr. Power, of Killaloe, reside at the Quirinal Palace, where apartments have been also reserved for the Primate, Most Rev. Dr. Kieran, on his expected arrival.

Peter Pence Offerings.

The several bishops of the different countries assembled at Rome, employed the occasion either of a private audience, or of a public audience given to all the bishops of a nation, to present the Pope with the munificent offerings of their faithful children, which they were commissioned to convey, and lay at the feet of their Holy Father. Those were tributes, not imposed on the people as a tax, nor extracted by compulsion, but the spontaneous tributes of reverential affection. The bishops of Canada, who came from beyond the seas, presented their people's tribute, in a silver ship of exquisite manipulation, fully rigged, with masts, shrouds, ropes, and every necessary nautical gear. The hull was freighted with a cargo of golden nuggets, and the passengers who crowded the first-class cabins were no others than sovereigns, or golden coins, with the very impress of royalty stamped upon their faces, just arrived from the mint! His Eminence the Cardinal Archbishop of Dublin, and the Irish prelates, were laden with the munificent offerings of Patrick's fervent disciples, to him, whose predecessor, Celestine, sent their Apostle from this very spot, to convey to them the more precious gift of faith. The English and Scotch prelates, presented ample testimonies of the invincible fidelity of British Catholics to Holy Faith and Peter's Chair. I was credibly informed that one English bishop presented the munificent sum of £100,000! The Archbishop of Mexico laid at the feet of the Holy Father the sum of 80,000 crowns. All the other bishops gave similar proofs of generosity and devotion to the Vicar of Christ. His Eminence Cardinal Mathieu, Archbishop of Besançon, presented a remonstrance of dazzling brilliancy, great height, and value, the disc of which was virgin gold, studded with rubies and diamonds of the purest water. One venerable pontiff, bent with a weight of years, whose bronzed complexion proved that the tropics marked him for their own, presented himself at the door of the audience chamber, with a stick in his hand. Monsignor Pacca politely signified to his lordship that it was contrary to the usages of the court to appear with a stick in presence of his Holiness. The Bishop still manifested a disposition to enter, but Monsignor Pacca was unyielding in his objection. The Pope heard of the difficulty, and directed that all the obstacles of court etiquette should yield before the Bishop's wishes. His lordship, on being introduced, presented the stick to the Holy Father, saying that that was all that he and his flock could afford as their humble offering. The Pope took the stick in his hand, and found it was a bar of the purest gold ! The accumulated sums presented by all amounted in the aggregate to twelve million francs, being little less than half a million of pounds sterling—the largest amount—the noblest tribute of affection, loyalty, and veneration—ever laid at the feet of mortal man !

Laudatory addresses, and presentations of silver and gold, are frequently offered to exalted and distinguished personages, as tributes of fame to perpetuate their celebrity; but the offerings of those Catholic prelates to the Vicar of Christ, were the external marks of that bond of unity, and that internal charity, by which all the dispersed members of the great Christian family, were united under the one head, and Father of the faithful. Worldlings may regard silver and gold as glittering and precious treasures, but when we contrast them with that exalted moral signification, with the treasures of Catholic unity and charity, which those offerings were intended to symbolize, then we regard the weight of those metals but as the down of a feather, and all their glittering and value, but as dull and worthless clods of clay ! We read that the ark of old, which enclosed the tables of the law, was covered with the skins of wild animals, to preserve it from external injury, as well as from the cupidity of the avaricious, rendering its appearance rough, and uncouth, to the strange tribes through whose country it passed, on its transit through the desert. But when placed in the sanctuary, those skins were removed, and then it displayed a covering of the most valuable, highly polished, and odoriferous woods, mounted with massive gold, and studded with precious stones. The gold and silver offerings of the prelates at the centenary, were but the coverings of the fealty and charity of the Catholic world ; and when they arrived in the sanctuary of the Vatican, in presence of the great high priest, and that these coverings were taken off, and laid at his Holiness' feet, they appeared more worthless in comparison with this unity, catholicity, and charity, which were then displayed, than did even the skins of old, when compared with the ark they covered !

FEAST OF ST. ALOYSIUS. 47

June 19*th*.—On this evening the first vespers of the great solemnity of Corpus Christi were solemnly chanted in the Vatican Basilica.

June 20*th*.—This was the solemn feast of Corpus Christi, and was celebrated with the grand procession, and usual august ceremonies, commencing at eight o'clock. In the processions on this solemnity, the Holy Father is usually conveyed on a low carriage; on this occasion, however, his Holiness walked in the procession, whilst bearing the Most Holy. The functions were attended by his Majesty the ex-King of the Two Sicilies—the Queen Dowager—the Princes of the Royal Family—her Royal Highness Donna Isabella Maria, the Infanta of Portugal—by all the ambassadors, cardinals, bishops, religious orders—and by an immense concourse of the faithful. Three hundred and three bishops assisted.

June 21*st*.—This was the twenty-first anniversary of the Pope's coronation, which took place on the 21st June, 1846. At early morning a Papal salute of 101 guns, was fired from the guns of the Castle of San Angelo. At ten o'clock, a "capella Papale" was held in the Sistine Chapel. The solemn Mass was celebrated by his Eminence Cardinal Mathieu, who was the first cardinal created by the present Pope. Immediately after, the Holy Father was received in the Royal Hall, by a dense crowd of dignitaries, with the most enthusiastic demonstrations of joyfulness. All pressed forward to express their warmest congratulations. Amongst the exalted personages who presented their reverential respects, were, his Majesty the ex-King of the Two Sicilies—Count Trapani—the ambassadors of foreign powers—the ministers of state—the princes assisting at the throne—superiors of colleges—the members of the municipality of Rome, who, in the person of the senator, expressed the attachment, and fidelity, of the people of Rome, to the see, person, and throne of his Holiness—the Noble Guard—the Generalissimo, or Commander of the Forces, General Kanzler, on the part of the army—and the officers of the Swiss Guards, and of the Palatine Guard, and many other dignitaries and officials.

The feast of St. Aloysius was celebrated with extraordinary splendour in the Church of St. Ignatius. The church was illuminated, and draped in graceful festoons of silk and gold lace. The ceremonies were very solemn, and the music of the most exquisite character. The ornaments of the shrines and altar of the saint, were of gold, silver, porcelain, and precious gems, and were gorgeous and glittering; and the marble basso-relievo, by Le Gros, never appeared more effective. A marble monument to Pope Gregory XV., by the same sculptor, stands near this altar. A young Jesuit, of grave, pious, and modest mein, evincing all the amenities of refined politeness and education, and of engaging appearance, a relative of the present Pope, introduced me into the room in which St. Aloysius lived and died, and from which he stepped to the threshold of heaven. He also showed me, in the adjoining oratory, the picture of the Madonna, before which the holy youth pronounced his vows. He also did me the honour of introducing me to the two celebrated Jesuit theologians, Padre Peronne, and Padre Cardella. Padre Cardella speaks the English language with great accuracy and fluency. At the Chamber of Commerce, a dowry was conferred on two young women, who were chosen by lot. In the same place there was a lottery, the proceeds of which were distributed amongst the poor.

Review of the Papal Troops.

In the evening there was a review of the Papal troops, numbering 12,000 men, in the Villa Borghese, by General Kanzler, and many general officers. The troops that formed line on the inspection ground, consisted of a battalion of the "Cacciatori," the rifle brigade, commanded by the distinguished officer, Lieutenant-Colonel Giorgi—the French regiment of the "Antibes Legion," commanded by Colonel Count D'Argy—ten companies of the "Carbinieri," the Carbineers, commanded by a brave veteran of the Holy See, Lieutenant-Colonel Jeannerat—three battalions of the line, each battalion containing eight companies, commanded by the hero of Castelfidardo, Colonel Azzanesi—one regiment of the Christian heroes, the "Zouaves," formed of fourteen companies, of 160 men each, commanded by Colonel Allet, so highly lauded in the dispatches of General Lamoriciere—

the "Grenattieri"—the grenadiers—one legion of the horse and foot "Gendarmea," numbering 2,000 men, and who are drilled to "line service," and commanded by Colonel Evangelisti—a corps of engineers under the command of Lieutenant-Colonel Laura—the cavalry regiment, "Dragoni Pontefici," the "Pope's own"—the "Scelta Compagnia," the chosen band—the "Caribinieri a Cavallo," the mounted carabineers—three batteries of artillery, supplied with rifled cannon, and mortars, and equipped with some very small but very efficient hand cannon, introduced by the Papal war department—there was a military train, and ambulance service. There was a corps of veterans, and other military contingents. The troops were armed with the "Stuttzen" gun, and the terrible sword bayonet. The guns have been lately superseded, by the most improved description of breech-loaders. The "Pompieri," the fire brigade, was not on the ground, nor the "Guardia del Senato," the Palatine Guard. The Noble Guard and the "Svizeri," the Swiss Guards, being household troops, and guards of honour to the Pope, are not subject to the ordeal of reviews. The commander-in-chief, his Excellency General Kanzler, was received with the usual salute, and amongst the officers of his staff rôde General Count de Courten, and General Marquis Zappi. The troops then deployed, and were put through a variety of manœuvres, which they executed with celerity and precision. There was no firing. The infantry, cavalry, and artillery, marched and countermarched, trotted and galloped by wings, and sections, wheeled into line, changed front to left, reformed column, retired, charged, fell back again by fours, changed position by wings, threw out skirmishers, were recalled, retired on columns, and after a variety of skilful moves, finally formed line with the artillery on the flanks, advanced in parade order, and gave the salute, the sun gleaming, accoutrements glittering, colours flying, and bands playing.

The "march past" was brilliant, and displayed a high condition of military discipline, and careful drilling. The order of precedence, was quite the reverse of that observed by British troops—with us, precedence is taken by the various batteries of field and horse artillery—next in order follow the heavy dragoons, the light dragoons, the guards, or household troops, and the various regiments of the line. Here the order was the contrary. When each band advanced it took "the left wheel," drew up in position before the General, and played whilst the regiment marched between, the General saluting the colours. The infantry marched in open quarter-distance columns; the step was steady and well-timed, the distances well preserved, and the lines well "dressed." The cavalry passed in "squadrons," and "columns of troops,"—the horses were small, but in good condition. The brigades of field artillery, and all the batteries, were very well appointed, and in very efficient condition. The martial music was very superior, and thrilling. The crowds were most overwhelmingly numerous, and, amongst other distinguished personages, I observed Monsignor Dupanloup. Some officers of the Irish Brigade still continue in the Papal service, and the gallantry, and distinguished services of Major O'Reilly, M.P., and his brother officers, and non-commissioned officers, and men, of the brave old Irish Brigade, will be long remembered, and appreciated by the Roman army. The spirit of discipline, magnanimity, and heroic bravery with which the Papal troops fought during the recent revolutionary war, and the signal victories they achieved, over the enemies of justice, and order, have crowned the Papal arms with military glory—but they have won a higher crown—they fought for the Holy Father, for religion, and for God—and God was for them, and "when God is for us, who shall be against us ?" Even Voltaire says that an army that fights for God is invincible ! All the streets and public buildings were brilliantly illuminated, after nightfall.

June 22nd.—On this day, at noon, his Eminence Cardinal Louis de la Lastra e Cuesta, Archbishop of Seville, was introduced into the pontifical apartments, by the Secretary of State, Cardinal Antonelli, where his Eminence was received in state in the throne-room by the Holy Father. On this day a telegram from Ireland to the Cardinal Archbishop of Dublin, arrived at Rome, announcing the death of the

Right Rev. Dr. Kilduff, Bishop of Ardagh. His lordship intended assisting at the celebration of the centenary, but was summoned to another "Eternal City," to celebrate it with St. Peter and St. Paul.

June 23rd.—On this day the Church of Santa Maria delli Angeli e Martiri, was consecrated by his Eminence the titular of the church, Cardinal Carafa de Traetto—all the bishops in Rome assisted at the function. This church is a portion of the ancient baths of Diocletian, and was adapted to its present sacred purpose, according to designs of Michael Angelo. On this spot, during the persecutions of Diocletian, forty thousand Christians shed their blood for Christ, and won the crown of martyrdom. Here are deposited the remains of the two great painters, Carlo Maratta, and Salvator Rosa ; and here stands the wonderful statue of St. Bruno, by Houdon, which is so lifelike, that Pope Clement XIV. said, " He would speak, were it not that his rule prescribed silence !"

ST. JOHN LATERAN'S—CARDINAL ALTIERI.

June 24th.—A "capella Papale" was held at St. John Lateran's. All the cardinals, princes, bishops, and dignitaries were present. The equipages were numberless and the pageantry was gorgeous. A vast concourse of people lined every avenue to the Basilica ; and on going and returning, the demonstrations of veneration, from the prostrate multitudes, overpowered the feelings of the Holy Father, who blessed the people as he passed in his brilliant equipages, surrounded by his guards of honour. Immediately after the Gospel of the Mass, the panegyric of the saint was delivered by M. Padre Giannobili, of the Roman College. The solemn Mass was celebrated by the Arch-priest of the Basilica, Cardinal Lewis Altieri, Archbishop of Albano. Alas ! he is no more ! Since then his Eminence departed this life a martyr of charity, under circumstances which surround his memory with a halo, that will long illustrate the Church. Not many weeks after the celebration of the centenary, a fearful visitation of cholera devastated the town of Albano, of which he was Archbishop. The good pastor was in Rome, but instantly hurried to the relief of his afflicted flock. This illustrious cardinal, the hereditary prince of the Altieri family, abandoned his palace for the dwellings of the plague—distributed his fine linen draperies to warm the limbs of the shivering—gave out the generous juices of his cellars, to propel vigour through bloodless arteries! We learn that his Eminence rose from velvet cushions, to support the head of the languishing, and to touch the gelid skin of the collapsed patient—that he left his mosaic pavement, to walk to the distempered, in his bare and tender feet, over the sharp stones of Albano, to appease the anger of the Omnipotent Avenger—and that he turned his eyes from the glowing portraits by Vandyke and Titian, to look benignly on the upturned gaze of the expiring—on the glaring eyes and pallid brow, the sunken cheeks, and livid hue, of the cholera victim! God accepted the sacrifice of the good shepherd's life for his people!—changed his downy couch for the grave—the bricks and mortar of the Altieri Palace, for a throne of sapphires, in the heavenly Jerusalem! "O death, where is thy victory? O death, where is thy sting?" His Eminence was sixty-two years of age—was consecrated Archbishop of Albano in the year 1840—and he was the last cardinal created by our late Most Holy Father of happy memory, Pope Gregory XVI.

June 25th.—On this day, according to previous announcement, all the priests in Rome assembled at the Vatican, in expectation of being received by the Pope. I was astounded at the vast concourse. Ten thousand obtained admission to the Hall of Consistories over the vestibule of St. Peter's, where the reception was to take place—but as many additional thousands were unable to obtain access. The hall was densely crowded, the heat excessive. The Holy Father entered, surrounded by his ministers of state—he read an allocution—the priests sang *Salvum fac Pontificem et Regem*, and the prayer for the Father of the faithful—they then defiled before him, and he gave them the Papal benediction as they passed. It was intended that his Holiness should present each with a printed copy of his allocution, and a medal, but the number of priests was so unexpectedly overwhelming, it was found impossible to strike off a sufficient number in time for distribution on that day. At this time a large steamship arrived at Civita Vecchia, conveying a great number of the members of the Society of St. Vincent de Paul, so precious to the Church, since those gentlemen, "urged by the charity of God," to exemplify, in their sanctified lives, every Christian virtue and work of mercy, desired to yield to none, in evincing their attachment, and veneration, to the person of the Sovereign Pontiff, and to the See of Peter.

Amongst the arrivals already announced were, his Grace Henry Edward Manning, Archbishop of Westminster—the Bishops of Birmingham and Beverley, who are residing at the English College; and Monsignor Dupanloup, who is the guest of the Prince Borghese. Monsignor Flavius Peter Matah, Bishop of Yesir, of the Syrian Rite; and Monsignor Languillot, Bishop of Serziopolis, and Prefect Apostolic of Nankin, have also arrived. Monsignor Languillot had never seen the Pope before, and was introduced by Cardinal Barnabo. He prostrated himself at the threshold, with tears of devotion trickling down his cheeks, and cried out, *Tu es Petrus*—" Thou art Peter!" The Syrian Bishop, on being introduced, saluted his Holiness according to the eastern custom. First, prostrating himself, then rising, took the Pope's hands in both of his, raised them to his head, in token of submission, then to his lips, then to his heart, signifying that in all he could do, speak, or think, he professed to be his Holiness' most submissive docile son. The ambassadors, and the entire diplomatic corps, were continually on the "qui vive" to obtain information, and convey the earliest intelligence to their various courts, of every ecclesiastical or political movement that may be projected by the Pope, cardinals, and bishops. The number of priests I met in the churches, palaces, museums, and the "trattorias," and in the streets, astonished me—chiefly French, in their soutanes, sashes, and cocked hats; other priests, from Lombardy, and Germany, wore round hats, black coats, and long clerical boots, such as were formerly worn by the priests in Ireland.

The College of the Propaganda.

EUNTES ERGO DOCETE OMNES GENTES.—MATT. xxviii. 19.
"*Going therefore teach ye all nations.*"

THE Sacred College of Cardinals manifested the deepest interest in the celebration of the centenary, and by the large number of its members that assembled in Rome round the Sovereign Pontiff, by their courteous attentions and hospitalities to distinguished strangers, the splendour of their equipages, by throwing open to visitors, all the institutions of art, or interest, under their control, and their constant attendance at all the processions, and solemn functions, evinced the most ardent zeal to employ every effort that could impart interest, edification, and brilliancy to the grand festivities. But if any one cardinal, more than another, could be regarded as pre-eminently distinguished for this interest, and solicitude, it was Allessandro Cardinal Barnabo. His Eminence is Prefect of the Congregation "de Propaganda Fide," which governs and bears the solicitudes of all the churches of the world, in missionary countries. This grand gathering, then, of pontiffs and people, from the most distant regions, was peculiarly his own festival—the children assembling round their father in their hereditary residence, and encircling their family hearth! Allessandro Barnabo was born at Foligno, in the year 1800, and after a distinguished collegiate career, was ordained, and occupied many most important and confidential positions, and was for a long time Secretary to the Congregation of Propaganda. He was eventually elevated to the cardinalate by our present Most Holy Father, and proclaimed on the 16th of June, 1856; and on the death of the venerated Cardinal Fransoni, whose memory is so endeared to the Irish Church, was appointed Prefect of the Congregation " de Propaganda Fide." This Congregation was originally instituted by Pope Gregory XV., and is justly regarded as one of the most important in the government of the Church. The Cardinal Prefect resides in the College of the " Propaganda." This College is sometimes called the " Urban College," as it was established by Pope Urban VIII., who, in the year 1627, published the bull " Immortalis Dei," constituting it an apostolic seminary, for the education of ecclesiastics from, and for, every missionary country. The building was formerly the Ferratina Palace, which, in the year 1606, was purchased by a zealous Spanish nobleman, of the name of Monsignor John Baptist Vives, who was minister of Isabella Chiara, Infanta of Spain, and Governor of Flanders, and devoted by him to the noble object it has so efficiently promoted. Since then, however, the edifice has been considerably enlarged and beautified, after the designs of Bernini. The government of the College was at first committed to a certain number of canons, and Padre Martha, a Theatine, was the first Rector: it was, however, withdrawn from their management by Pope Urban, and, in 1641, by the bull " Romanus Pontifex," was entirely subjected to the jurisdiction of the Congregation of " de Propaganda Fide." The Rector is "parochus" of the College, by the ordinance of Pope Clement XI. The rules which guide the studies and discipline of the College, were drawn up in the year 1732, and finally sanctioned by Pope Clement XII. The endowments which maintain the College amount annually to £8,000. The students are educated, and supported, and forwarded to their distant missions, free of all expense; and at the time of the centenary they numbered 118, and represented very many foreign countries, climes, features, complexions, rites, and languages. The Rector was then the prudent, learned, sanctified, and venerated Canon Tancioni.

The priests educated in this College are bound by oath to stability in their respective missions, and make an annual report of their proceedings, and the success of their labours; and their number all over the world was then 450. The museum contains many objects of the deepest interest, and the library contains 45,000 volumes, in every language; and the printing press and publishing department, under the direction of Don Pietro Marietti, of Turin, have issued books, which, for the exquisite character of paper, typography, and binding, have been unrivalled in the world, and won the prizes at the great London and Dublin Exhibitions; and these successful specimens were afterwards liberally presented by the Pope to our Cardinal Archbishop, and to the Catholic University, where they may now be seen, and will delight every visitor of taste. The College possesses a beautiful villa, at Montalto, near Frascati, where the students enjoy their annual vacation during the summer months—it was formerly the Odescalchi Palace. During the French Revolution, and in the year 1798, the College of the Propaganda suffered severely—the students were dispersed—some were imprisoned—the property confiscated—and, amongst other depredations, the invaders carried off twenty-five founts of rare and valuable type, in letters of twenty-five different languages! This is no very convincing proof that the obstacles to progress, education, and learning, are erected on the side of the Catholic Church! This College has rendered inestimable services to the foreign missions, and given to the Church many distinguished, learned, zealous, and sanctified ecclesiastics, some of whom had the honour of suffering for the name of Christ, sealed their faith with their blood, and won the palm of victory—it has given an Archbishop to Dublin—an Apostolic Delegate to Ireland—a Cardinal to the universal Church, in the person of his Eminence Paul Cardinal Cullen.

The Cardinal Archbishop of Dublin.

His Eminence was born on the 29th of April, in the year 1804—received his primary education at Mr. Sheckleton's seminary near Ballitore, famous for the many celebrated characters who there made their early studies, amongst them was Edmund Burke. He was afterwards transferred to the solicitous care, of the superiors of St. Patrick's College, Carlow, the nursery of learning, and of every virtue. Here he became quite a favourite, with the great Bossuet of the age, the renowned J. K. L., Right Rev. Dr. Doyle. In the year 1820, his Eminence left Ireland, and entered the Propaganda College—he was ordained priest in 1829—succeeded Dr. Boylan, and Dr. Blake, as President of the Irish College at Rome—became successively Professor, and Rector of the Propaganda. He was honoured with the esteem and confidence of the late Pope Gregory XVI. He was consecrated Archbishop of Armagh, by Cardinal Castracani, and appointed Apostolic Delegate in 1850—was translated to Dublin on the 3rd of May, in the year 1852—was created cardinal by Pope Pius IX., under the title of San Pietro in Montorio, on the 22nd of June, 1866.

At the time of a former visit I made to Rome, in the year 1845, the Rector of the College of the Propaganda, was Padre Rillo. He was a Jesuit Father, and laboured much and effectively, to extend the kingdom of Christ. In his labours of zeal, and love for souls, he penetrated into Persia, and Abyssinia. He and his heroic companions were forwarded in two ships, chartered by the Austrian branch of the Society for the Propagation of the Faith. He was accompanied by a magnanimous Propagandist, named Father Knobliger. They established a mission far up on the banks of the Nile, at a place called Cartoun, in Upper Egypt. Here they purchased the freedom of many slaves and their children—instructed them in the rudiments of Faith—baptized them—and sent them to an establishment in Leghorn, where they were educated, and became edifying Christians. Padre Rillo was succeeded as Rector, by another Jesuit, distinguished for his profound learning in theology, ecclesiastical history, and all the polite literature of the age—he was the author of many valued works, amongst others, of "Lionello," and "The Jew of Verona"—his name was Padre Bresciani. Both those Fathers have since then gone to join the members of "the society," who "sit under the shadow of Him whom they desired!"—*Sub umbra illius quem desideraveram sidi!*

During the centenary, thirty-six of the former students, from all quarters of the globe, re-assembled in its halls, of whom twenty-three were priests, and thirteen were bishops, including the Cardinal Archbishop of Dublin, the Armenian, Maronite, and Melchite Patriarchs; the Archbishops of Marden, Tarnovia, Arichat, Antivari, and Baltimore. Amongst the distinguished assemblage, was his Eminence Cardinal Reisach, who formerly was Rector of the College—and is connected by consanguinity with the noblest blood of Bavaria—he is a cardinal of profound learning—possesses many accomplishments—and speaks the English language with the accuracy and elegance of a native of the British isles. There were also present Monsignor Capalte—and the learned Irish Benedictine, Very Rev. Professor Don Bernardo Smith, a native of Cavan—a distinguished theologian, ecclesiastical historian, and antiquarian, who was long a Benedictine Father of the great monastery of Monte Casino, and at present, is associated with the Fathers of St. Calistus', at Rome; and also Professor Conti, and the other learned professors—and they were all received with courtesy and joy, by the hospitable, noble-minded, and paternal Cardinal Barnabo. Some of those who here once were young, but who now were advanced in years, at the close of life's labours, wished to remain and die there—*Mane nobiscum quoniam advesperascit* (Luke, xxiv. 29). "Stay with us, because it is towards evening!" But Christ wished them—*longius ire*—"to go farther!"—and they went!

June 26th.—A public consistory was held in the Hall of Consistories. In it the Holy Father conferred the red hat on his Eminence Cardinal Louis de la Lastra e Cuesta, Archbishop of Seville, who was created and proclaimed cardinal at the consistory held on the 16th of March, 1863. After the ceremony his Eminence drove in state to St. Peter's. During the consistory, the Consistorial Advocate, Monsignor Ralli, pleaded, for the second time, the cause for the beatification of Venerable Mother Mary Rivier, foundress of the Sisters of the Presentation.

The Pope's Allocution to the Assembled Bishops.

ET CONVENIENTES APOSTOLI AD JESUM, RENUNTIAVERUNT EI OMNIA, QUÆ EGERANT ET DOCUERUNT. ET AIT ILLIS: VENITE SEORSUM IN DESERTUM LOCUM ET REQUESCITE PUSILLUM . . . ET CŒPIT ILLOS DOCERE MULTA.—MARK, vi. 30, 31, 34.

"*And the Apostles coming together unto Jesus, related to him all things that they had done and taught. And he said to them: Come apart into a desert place, and rest a little . . . . and he began to teach them many things.*"

ON this day the Pope invited all the bishops at Rome, to assemble in the Sistine Chapel, in the Vatican. His Holiness, on ascending the throne, was received with the most profound respect and veneration, by the assembled prelates. He addressed to them an allocution—expressed his pleasure at seeing them assemble, in such large numbers, from the most distant regions of the world, around the shrines of the Apostles—and in witnessing the proofs of unity, catholicity, and vitality, in Holy Church, which such a demonstration presented to the world. The Holy Father expressed his intention of convening an œcumenical council, an announcement which was received with enthusiastic and respectful manifestations of joyfulness, by that venerable assemblage.

The number of bishops who received the Pope in the Vatican on that memorable day, was five hundred and six.

With the exception of some very few occasions, this was the largest number that had ever assembled since the foundation of the Church. The most intense anxiety was evinced by the bishops, the city of Rome, the ambassadors representing foreign courts, and the entire Christian world, to hear the terms in which the Holy Father would address that most august assembly. The sentiments and words, constituted a discourse fully equal to the importance of the occasion, and exceeded the most sanguine expectations— it was grand—it was sublime—it was drank in with avidity by every ear in silent rapture. He spoke in the Latin language. The following, in an English version, is the purport of the allocution of the Holy Father :—

VENERABLE BRETHREN,
It is a singular pleasure and consolation to Us, amid our great sorrows, once more to enjoy your welcome presence, to see so many of you here, and to address you in this august assembly. You have been brought to this city, from all parts of the world, by the expression of Our desire, and by the instinct of your piety ; and eminent as you are by your religion, and called as you are to share Our solicitude, you have no dearer object than to lend Us every assistance in these days of calamity for the defence of the Catholic cause, and for the salvation of souls, to assuage Our manifold afflictions, and to afford even nobler proofs of your fidelity, your good-will, and your obedience towards this Chair of Peter. We are deeply rejoiced at beholding you, and this new mark and proof of your piety and affection recalls the pleasing remembrance of all those proofs, which, up to this day, you rivalled one another in giving with such unanimity, with such diversified good offices, without ever relaxing your zeal, without ever losing heart in adversity. The sweet remembrance of these things is deeply impressed on Our soul, and will for ever dwell there, and it causes Our grateful affection, far more glowing and vivid now than heretofore, to insist upon openly and publicly manifesting itself towards your whole order, by a conspicuous attestation and by the most striking proofs.

But if this remembrance of other days, thus slightly and

briefly alluded to, so moves and consoles Us, you will easily understand, Venerable Brethren, with what joy our heart exults, with what love it burns to-day, when We once more reap the benefit of your devotion, and see how many of you, on the intimation of Our desire, have come to Us from the remotest parts of Christendom, all under the impulsion of a common piety and affection.

Nothing can be more desirable and more pleasing to Us, than to find Ourselves among you, and to enjoy the benefit of your co-operation with Us in the performance of those solemn rites in which everything that meets the eye speaks of the unity of the Catholic Church, of the immovable foundation of that unity, and of the noble desire and glory of defending and preserving it. This is that admirable unity, by which, as through a vein, the graces and gifts of the Divine Spirit flow into the mystical body of Christ, and excite in each of its members those wondrous proofs of faith and love, which command the admiration of the whole human race. For the work now in hand, Venerable Brethren, is to decree the honours of the Saints to many illustrious heroes of the Church, most of whom, fighting the glorious fight of martyrdom, have gladly sought and obtained a precious death, some for the defence of the supremacy of the Apostolic See, in which is the centre of truth and unity, some for the maintenance of the integrity and unity of the Faith, some for restoring to the Catholic Church men who had been torn from her by schism; that so the wondrous design of Divine Providence may be shown forth, which gave these examples of attachment to Catholic Unity, and these triumphs to its adherents, when the Catholic Faith, and the authority of the Apostolic See, were most violently assailed by the machinations of enemies. We have also to celebrate, by a solemn rite, the memory of that auspicious day, on which the blessed Apostle Peter and his co-Apostle Paul, eighteen hundred years ago, fulfilled in this city their illustrious martyrdom, and consecrated by their blood the immovable citadel of Catholic Unity. And what could we more desire, Venerable Brethren, and what could be more congruous to the triumphs of so many martyrs, than that, in the honours paid to them, the fairest proofs and evidences of Catholic Unity, should be made to shine with the greatest significance and brilliancy? What could be more meet than that this rejoicing over the triumphs of the Princes of the Apostles, which is a part of the religion of all Catholics, should be enhanced by your presence and zeal? What could be more fitting than that the splendour of so many, and such great events, should be made more glorious by the addition of your piety and your joy?

But, Venerable Brethren, your piety and cordial union with the Apostolic See, are not only apt to the times and pleasing to Us, but they are a thing of such moment, that very great, and very salutary fruits must necessarily spring from them, both towards the repression of the audacity of the impious, and towards the common advantage of the faithful and of each of you. It cannot be but that the enemies of religion must perceive from them, how the Catholic Church flourishes and what vitality it has, while they cease not to pursue her with enmity. They must needs perceive how vainly, and foolishly, they railed against her, as if her strength were exhausted, and her time past. They must needs learn how ill-advised they are to applaud their own triumphs, and to trust in their own devices and efforts, when they see that it is impossible to rend asunder this union of forces, which the spirit and divine virtue of Jesus Christ, have concreted together in the rock of the Apostolical Confession. Surely, Venerable Brethren, now, if ever, it must needs be clear to all, that souls can be held together in close conjunction only when one and the same Spirit of God dominates in all; but that when God is forsaken, and the authority of the Church despised, men miss the happiness which they seek by crime, and are miserably tossed by angry storms and dissensions.

On the other hand, Venerable Brethren, if We look to the common advantage of the faithful, what can be more opportune and more useful, to increase the obedience of Catholic nations to Us, and the Apostolic See, than for them to see what value their pastors set upon the rights and holiness of Catholic Unity; and how, for its sake, they traverse sea and land, and are deterred by no difficulties from flocking to the See of Rome, and reverencing, in the person of Our humility, the Successor of Peter, and Christ's Vicar on earth? By the influence of this example, far better than by any more recondite teaching, they will learn what reverence, obedience, and deference they ought to show Us, to whom, in the person of Peter, Christ, our Lord, said, "Feed my lambs, feed my sheep," and by those words entrusted and delivered the supreme solicitude and sovereignty over the Universal Church.

Even you yourselves, Venerable Brethren, even you, in the performance of your sacred ministry, will derive great benefit from this act of devotion to the Apostolic See. For, in proportion as stronger bonds of the intimacy of faith and love unite you with the corner-stone of the mystic edifice, all the more, as the history of the Church in all ages teaches, will you be clothed with that fortitude and strength, which the greatness of your office requires against the attacks of enemies and adverse circumstances. What else did Christ our Lord mean, when appointing Peter to sustain the firmness of his brethren, He said, "I have prayed for thee, that thy faith fail not; and do thou when converted, confirm thy brethren." Indeed, as St. Leo the Great intimates, "Special care of Peter is taken by our Lord, and prayer is made for the faith of Peter in particular; for the state of others will be more secure if the mind of the Prince be not overcome. In Peter, therefore, the strength of all is fortified, and the help of divine grace is so ordained, that the firmness which is given by Christ to Peter is conferred by Peter on the other Apostles." Wherefore we have always been persuaded, that of the strength with which Peter was enriched by our Lord's special gift, a considerable share must needs accrue to you as often as you present yourselves before the person of Peter, who lives in his successors, or only tread the soil of this city, which was watered by the sweat and triumphal blood of the Sacred Prince of the Apostles. Nay, we have never doubted, Venerable Brethren, but that even from the sepulchre where the ashes of Blessed Peter, lie for the perpetual religious veneration of the world, there goes forth a certain secret and salutary power, which inspires the pastors of the Lord's flock with hardy resolves, mighty spirits, and magnanimous feelings, and, by renewing their

ALLOCUTION TO THE BISHOPS.

strength, makes the shameless audacity of the enemy yield and collapse in the unequal conflict, when matched against the strength and power of Catholic Unity.

Why should we disguise it, Venerable Brethren? We have long been actually engaged in battle for the defence of justice, and religion, against crafty and bitter enemies. So protracted and so severe is the struggle, that the united forces of all who are enrolled in the sacred militia, does not appear to exceed what is necessary for resistance. True it is that, while defending the cause, the liberty, and the rights of the Church, according to the duty of Our supreme office, We have unto this day been preserved by the help of Almighty God from mortal danger, but We are still harassed and tossed by adverse winds and waves. We fear not shipwreck, because the present help of Christ our Lord forbids Us to fear, but we are deeply grieved by many monstrous and new doctrines, and many crimes impiously committed against the Church, and against this Apostolic See. We have condemned and reprobated them already, and in the discharge of Our sacred office We now once more publicly reprobate, and condemn them. But, on the present occasion, and in the gladness which your presence brings Us, We abstain from relating the anxiety, care, and anguish, which torture and excruciate Our heart with cruel and enduring wounds. Rather We will bear them all to the altar which We daily load with our prayers, and water with our tears; We will once more unfold, and reveal them all to the most clement Father of mercies, with renewed supplications, wholly relying upon Him who knows the way, and has the power to defend the safety and glory of His Church, and who, doing justice unto all who suffer wrong, will judge with a just judgment, on a day that will surely come, both our cause and the cause of our enemies.

In the meanwhile, however, Venerable Brethren, your proved sagacity will duly appreciate of what vast moment it is, in order to thwart the designs of the wicked, and to repair the disasters of the Church, that your concord with this Holy See, which is so conspicuous, should strike ever deeper roots, and be ever strengthened. The love of Catholic union, which, once impressed upon the soul, diffuses itself widely for the benefit of others, assuredly will not permit you to rest, without endeavouring to unite your efforts, to bring into the same universal concord and undivided agreement of Faith, Hope, and Charity, all the ecclesiastics of whom you are the leaders, and all the faithful entrusted to you. Truly, there will be no fairer sight, in the eyes of men and angels, than if in this our pilgrimage, proceeding from exile to our country, we reproduce the likeness and order of that pilgrimage in which the twelve tribes of Israel marched together to the happy Promised Land. All entered, all under their own rulers, distinguished by their own designations, and appointed to different districts. Every family obeyed its father, every band of warriors its general, and the multitude obeyed their princes. Yet it was one people out of so many tribes, and it prayed to one and the same God, at one and the same altar. It was one people, and it obeyed the same laws, the same high priest, Aaron, and the same messenger of God, Moses. It was one people following one law, in the toils of war, and in the fruits of victory. It was one people, who, living together in tents, and fed by miraculous sustenance, aspired with one common wish to one common goal.

From the many pledges of your fidelity which We have received, We feel sure that you will endeavour perpetually to maintain this union. We are assured of it by your proved integrity and conspicuous virtue, which has shone forth always and everywhere equal to itself, and superior to every danger. We are assured of it by the great zeal, and ardour, which urges and impels you to strive for the salvation of souls, and to magnify the glory of God. We are assured of it, and most certainly assured of it, by that sublime prayer which Christ Himself, before His last Passion, offered to the Father, beseeching Him "that they all may be one, as Thou, Father, in Me, and I in Thee: that they also may be one in Us."—St. John, xvii. 21. A prayer to which the Divine Father will never refuse a hearing.

We desire nothing more, Venerable Brethren, than to derive from this, your union with the Apostolic See, such results as We consider most beneficial, and salutary to the Universal Church. We have long revolved in Our mind—it has been made known, as occasion arose, to many of Our Venerable Brethren, and We trust hereafter to be able to effect it as soon as the desired opportunity shall present itself—to hold a sacred Œcumenical and General Council of all the Bishops of the Catholic world, whereby, through collected opinions and united efforts, necessary and saving remedies may, with the aid of God, be applied especially to the many evils by which the Church is oppressed. The result will be, as We greatly hope, that the shades of error which obscure the minds of men will be dispersed, and that the light of Catholic truth will diffuse its saving radiance, and teach them to know and to pursue, by the grace of God, the true path of salvation and justice. Another result will be that the Church, like an invincible army in battle array, will defeat the hostile attempts of her enemies, will break their attacks, and, triumphing over them, will propagate and spread far and wide the reign of Jesus Christ upon earth.

And now that our prayers may be fulfilled, and that your and Our cares may bring abundant fruits of justice to all Christian nations, let us uplift our eyes to God, the Fountain of all justice and bounty, in whom resides, for those who hope, all fulness of protection and abundance of grace; and since we have, as our advocate with the Father, Jesus Christ, His Son, the High Priest, who penetrated the Heavens, who always living intercedes for us, and who, in the admirable Sacrament of the Eucharist, is with us all days until the consummation of the world, let us place this most loving Redeemer, as a seal upon our heart, as a seal upon our arm, and let us assiduously offer up our prayers with all confidence at that altar, where the Author of grace Himself has fixed His throne of mercy, and where He awaits all who labour and are heavy burthened, longing to refresh them. Let us humbly and unceasingly beseech Him to rescue His Church from its calamities, and from all peril, and to grant it a happy peace and victory over its enemies, to give us and you new strength, that we may promote the glory of His name, to inflame the minds of men with that fire which He came on earth to enkindle, and by His mighty power to turn to saving counsels all who are astray. It will be for your piety, Venerable Brethren, to take every pains that the faithful intrusted to you, may daily increase in the knowledge of our Lord Jesus Christ, and may with constant faith venerate, love, and frequently visit Him present in the august Sacrament. And nothing will be more worthy of your zeal and care than that, as the lights burn before His altar, so a grateful sense of piety, and an unfailing flame of charity, shall burn in the hearts of the faithful.

And in order that God may graciously incline His ear to our prayers, let us ever strenuously seek the suffrage, first of the Immaculate Virgin Mary, Mother of God, for no patronage is more powerful with God than her's; next of the holy Apostles Peter and Paul, whose birth in heaven we are about to celebrate, and also of all the Saints in heaven who reign in heaven with Christ, and by their prayers gain for men the gifts of His divine bounty.

Lastly, Venerable Brethren, to yourselves, and to all other our Venerable Brethren the Bishops of the Catholic world, and also to all the faithful entrusted to your and their care, of whose piety and love We have always received and are daily receiving brilliant proofs—to each and to all We give lovingly and from Our very heart, Our Benediction, with every wish for their happiness.

A most edifying and prepossessing English young lady, Miss Corby, who had lately returned to Rome, from an excursion to Naples, died about this time, from typhoid fever. She was deeply regretted, and the liveliest feelings of sympathy were manifested by the Roman nobility, and the English residents, for her father, Mr. Howard Corby, at his afflicting bereavement. The funeral obsequies for her repose, were celebrated with great solemnity, in the Church of Santa Maria del Popolo, at which many of the English bishops assisted.

ILLUMINATION OF THE COLISEUM.

On this evening the Coliseum was illuminated interiorly and exteriorly—the spacious area inside, and all the grounds, and approaches outside, were densely crowded, by congested masses of people—the spectators must have fully amounted to one hundred thousand. Here acquaintances met from opposite extremes of the world, from Canada and Madras, from Chicago and India : amongst others, I met some of the gentlemen of the Irish Augustinian convent, and Very Rev. Dean Hayes, and Right Rev. Dr. Goold, of Melbourne. Two francs were charged for admission to the interior—and this was the only exception of a charge having been made for admission, to any of the entertainments during the festivities—and it was occasioned, in this instance, by the illumination having been got up by private speculation. Military bands entertained the visitors till after nightfall, when the darkness became impenetrable. Instantly the entire extent of the vast ruin, was lit by a crimson flame of the most glowing tinge—it was next lit up with a brilliant hue of delicate blue—then yellow, and vermilion, and purple colours, produced by Bengal lights, of ever-varying dyes—the collossal columns, extensive corridors, gigantic arches, spacious chambers, and gloomy recesses, receding one behind another, encircling an area of six acres, and once affording accommodation on the structure itself, for 90,000 spectators, all lit up to-night by those mystical colours, threw out to view, that old Flavian amphitheatre, with a grandeur and sublimity of effect, which must ever remain unrivalled! Myriads of birds, swallows, pigeons, bats, and owls, that had retired to rest, in crevices, never before intruded upon, were scared by the sudden invasion of these glowing colours—started from these impenetrable recesses—and affrighted, flew round and round the amphitheatre—and as they flitted over the various lights, their plumage was tinged with all the changing colours of the chameleon—crimson and blue, green and yellow, purple and vermilion, and seemed as if a flock of gorgeously plumed winged visitors, parrots, humming birds, or birds of paradise, just arrived from Guatemala, the Indian isles, Ceylon, or sunny regions in tropical climes. The cheers of the tens of thousands of delighted spectators, were vociferous. I thought of early Christian times, and of the thrilling cheers, echoed by these gigantic piles from 90,000 spectators, expressive of the delight which regaled their eyes and their ears, at seeing the tortuous writhings, and hearing the agonizing groans of the dying gladiator, wounded in brutal conflicts on that very arena, and that in the very presence of his wife and children!

> "There were his young barbarians all at play,
> There was their Dacian mother—he, their sire,
> Butchered to make a Roman holiday!"

Every fibre of my heart vibrated with enthusiasm, when I remembered I stood on the very earth, that was saturated with the seed of Christians—the blood of martyrs!—and almost imagined if I heavily pressed the holy soil, I should see the sacred crimson oozing! Here many heroic youths, and tender virgins, encountered the fangs and tusks of panthers, and other ferocious wild beasts—on this spot the venerable St. Ignatius of Antioch, was exposed to these raging lions, that by tearing the flesh from his limbs broke down the reservoirs of life's tide, and wafted his soul to the palm of victory—and, to use his own expression, ground his bones as the wheat of Christ!—amidst these shouts, I fancied God stretching down His hand, to lift the venerable Pontiff to the martyr's throne, of a blessed immortality! Alas! we live as though heaven were to cost us nothing! *Ubi multæ coronæ, multa certamina!* No cross, no crown! When the interior illuminations had terminated, the word *Esterno*, "outside," suddenly appeared in large glowing letters of fire, over each of the two openings for egress—which, besides presenting a most beautiful pyrotechnic display, signified to the spectators, that the exterior illuminations were about to commence. The exterior was then similarly illuminated—and the multitudes streamed in through every avenue to the city.

Audiences to the Irish Bishops and Priests.

June 27th.—On this day a solemn requiem Mass was celebrated for the repose of the soul of the Right Rev. Dr. Kilduff, late Bishop of Ardagh, in the Irish College in the beautiful Church of St. Agatha. It was in an especial manner an Irish function—the Mass was sung in the melodious, and plaintive musical strains, of his Lordship of Limerick, Right Rev. Dr. Butler. The choir comprised the young gentlemen the students of the Irish College, the greater number of the Irish priests in Rome, and fourteen bishops, all of whom were Irishmen, the greater number of them from Irish sees, and the others from sees at the utmost extremes of the world—California and the United States, Newfoundland and Australia, Bombay and Madras, Canada and South Africa—all congregated to supplicate for the repose of the soul of an Irish bishop—and presided over by an Irish cardinal—and over the very spot where reposes the heart of O'Connell! Amongst the prelates who assisted were the Bishops of New Brunswick and of New Chatham, North America, Dr. Sweeney and Dr. Rogers. Immediately after the solemn function, the Cardinal Archbishop and suite drove off in two state equipages, followed in carriages by the Irish bishops, and a lengthened line of Irish priests, for the Vatican Palace, where, upon this day, the Holy Father was to honour them with an audience. The bishops entered the Palace, and were introduced to the Pope, by the Cardinal Archbishop of Dublin. His Grace the Archbishop of Cashel, Most Rev. Dr. Leahy, on the part of the Irish hierarchy, expressed, in the most felicitous terms, their homage and obeisance to his Holiness—their attachment, obedience, and submission to the See of Peter—their sympathies in his sufferings—and their ardent aspirations for a lengthened continuation of his Holiness' auspicious reign —and made his most respectful acknowledgments, that under his weighty solicitude for all the churches, he ever evinced an especial interest, in the welfare of the Irish Church. His Holiness expressed his assurance of the obedience and attachment of the Irish bishops, of their zeal in opposing error, and in promoting the interests of the Church. His Grace of Cashel, again begged to express the thankful acknowledgments of the Irish hierarchy to his Holiness, for the exalted honour conferred on them, and on the entire Irish Church, by the elevation of one of their body to the Sacred College, and to the princely position of the Cardinalate, and their acknowledgment of his great wisdom, in selecting for that dignity, a prelate so illustrious for his prudence, erudition, zeal, and sanctity, as the Cardinal Archbishop of Dublin. The Holy Father said, that on all such occasions, he supplicated the infallible guidance of the Holy Ghost, to direct him in his selection, and he had every reason to believe, that the Holy Spirit had so guided him in the instance of the selection of the Cardinal Archbishop of Dublin. All the distinguished personages within that apostolic chamber, on that day, expressed the most cordial concurrence in the justice of these sentiments. I should not have said all—the overwhelmed feelings of one, evinced too forcibly, that a profound humility made that one, an exception. The bishops then presented the Peter pence offerings of the faithful of their respective dioceses, which, exclusive of the amount previously forwarded, amounted in the aggregate to £13,000. The Cardinal, in a private audience on a former day, presented £2,230; and his Lordship Dr. Delany, of Cork, in addition to former contributions, gave £300 immediately after his arrival at Rome. The Irish priests entered the Vatican Palace after the bishops. From the foot of the Sala Regia, where I first entered the palace, to the state chamber, where I came in presence of the Pope, I counted the number of paces I took, and they amounted to 874. I measured in Dublin a distance by the same number of paces, and it extended from the Exchange, through Dame-street and College-green, to D'Olier-street! The guards received us with a military salute as the Pope's visitors. We assembled in a gorgeous saloon, paved in mosaics, the walls and ceiling panelled, and above, the Papal arms, highly relieved and brilliantly gilded. The hall was crowded with foreigners, all anxiously awaiting their admission, to the presence of his Holiness. After a considerable interval, the Pope's senior Chamberlain, Monsignor Pacca, came forth, and announced to the thronging multitudes that, in the audiences of this day, the Pope directed that precedence should be given to the Irish priests. Many pressed forward, expecting to obtain admission with the Irish priests, but a double line of soldiers was formed; and as in the days of ancient Rome, privileges could only be secured by the cry, "I am a Roman citizen!" so to-day the only passport that could secure admission through this passage, was the cry, "I am an Irish priest!" We passed through some grand saloons—and through companies of gentlemen-at-arms, "camarieri," and Noble Guards, till we reached a room decorated with a large ivory crucifix, china vases, and marble and ormolu tables. Here we were all arranged, kneeling in lines. The Pope entered, accompanied by some ecclesiastical dignitaries. The Irish priests numbered about sixty, and were introduced to the Holy Father, by Monsignor Kirby, Rector of the Irish College. He addressed us in French, expressing his pleasure at our visit to the seat of Catholicity, and presented each with a copy of his allocution, and a bronze medal. The Holy Father looked very well and benignant, manifesting great activity, and vivacity of character. He was dressed in a white soutane, white shoes, white silk sash, terminating in gold tassels, and a gold pectoral cross, suspended from his neck by a golden cord. With the enthusiasm characteristic of our countrymen, in their ambition to obtain a medal, all stretched forth their hands together—the Holy Father, with a gracious smile, said in English, "Have patience!" He expressed his pleasure at their zeal for religion, and their attachment and devotion to the Holy See. He imparted the Pontifical benediction to us, to our flocks, and to our relatives, and we retired.

CARDINAL ANTONELLI AND THE IRISH BISHOPS.

Soon after, many of the Irish bishops assembled in the Sala Regia, and proceeded to pay their respects to the Secretary of State, Cardinal Antonelli. Right Rev. Dr. O'Hea, Bishop of Ross, invited me to accompany them. I declined, fearing my presence might appear obtrusive. His Lordship said, "Come—I appoint you my chaplain, and now you can enter in an official capacity." I thanked his Lordship for his thoughtful courtesy, and accepted of it. The Cardinal's saloons were furnished with simplicity and elegance—some oil paintings, large china vases, a likeness of the Pope, and a large ivory crucifix, being the chief ornaments. His Eminence was dressed in a purple soutane, trimmed with scarlet, a scarlet cap, scarlet stockings, patent leather shoes with gold buckles, and round his waist a scarlet sash, terminating in gold tassels. He is tall, of easy carriage, dark complexion, aquiline nose, high forehead, exhibiting indomitable determination, and his dark, penetrating eyes are beaming with intelligence. He was born on the 2nd of April, 1806, at Sonino. He was highly esteemed by Cardinal Lambruschini, who introduced him to the notice of Pope Gregory XVI., and whilst yet young, was appointed delegate at Orvieto and Viterbo. Pope Pius IX. created him cardinal on 14th of June, 1847. His Eminence received us standing. He was at intervals calm and excited, serious and animated, facetious and thoughtful, laughed heartily, and spoke with volubility and expressiveness, and displayed all the capabilities, and versatility, of an accomplished diplomatist. The conversation was conducted in the French language, and was principally confined to his Eminence and Right Rev. Dr. O'Keane, of Cloyne, who spoke French with great fluency and elegance. The subjects of the conversation embraced topics of the greatest ecclesiastical and political interest, and importance to these countries—but fearing I might violate the privilege conferred on me, in being associated with the prelates present, by publishing the conversation without permission, I deem it more prudent to observe silence. His Eminence courteously bade us farewell, and we retired.

Address of the Bishops to the Pope.

On leaving the hall of audience, the Right Rev. Dr. Donnelly, Bishop of Clogher, invited me to take a seat in his carriage, and accompany his Lordship, to the Altieri Palace, where the address of the prelates to the Pope, was awaiting the signatures of the bishops. The Altieri Palace was built by Cardinal Paluzze Altieri, in the year 1670, during the pontificate of Clement X., after the designs of Giovanni Antonio Rossi. It is grand, and sumptuously decorated, and has the most extensive façade of any palace in Rome, and once possessed a most valuable library, rich in the rarest manuscripts, and its galleries were hung with paintings by the most celebrated masters. Its portals and hospitable halls were ever thrown open by his Eminence, of happy memory, its late possessor, for the promotion of every work of charity or religion. Here very many Irish and foreign prelates were assembled, to attach their signatures to the address. The address was drawn up by a select number of bishops, constituting a commission, and elected by the general body. This commission consisted of thirty-two prelates, of whom two were for Ireland, two for England, three for Spain, three for Austria, four for France, three for Italy, one for Belgium, one for Holland, two for Prussia, one for Bavaria, one for Switzerland, one for Portugal, three for North America, one for Brazils, one for Mexico, and three for the Eastern Churches. The prelates chosen as the representatives of the sixty French bishops, were the Bishop of Orleans, the Archbishop of Cambrai, the Cardinal Archbishop of Besançon, and the Cardinal Archbishop of Rouen. His Eminence the Cardinal Archbishop of Dublin, was solicited to lend the favour of his assistance, on the part of the Irish hierarchy. One of the prelates elected by the English bishops, was Henry Edward Most Rev. Dr. Manning, Archbishop of Westminster. The commission elected his Eminence Cardinal de Angles, as their president, and charged six of the episcopal members to draft the address, and then present it to all for approval; and these six appointed Monsignor Haynald, Bishop of Colocza, as their draughtsman and secretary. The number of bishops who actually attached their signatures to the address to the Pope, was 499. This number, however, did not include all the bishops then assembled in Rome. Some few declined to sign, from motives of strict etiquette, either because they derived their titles solely from localities within the city, or because they were not in actual possession of episcopal sees—and one Portuguese bishop, in declining to attach his signature, was influenced by prudential motives, arising from political movements in his own country. These exceptions, although they detracted some few from the number of the signatures to the address, added materially to the moral effect of the sentiments expressed, as they afforded the strongest evidence, even in the face of so august an assemblage of prelates, and in the very presence of the Pope, of the perfect freedom, which every individual could command. The bishops who formed these exceptions, were seven in number, so that the entire number of prelates who assisted at the celebration of the centenary, amounted to 506. This is a number greater than ecclesiastical history records to have been congregated on any former occasion, with some few exceptions. At the Council of Chalcedon, the Fourth General Council, held in the year 451, according to Tillemont, 560 bishops assembled—Bellarmin says 600 were present, though other writers make large deductions, from these high figures. At the Second Council of Lateran, which was held during the pontificate of Pope Innocent II., and in the year 1139, history asserts that the bishops assembled, closely approximated to the number of 1,000. For obvious reasons we shall not notice the Council of Rimini, held in the year 359—Bellarmin states that 600 bishops attended that Council.

On the two last evenings, Cardinal Louis de la Lastra e Cuesta, Archbishop of Seville, held levees on the occasion of his having received the cardinal's hat, when his Eminence was waited on by all the cardinals, the Roman nobility, the ministers of state, the senators, the bishops, the principal functionaries—civil, military, naval, municipal, and ecclesiastical, and by all the Spanish priests and residents at Rome. The levees were held in the palace of the Spanish embassy, which was decorated and illuminated for the occasion, and was surrounded by guards of honour and military bands of music.

Vigil of St. Peter and St. Paul's Day.

O Roma felix, quæ duorum Principium
Es consecreta glorioso sanguine :
Horum cruore purpurata cæteras,
Excellis orbis una pulchritudines.
—VESPER HYMN.

O Rome, how happy is thy lot,
To be these martyrs' hallow'd spot !
Their purple blood within thee dwells ;
Thy city, then, all lands excels.

THIS was the feast of the Sacred Heart of Jesus, and I assisted at the solemn celebration in the church of the nuns of the "Sacre Cœur," at "Trinita de' Monti," on "Monte Pincio." After the ceremonies, I stood before the vestibule, before the lofty balcony ascended from the Piazza di Spagna, by a flight of marble steps numbering 135, and here I was enjoying a commanding view of the entire city and environs. It struck twelve o'clock, noon—I was startled by a thundering cannonade from the fortress of San Angelo, which I could discern in the distance, and by the booming and ringing of all the bells of the 400 churches of Rome ! I remembered it was mid-day, and we were now entering on the eve of the glorious festival of the eighteenth centenary of the martyrdom of the Princes of the Apostles, and the first hour was thus saluted by chiming bells, and salvoes of artillery ! The first vespers of the feast were celebrated in the Vatican Basilica, with transcendent grandeur, and extraordinary solemnity of ceremonial, combining military pageantry, thrilling music, booming guns, regal suites, exalted dignitaries, tens of thousands of people from every clime, thirty-eight cardinals, and 368 bishops, clothed in vestments of the most costly textures, and glowing dyes, embroidered in golden threads, and studded with bullion, and precious stones. The assemblage congregated in that stupendous Basilica, which was decorated with flowers, and ample graceful folds of scarlet draperies, seen amidst myriads of flickering lights—and the declining rays of the parting Italian sun streaming through the silken curtains, and colouring every object with the most delicate golden and crimson tints, culminated in the climax of the presence of the Vicar of Christ! Oh, it looked like a glimpse into the heavenly Jerusalem! *Gloriosa dicta sunt de te civitas Dei!*—" Glorious things are said of thee, O city of God!" Immediately after vespers, the Pope blessed the palliums, worn by all archbishops, and which are conferred on them soon after their elevation.

The Pallium.

I deem it may be of interest to my readers to learn the origin of the pallium—what the pallium is—the ceremonies employed in blessing the pallium—the dignity and jurisdiction represented by it—and the episcopal virtues which it symbolizes.

The usage of conferring the pallium, and employing it as an emblem of ecclesiastical dignity, and jurisdiction, dates its origin from a very early period of the Church's history, and we find its first mention made in connexion with the oriental churches. St. Isidore writes very diffusely of it, and proves its origin, particularly in the East, to be of very great antiquity. Even in the Western Church, the history of the pallium may be traced to the very early ages of Christianity. We find that Cosarius, who had been the Archbishop of Arles, in the beginning of the sixth century, was honoured with the pallium by Pope Symmachus.

In the days of ancient Rome, and Greece, the special toga

or pallium was a long flowing mantle, which fell in graceful folds from the shoulders, closed in front, and covering the entire person, and was worn by emperors, and eastern potentates, as significant of their imperial dignity, as the toga was worn by the noble Romans, as emblematic of their nobility. Spelman and others, attribute its origin as a mark of ecclesiastical dignity, to the early Christian emperors—having conferred it on the more exalted, and eminent of the prelates of their empire, as a token of imperial pleasure, distinguished merit, and symbolical of the royal character of the Christian priesthood which characterized them. This, however, is quite an error; for though the name may be derived from Greece and Rome, the pallium worn by archbishops, is decidedly ecclesiastical in its very origin, and is significant of the authority emanating from Christ, and conferred through His Vicar on the Church.

It is believed that the pallium at first was worn exclusively by the Popes, to represent their precedence over all other bishops. It was subsequently conferred upon other prelates, who were distinguished for virtue, learning, or zeal in promoting the interests of the Church; it was, however, never conferred upon all bishops promiscuously, nor even upon all metropolitans, as is clearly proved by Peter de Marca, until the time of Pope Zachary, who decreed that it should be conferred upon all metropolitans, to signify their superiority over their suffragans. There are some exceptions even at present, where suffragan bishops are honoured with the pallium. It is worn by ecclesiastical dignitaries alone, and never worn except in the church, and at solemn episcopal functions.

The modern pallium has, no doubt, undergone great modifications from the pallium of old, both in size and fashion, and in the materials of which it is composed. The modern pallium is a circular band, or collar, with two pendent lappets, one hanging before and another behind, woven of white lamb's wool, and ornamented with crosses of a different colour. The wool of which it is made, is shorn every year from two lambs without blemish, of a year old. These lambs are blessed every year on the festival of St. Agnes, and in the Church of San Agnese outside the walls. This church is situate about two English miles from Rome, and is approached from the city through the Porta Pia, by the Via Nomentana of the ancients. The external architecture of this church, presents nothing particularly prepossessing, but internally it is replete with objects of the deepest interest to the Christian, the artist, and the antiquarian. It was built by Constantine, in the year 324, at the request of his daughter Constantia, on the spot where the body of the youthful and heroic virgin, St. Agnes, was found, who crowned a short but glorious career of 17 years, with the palm of chastity, and martyrdom.

In this church, on the festival of St. Agnes, the writer of this book had the pleasure of being present at the ceremony of the blessing of the lambs. The ceremony took place immediately after the High Mass, which was celebrated with great solemnity. A long procession of pious youths, wearing surplices, and proceeded by a thurifer, and acolytes, issued from the vestry, wound round, and through the centre of the church, to the high altar, and was followed by two ecclesiastics bearing the lambs, which reclined gracefully on two cushions of scarlet velvet, trimmed with gold lace, and pendent tassels. They were as white as snow—their heads ornamented with fillets of artificial flowers, and their bodies adorned with rosettes of crimson silk ribbons, and other ornaments. The procession was closed by the officiating dignitary, who, on this occasion, was Barduani, the mitred abbot of the monastery, attached to the church, "San Pietro in Vincoli." He wore his precious mitre, and red cope, and was assisted by his deacons at either side. The lambs were then laid, one at each side, on the high altar, the abbot standing between, when a very sweet hymn was executed by a superior choir. The abbot then chanted an oration, to the following effect :—"O holy God, who, through Moses, appointed vestments for Aaron, and the priests of the old law, and who hast mercifully provided vestments for Thy Apostles, and their successors; bless, we beseech Thee, these lambs, of whose wool are to be made the palliums for the Pope, patriarchs, and archbishops, who shall be appointed to rule Thy people, that they may obtain grace, prudently to govern those commited to their care, and guide them to eternal salvation: through Christ our Lord. Amen." He then invoked the intercession of our Blessed Lady, and St. Agnes, incensed them, sprinkled them with holy water, and after giving his benediction to the congregation in the usual form, the procession formed, and retired in the same order to the vestry. The lambs are subsequently committed for twelve months, to the care of the community of religious ladies, who dwell in the convent of San Antonio, and the community so selected, is deemed as especially complimented by the Holy Father. At the expiration of that time, the wool is shorn off, and woven into palliums, and on the vigils of SS. Peter and Paul, they are laid the entire night over the tomb of these Apostles, and on the following festival are blessed at the high altar, during the Papal Mass, and are afterwards sent to the various prelates through the Christian world who are to be honoured with the pallium.

The pallium, like the vestments, and other ornaments, employed by the Church in our solemn ceremonies, is a mystical emblem, and replete with edifying signification. Its being laid on the tomb of St. Peter, and blessed at the Mass of his festival by the Pope, and transmitted by him to the princes of the Church, dispersed through every clime, is intended to signify that all ecclesiastical authority, and jurisdiction, have emanated from the divine fountain, Jesus Christ, and transmitted through Peter, the Prince of the Apostles, to his legitimate successors, and shall uninterruptedly descend to the rulers of his faithful people, to the end of time. It is made of the whitest wool, shorn from lambs without blemish, and reared by religious virgins, to signify the spotless innocence—the eminent sanctity—the unimpeachable integrity—the unsullied purity, and chastity, which should characterize the Christian bishop's life, who should be a secure guide to lead his people, through the darkness of this world, to the most exalted perfection, and to heaven, and be, as it were, the focus, and mirror, which should reflect all the virtues of Jesus Christ, and dazzle the eyes of his admiring flock, as Moses did the eyes of the Israelites of old, after descending from the mount, where he held his intimate converse with God. It is composed of many weak fibres, woven into one strong band, to exemplify the necessity, and powerful efficacy of Christian unity, by which the faithful, no matter how widely dispersed over the world, are, through one head, bound together by the bonds of charity, which can never be snapped asunder, and renders them invincible over all the powers of darkness. It is soft and pliable, to denote the gentle manners, the mildness, and condescending courtesy, by which he should accommodate himself to the dispositions of his people, and make himself "all to all, to gain all." The honorary collars, and stars of worldlings, their badges of knighthood, or the various orders of the Bath, and the Garter, are made of gold, and of the most precious silks and metals, and studded with precious stones, and diamonds of the purest water; the pallium—the badge of the royalty of the Christian priesthood, is adorned with no other ornament than the sign of the cross; but an ornament, in the eyes of a Christian bishop, and a Christian people, more dazzling than the most glittering jewels, and more precious than the united produce of all the diggings of Australia, or the auriferous regions of California. As the pallium is conferred on the archbishop, by the legitimate successor of St. Peter, it should serve to remind the faithful of the respect, obedience, and reverence which they owe to their prelate, who is their teacher, their guide, their model, the guardian of their faith, the dispenser of God's gifts, and the representative of Christ.

The Holy Father, accompanied by the grand procession, then passed down the nave, and returned to the Vatican.

St. Peter's Chair.

The next ceremony, and one which elicited the most lively interest and devotion, was the removal of the chair of St. Peter, which was to be exposed for the veneration of the faithful during the octave. The removal of the chair of St. Peter took place under the superintendence of the Dean of the Sacred College—it was borne on a trestle, by four

ST. PETER'S CHAIR. 83

deacons and four priests, the cords being held by four archbishops. It was conveyed processionally from the elaborately wrought bronze case, at the end of the tribune where it usually remains, to the chapel of "Madonna del Soccorso," and was accompanied by lines of ecclesiastical dignitaries, and by a guard of honour of that distinguished corps, the "Zouaves." Two hundred years have elapsed since it was similarly removed, and exposed for the veneration of the faithful. It is an arm-chair, made of wood, inlaid with ivory. This chair is no doubt of great antiquity; and the faithful believe it to be the identical one, upon which Christ's Vicar, the Prince of the Apostles, sat, when he laid the foundation of the Roman Church. St. Peter arrived in Rome during the reign of Claudius, and was received, and hospitably entertained, by the Senator Pudens. Pudens was soon favoured with the grace of conversion to holy Faith, was baptized, and became a most fervent Christian. The character of the chair identically corresponds, with that of one, which historians assert formed the principal article of furniture of every family of exalted social position in those days. Now Pudens was a senator, and it is then most probable Peter sat in that chair in Pudens' house, when he ruled his infant Church, and that Pudens felt but too highly honoured, in being allowed to present it to Peter, to be in future his own. The chairs of the Apostles, and early Christian bishops, were most carefully and religiously preserved, by the faithful, as sacred relics, and emblems of jurisdiction, and were frequently visited by crowds of fervent pilgrims. Of this fact we are supplied with convincing testimony by Nicephorus, and by Eusebius, who lived at so early a period, as the fourth century. If the chairs of other Pontiffs, were so appreciated and transmitted so solicitously and traditionally, it is not possible that the chair of the Sovereign Pontiff, Peter, could have been regarded with such indifference, as to have been lost, or become a subject of disputed identity. Evodius of Pavia, St. Optatus, and Tertullian, emphatically deny the possibility of such a contingency. Chair upon which Peter sat! What a throne!—the seat of Christ's Vicar!—the throne of thrones!

Illumination of St. Peter's.

SURGE, ILLUMINARE JERUSALEM, QUIA VENIT LUMEN TUUM, ET GLORIA DOMINI SUPER TE ORTA EST.—ISAIAS, lx. 1.

"*Arise, be enlightened O Jerusalem! for thy light is come, and the glory of the Lord is risen upon thee!*"

THE sun, the radiant orb, which illumined the recent grand ceremonial, has now nearly completed its course; and, as we approach its vesper twilight, Rome, in anticipation of tomorrow's festival, prepares to display that most transportingly beautiful spectacle, the exterior illumination of St. Peter's. As she employs the meridian beams of an Italian sun, to reflect splendour on her sublime mid-day ceremonies, and tinge the vari-coloured, and gorgeous costumes, of her ministers, with all the glowing dyes of the rainbow; so she now economizes the darkness, to afford a contrast, that may impart additional effulgence to the artificial lights she employs in that most fascinating spectacle, so expressive of her exultant joyfulness. *Sicut tenebræ ejus ita et lumen ejus.* (Psalm cxxxviii. 12.) "The darkness thereof and the light thereof are alike."

The streaming crowds, that were now congregating, before the façade of St. Peter's, to witness the interesting spectacle, seemed countless, and being dispersed over, seemed completely to fill the vast piazza. The numberless moving figures, were draped in costumes of every brilliant dye—and displayed the gorgeous liveries of footmen, valets, and majordomos—the dazzling embroideries of the diplomatic corps—the scarlet and blue of military and naval officers—the crimson of cardinals—the violet, and purple, of so many ecclesiastical dignitaries and numerous officials, moving about in complicated mazes—the tossing plumes of cavalry helmets, and ladies draped in the national costumes, and colours of every country in Europe and Christendom, their head-dresses decorated with waving feathers, and their persons clothed with glowing shawls, fringed with eastern dyes, and rolled out from the looms of Brussels or Berlin, Turkey or Cashmere! There they were—and all the colours were as decided as ever; but the orb that lighted them, was fast declining beneath the horizon, and as its radiance became fainter, so their lustre became more languid, and sombre, and assumed an air of sadness. The showering drops of the two playing fountains, which, in the noon-time light, sparkled like dripping diamonds of the purest water, were now coloured by the various glows of the evening sky: in one instance, blood-coloured like the ruby, again blue like the sapphire, and azure like the amethyst; and between them rose the venerable old Egyptian obelisk casting its longest shadows, and calmly looking down upon the scene! That Egyptian obelisk is believed by antiquarians, to have been quarried about the time that Merrhis, Pharaoh's daughter, with her maids, found the child Moses in the basket amidst the rushes, in the year 1571 before the coming of Christ! It was erected most probably with two others, which were erected to ornament the Temple of the Sun, at Heliopolis, one of which now stands in the Piazza del Popolo, the other still standing on the site of the ancient Temple, and which were placed before that temple by King Rameses! Perhaps that obelisk, may have been fanned by the wings of the destroying angel, as he flitted by to slay the first-born of men and beasts, over the land of Egypt, at the command of the Omnipotent Avenger! Perhaps Moses, at the head of the tribes of Israel, as he led the multitudes towards the Red Sea, may have passed beneath that very obelisk! What an interesting relic of antiquity! It was conveyed to Rome by Caligula, in a ship of 300 oars. It was discovered in the circus of Nero, on the spot where the vestry now stands. It was raised from its grave, and was erected, in the year 1586, in honour of Christ and His cross, which it supports, by the fisherman's successor, Pope Sixtus V. It is the only one of the obelisks of Rome, which is entire and unbroken.

The sun has gone down behind Monte Mario, and the pinnacle of the Egyptian obelisk, and the orb, and cross, over the towering dome of St. Peter's, are the last objects to which it communicates its rays; and as a parting gift, irradiates them with a glowing coating of golden hue—it has departed, and has totally disappeared, and has left all shrouded in obscurity. The moving crowds are still there —the colours and stately architectural fabrics are still there —but the sun has gone, and they have lost their brilliancy, and beauty, and are all enveloped in a gloomy darkness. Even so is it with all the most refining accomplishments, and the most elegant education, with our studies, our professions, and avocations of life—if the beaming sun of religion irradiate them not with a genial and brilliant ray, they are dim and unproductive; the literature, the history, the sciences may remain, but they lose all their bright colours and beauty; their exquisite symmetry is unseen, and they mingle into a confused mass of impenetrable darkness—without the light of religion, the most profound philosophy is indiscernable from ignorance and folly!

What means that commotion yonder?—cries of "avanti! avanti!"—you, forward, clear the way!—the crowds divide, and clear a passage between! Ho! here comes an Austrian "aide-de-camp," sent from the Palazzo Venezia by the Austrian embassy, with despatches to Cardinal Antonelli! The despatches he bears are perhaps drafts of a Concordat, and big with the destinies of empires! He wears the costume of an Austrian staff-officer, green, embroidered in gold, long military boots, cocked hat, and ostrich plumes, and rides a steed of Arabian blood. How martial he looks as he canters past the colonnade to the foot of the "Scala Regia!"—there is an air of romance, poetry, and chivalry about him, worthy the pencil of Salvator Rosa! See the scintillating sparks, how they fly from the violence with which his iron shoes strike the marble pavement. These we could not have seen under the brilliant rays of the meridian sun. How many an inspiration of divine grace, to a holier life, is clearly seen in the gloomy darkness of affliction and sorrow, which is unheeded, and unobserved, in the bright noontide of prosperity, and pleasures!

> "Then sorrow touched by thee grows bright,
> With more than rapture's ray;
> As darkness shows us worlds of light,
> We never saw by day."

This military courier, seen after sunset, in the dusky, dreamy-like indistinctness of an Italian eve, seemed like the spectre of some mailed knight of olden days, viewed through the hazy, dim vista of past centuries, returning from Palestine, with despatches from Peter the Hermit, to Pope Urban II., announcing that, after many sanguinary engagements, and the slaughter of numberless hordes of Saracens, the soldiers of the cross, led by Godfrey, Hugh Raymond, and Tancred, were conquerors, and that Jerusalem was delivered! How many ages and generations have since flowed by! They were but as surges, that undulated over the surface, and were again absorbed in the tide. The Hermit Peter and Godfrey, Raymond and Tancred, and the mighty hosts of the gathered Crusaders, whom they led to victory, have all passed away. Religion swayed their charging battalions—its reflection may have appeared disturbed on the undulating vicissitudes of human events, like the rays of the sun reflected on a lake when a breeze agitates the waters. But though the light appear disturbed, and flickering over the rippling surface, the radiant orb is still steady, and unchanging. Even so the Vicar ever steadily presides, and unchangeably transmits light from the Sun of Righteousness, cheering, cherishing, vivifying all beneath its genial gleaming.

> "As a stream
> Glasses a star, so life the eternal love;
> Restless the stream below—serene the orb above."

It is now near eight o'clock, long after sunset, and all is darkness around! In southern climes, the twilight is of much shorter duration than in our latitudes, and the darkness of the night more impenetrable. Yet, even here, darkness does not rudely rush in abruptly ; but with true politeness, and an easy deportment, introduces itself with a gentle, courteous gait. The darkness increases—everything is lulled into calm and quietude—the bleating sheep and lambs, on the grassy slopes, and over the Campagna, are now silent, and sink on the herbage in repose—even the shepherd's pipe has exhausted its gentlest cadences, on the stillness of the eve—the warbling birds are gone to nestle, in their little downy homes—not a pulse of nature is beating—not even an aspen leaf, in the neighbouring Vatican gardens, is quivering. Hush!—you fancy you hear the rippling of the playing fountains, and the purling of the limpid streamlets, as they fall over the marble rocks, in artificial cascades. See! Monte Mario, and the Sabine hills, are fading away like a dissolving view !

> "Now fades the glimmering landscape on the sight,
> And all the air a solemn stillness holds ;
> Save where the beetle wheels his droning flight,
> And drowsy tinklings lull the distant folds !"

They are gone !—the vast fabric of St. Peter's, has become engulfed in the darkness—you cannot see your hand before you ! A lengthened interval elapsed, one of awe, of nervousness, and intense anxiety—every eye is peering, endeavouring to penetrate the gloom. Oh! what is that ?—a hissing, scarlet, lambent flame, meteor-like, has shot up into the heavens from the top of the cross on the dome, which is little less than 500 feet high ! Immediately after—astonishing spectacle !—all the great architectural features, and every minute outline of the vast mole of the Basilica, are all instantly delineated in thousands of flickering lights ! There it is, the mightiest fabric that was ever erected by the hands of man, to the worship of God ; and which, lost just now in darkness, is reproduced in light ! That gigantic creation of architecture, with foundations of rock, and pillars like colossal moles of masonry, to support its towering arch, is now, as an aerial phantom, erected in a firmament of fire ! Every arch, entablature, architrave—

every pillar and pilaster, every cornice and frieze—every band of the dome, every minute detail, to the very arms of the lofty orb, and cross, stand brilliantly relieved, on the sombre curtain of the dark sky! Thus did the white or silver lights, continue burning for an hour, to the delight of the gazing multitudes, when the striking of the hour of nine o'clock was the signal for an instant transition, from the silver lights, to lights of a rich, golden hue, and of a much larger and more glowing character. This sudden transition was transportingly beautiful and astonishing! The first is called the silver illumination, the second the golden illumination. The number of men employed in lighting the lamps is 120—their position is often apparently of the most critical, and precarious character: though fatal accidents are of very rare occurrence. They all approach the sacraments, previously to undertaking the duty. They are carefully trained, to act in concert with the greatest precision, according to preconcerted signals, so that every region of the vast fabric, may be lit up simultaneously, and instantaneously. The number of lanterns employed in the first or silver illumination, amounts to 4,520—in the second, or golden illumination, 1,475 additional lamps are lit. The cost of the illumination amounts to 1,000 crowns. It is regarded as one of the most charming objects that this whole world can present to the human eye—the instantaneous effect—the contrast of light and darkness—the diversified accidents of the "chiaro-scuro"—and the multitudes moving in the sombre perspectives, triumphantly challenging all the efforts of science or art, to produce any spectacle of such unparalleled beauty and magnificence! The illuminations continued till an advanced hour in the night.

Thus, thought I, shall it be with Holy Church, that glorious fabric, without spot or wrinkle, towering and extensive, into which millions and millions have congregated from every age, and country, and clime, when for me the day of time shall be declining, and on my journey to eternity I shall see it fading from my view, till having reached the confines of time, passed the "eternal portals," and landed on the ethereal plains, I shall, with astonished vision, behold the same Church glorious and triumphant, as a vast repository of light, illuminated with dazzling effulgence, by the saints, the glorified citizens of the heavenly Jerusalem, who will irradiate it with a lustre, in whose light not merely the lanterns of St. Peter's, but the lustre of the amethyst, sapphire, and topaz, shall be totally extinguished ! There we shall see God !—see God, face to face ! " Glorious things are said of thee, O city of God !"

The Ceremonies of the Church.

Religion to be true must be interior. But religion employs external signs, to convey internal impressions to the soul, through the medium of the senses, usually through the organs of hearing or seeing, either by the voice of the preacher, or by the written Word. Other signs, directed to the eyes or ears, may also be efficacious, in conveying these salutary interior impressions, and amongst them she employs certain rites, which she calls " ceremonies." To confine ourselves exclusively to external rites, or ceremonies, irrespective of the interior worship of God in the soul, she regards as useless, pernicious, and hypocritical. But when ceremonies are employed, either as external manifestations of our interior sentiments of religion, or as a means to enliven our piety, and inflame our charity, these are regarded by her as most useful, most precious, and most venerable. Behold the wisdom of Holy Church, in instituting her ceremonies, and in employing the efforts of that art in painting, sculpture, music, architecture, and decorations, which she herself nurtured, and educated, as auxiliaries to promote her interests, to produce religious impressions, and elicit from the soul sentiments of sorrow, compunction, gratitude, and adoring love. When the Son of God consummated the sacrifice, and died the bleeding victim for our sins, that sacrifice was made, not in the peaceful attitude, and stillness of all nature—not in the brilliant rays, and under the genial heat of a summer's sun—not amidst beautiful scenery, amidst rippling fountains, verdant meads, and enchanting sylvan glades. No ! it was made on the barren, and rugged mount of Calvary ! A tempestuous storm convulsed all nature—the veil of the temple was rent to pieces—the flinty rocks were riven asunder—the dead started from their graves, and, in their winding-sheets, walked about in the very daylight—in the streets of Jerusalem, in the very sight of affrighted, withering, shivering, living men—the sun veiled its light, and a gloomy darkness enveloped the whole world! Why all these miracles, and writhing convulsions of nature! They were intended by the Omnipotent as external means, to affect the senses; and unless our hearts are more insensible than the very dead in their graves, who heard His voice—than the very veil that exposed the sanctuary—than the very rocks as hard as flint that were riven to pieces—those convulsive revolutions, were intended to elicit from our hearts sentiments of terror, compunction, and devotion, and oblige the most insensible amongst us, to strike our breasts, and acknowledge at last, that the God of Nature was dying. And this proves most convincingly the efficacy of sensible representations, either by the aid of art or ceremonies, to harmonize the feelings of the soul to the glorious triumph and mysteries which Rome and we are commemorating, on this eighteenth centenary of her Princes' victory!

Eighteenth Centenary of the Princes' Victory!

Hodie Simon Petrus, ascendit crucis patibulum: hodie clavicularius regni, gaudens migravit ad Christum: hodie Paulus Apostolus, lumen orbis terræ, inclinato capite, pro Christi nomine, martyrio coronatus est.—Anthem 2nd Vespers of SS. Peter and Paul.

"*This day, Simon Peter ascended the gibbet of the cross: this day, the key-keeper of heaven, went with joy to Christ: this day, Paul the Apostle, the light of the world, laid down his head, and for the name of Christ, was crowned with martyrdom.*"

AT early dawn on this memorable anniversary, a delicate tinge of crimson hue, and ruddy streaks, tinted the firmament; and as the fleecy clouds passed over the horizon, it seemed as if Nature, at Religion's bidding, were drawing aside the floating curtains, from those eastern chambers, to hasten the radiant orb of Italy to come forth, and shed his brightest effulgence on this eighteen-hundredth anniversary of the Princes' victory. Sentinels on the ramparts of old Adrian's Mole, the citadel of Rome, were long peering through the grey twilight; when they announced that the first rays, the harbingers of his approach, had appeared over the groves and cascades of Tivoli, those early rays were saluted by a salvo of 101 guns, from the Castle of San Angelo. Away went the thundering volleys from those heavy pieces of artillery placed in position, on the ramparts of the castle—

away they went, sometimes booming in quick succession, sometimes at lengthened intervals, electrifying the citizens, and shaking the foundations of the old palace of the Cæsars. They reverberated from the mountain dome of St. Peter's, over to Monte Mario, and were re-echoed back again from the classic Sabine hills in the distance, across the Campagna, till the homage of a salute of 101 guns was duly paid. These repeated volleys of thundering artillery, seemed to me to proclaim, that, after a bloody battle, the victory was on the side of the just one—like the demonstrations of a triumphant general, over his prostrate foe—each volley seemed to roar out to the mount of yonder Janiculum, on which, upon this day eighteen hundred years, Peter's gibbet was erected. "Death is swallowed up in victory!" He reclined in death for a moment, but it was merely as a warrior taking his rest, who, after a short slumber, rose up more powerful than Samson, and wielding the keys in his hand, burst open the gates of death, stronger than those of Gaza, through which, after Christ, he led the canonized saints, and all his followers, from regions of darkness, to realms dazzling with the brilliant effulgence of eternal day! Each deafening report seemed like an archangel's trumpet, proclaiming "He has arisen!—He has arisen!—He dieth now no more!" Having communicated the triumphant tidings to the city, those thundering volleys went off to sea, in an attempt to convey the report to the distant countries of the world beyond the seas. *Urbi et orbi!*—futile effort!—their noisy and evanescent efforts were exhausted ere they had travelled a league! *Urbi et orbi!*—presumptuous thunderings—little tinkling cymbals—they thought within themselves, "we will be like to the whisper of the Vicar of the Most High!"

This alarm for Rome was unnecessary—all Rome was long before awake, and in commotion. Toil herself seemed to have dispensed on last night with the necessity of sleep and repose; and the balm of the atmosphere, rendered genial by Him, "who tempers the wind to the shorn lamb," dispensed with the necessity of hotel accommodation, and as many of the peasantry carried sufficient provisions for several days, all their commissariat requirements were amply supplied.

It was advertised, in all the public places in the city, that the doors of the Basilica would be thrown open the next morning at five o'clock. Many pilgrims from distant countries, and hundreds of the children of labour, spent the night, on the vigil of that memorable day, either praying before the porches of St. Peter's Temple, or reclining on the marble pavements, under the porticoes, the covered galleries, or between the columns of the piazza, that they might secure an early entrance, and a favourable position, at the august ceremonies on the next day's centenary. The people, coming forth from their houses, and streaming through every leading avenue, were assembling at every corner—excitement agitated every bustling group—silk flags, of various colours, were suspended across the streets, from the tops of opposite houses—windows were thrown up, and extended hands were actively employed in decorating the fronts of the houses with pendent brilliant tapestries—the entire city, with its numerous inhabitants, and with its 100,000 strangers, were all attired in their gayest gala habiliments. Excited aides-de-camp, cantering orderlies, and dragoons conveying despatches from the commander of the forces, were flying in all directions. Sharp bugle calls, and rolling drums, were summoning the military detachments, from their various cantonments, to the appointed place of rendezvous. The booming notes of the great bell of St. Peter's, and the numberless bells of the other churches, were chiming merrily over the city—soldiers of the Palatine Guard were issuing from every street—richly caparisoned horses were led by their grooms, and gorgeous equipages—and valets with glittering liveries, were driving to receive the cardinals, the princes, and other noble and distinguished intended occupants, military, naval, and diplomatic officers—Franciscans and artists—Turkish and Grecian costumes—and foreigners and ecclesiastical students—and pupils of the German College in their red cassocks—generals, Capuchins, monks, advocates, and admirals, all moving through each other in inextricable mazes, seemed like coloured threads of various dyes, imported from distant tropical climes, driven by the shuttle of some loom of complicated machinery, through their intricate evolutions, but which in a short time were to be rolled out into a lengthened floriated texture of the most exquisite pattern. It was now five o'clock, and the ceremonies were to commence at seven o'clock. Every vehicle in the city, from the most respectable equipage, and "turn-out," to the humblest "caleche" for hire, was held in requisition for many days, and at extravagant charges; and as they rattled past on the pavements, the noisy din was deafening. As the morning advanced, they became more and more numerous, and more brilliant in character, till, at about six o'clock, came the superb equipages of the magnates. Nobles and counts, the ex-King of Naples, princes and princesses, monsignori, ecclesiastical dignitaries of every grade, generals and notabilities from every country, with their *suites*, rolled by in quick succession, in glittering liveries, the footmen of some being dressed in scarlet coats, with gold lace belts, and swords, cocked hats, and ostrich plumes. How dashing they looked! Now come the ambassadors, each vieing with the other in the splendour of his retinue and *suite*, that by these external demonstrations they might exhibit the superior respect of the countries and courts, and the royal masters they represented, for the Vicar of Christ. A tear of delight started to my eye, and every fibre of my heart thrilled with joy, to see the great ones of this world exhibit such respect for our Holy Father! The ambassador whose state equipages and retinue eclipsed in brilliancy all the others, was the Austrian ambassador. His Excellency, and the ladies attached to the embassy, and their *suite*, were conveyed in three full dress coaches, of exquisite finish and decorations, brilliant liveries of blue, white, and gold, and pendent tassels—the hammer-cloths—the stately horses richly caparisoned, the glittering harness, and the lace trimmings pendent from the traces, and housings, were superb. At lengthened intervals before the ambassador's carriage, in the centre of the street, ran two "running footmen," dressed in yellow silk small-clothes, scarlet vests, yellow loose silk jackets, and yellow silk helmets, decorated with plumes, white silk stockings, patent leather shoes, and buckles, and in their hands they held aloft canes, with gold heads, and tassels, which they carried high above their heads, as they ran along. The coaches, horses, and entire retinue, displayed such untarnished beauty and brilliancy, such delicacy and refinement, they seemed as if they were on that morning for the first time unpacked from tissue paper, and rolled out of a band-box! Austrian Empire! so long the right arm of the Holy Father's temporal power, how much I regret your recent humiliations, and the disastrous fate of the Emperor Maximilian, and his amiable Empress Charlotte, which has elicited the sympathy of the whole world! May the departed rest in peace!

The cardinals are coming!—oh! see their glittering lines of carriages in the distance! A cardinal's state equipage still retains all the gorgeous splendour of the full dress coach of the courtly days of Louis XIV. The swollen sides and general outlines present wavy and graceful curves. It is delicately suspended from C and elliptical springs—the upper quarter panels, are painted black, the lower quarter panels, and doors, and wheels, are painted a bright purple, or red colour, picked out with vermilion, and gilded lines—all blending in harmony—the edges, and panels, are surrounded by highly burnished mouldings, and the roof of the carriage is surrounded by chased open-worked ormolu cornices—the axles terminate in highly burnished brass cylinders—how the wheels glitter as they roll! The hammercloth is made of crimson cloth, falling in ample folds, with brass monograms and escutcheons, and the heraldic emblazonments painted on the panels of the doors, are specimens of the highest order of artistic skill. The interior is upholstered in the highest style of elegance—the cushions being covered with crimson brocade. The housings, copious trappings, and harness, are all covered with crimson velvet, studded with brass ornaments, and the horses' heads are decorated with tall scarlet plumes, and waving wreaths of silk, their manes and tails platted with silk ribbons of various colours, with a rosette at the end of every falling fold. The coachman wears a dress coat, all embroided with lace, scarlet vest, blue or white small-clothes, silk stockings, and buckles in his shoes, a powdered head, and a cocked hat, with gold lace. Three footmen, attired in corresponding liveries, always stand behind. The horses are always black, tall, stately, and high stepping—their noble bearing seeming to indicate, that they are conscious they are cardinals' horses, and are expected to display a corresponding majesty of deportment. Every cardinal requires two such state coaches for the conveyance of his Eminence, and suite, and sometimes three. On this occasion of the centenary, there were forty-five cardinals in Rome, who required more than one hundred such state equipages, and this will convey some idea of the splendour displayed in this one department alone. They, however, constituted but a small portion of the entire number of grand equipages, when we take into account the number employed by the other exalted dignitaries, the judges of superior courts, the princes, the five hundred bishops, and other numerous celebrities, rolling on, on that day, in one surging tide of regal magnificence, to the shrines of the Apostles!

See, this is the Senator! a lay dignitary appointed by the Pope, lay Governor of Rome,—he and his retinue, always occupying three state coaches, more gorgeous, if possible, than those I have described. He is dressed in crimson silk, with a massive gold chain, and over all a mantle of cloth of gold, lined with scarlet silk, furnished with an amazingly long train, supported by four sweet little boys, dressed in little silk small-clothes, crimson tunics, and silk bonnets, which they wear rakishly on one side of the head, and are adorned with feathers, similar to those of the Prince of Wales' plume—angelic looking little beauties! The Senator commands a superbly appointed regiment, called the "Senator's or Palatine Guard." He is followed in his suite by eight "conservatori," who are prefects, or puisne judges, all dressed in lengthened garbs of yellow silk. We cannot delay, however, to observe the various personages, but as the morning is advancing, we must hasten on to the bridge of San Angelo—beautiful bridge! The architecture of this bridge is very much, and very justly admired. It is very ancient, and was built by Adrian, probably about the year of our Lord 130. The present parapets were built by Clement IX., who erected on them the ten large marble statues of the angels, which now stand on them, in every variety of graceful position, each holding either the nails, the lance, the cross, or some other instrument of our Lord's passion, and presenting them to the observation of the passers-by, with the most affecting expression of countenance.

> "Fac me plagis vulnerari,
> Cruce hac inebriari!"

Many streets, which are the leading avenues of Rome, here converge on an open space, in front of the bridge, and here there was now quite a "block up"—and dragoons were actively engaged in liberating the congested masses, by allowing only three equipages at a time, from each street, to pass over the bridge. When I looked down from a height on this congregated assemblage of people, from all parts of the world—from Italy, Dalmatia, Albania, and the isles of Greece—attired in every variety of picturesque and lively, brilliant, glowing costume, on so many gorgeous equipages, and liveries, military uniforms, gleaming bayonets, swords, and on the helmets of the soldiers, and their waving plumes, cardinals in scarlet robes, glowing in the sun, ambassadors sparkling with diamonds and jewelled decorations, they seemed to me like a vast parterre, embroidered with the most charming flowers, sparkling with the jets of the morning dew, and painted in all the coloured charms of the fluid firmament's ethereal bow! The Papal banners were run to the flag-staffs on the ramparts of San Angelo at dawn of day, and floated buoyantly in the morning breeze, in every variety of graceful curve. The detachment that mounted guard at the portcullis of the fortress, was indeed on active duty. The instant a cardinal's carriage was descried approaching the bridge of San Angelo, the sentinel roared hoarsely, "Turn out the guard!"—immediately the entire company turned out in "review order"—the soldiers "dressed up" in two lines, rank and file, taking "close order"—the officer gave the command—arms were presented—colours drooped—drums rolled, and trumpets flourished—the cardinal returned the salute by a wave of his hand, and by raising and letting down the window of his carriage—his Eminence passed on—the guard recovered arms—broke, and returned to quarters. A similar military salute was given when the next and the next cardinal prince or general officer made his appearance. Soon after passing the bridge and castle of San Angelo, then the Vatican Palace, the great façade of St. Peter's, the vast piazza and colonnade, are thrown open to view. Few structures have ever impressed me with a higher idea of the genius of design, than the beauty and originality of the conception that erected this colonnade. I consider it never can be fully appreciated, unless we had the capability of removing it and then replacing it again, and judging by the contrast what the appearance of the façade would be without it. The talent of Bernini created it. It consists of two semicircular porticoes supported by four rows of columns, numbering in all 284 columns, and 64 pilasters, and the entablature supporting 192 statues, each 11 feet high, and the piazza the colonnade encloses is 777 feet in diameter. In the centre stand the Egyptian obelisk, with the two playing fountains, which throw up their crystal waters, falling like showers of sparkling diamonds, into the two spacious basins of Egyptian granite, of most graceful outline. We have now arrived at the extreme end of the colonnade to the right, and here we reach the covered gallery, and that staircase, the grandest in the world, and which is called the "Scala Regia," and leads to the "Sala Regia," a superb hall of audience, whence you enter into the Sistine Chapel, where the ceremonies take place during Holy Week, and on some other festivals, in presence of the Holy Father, and the College of Cardinals. The gallery leading up to the "Scala Regia" is 23 feet wide, and 360 feet in height, and at the entrance were congregated splendid equipages, and brilliant liveries, and crowds of every grade, profession, and clime thronging to the ceremonies. They ascended the "Scala Regia" in different groups, and in quick succession. There were princes and several members of the royal families of Europe, several members of the house of Austria, and of the royal family of Naples, and some Turkish notabilities, and the Princess of Portugal. There were there the ambassadors of Spain, France, Austria, and Bavaria, with many other courts of the world, with their attachés and suites, accredited to the court of Rome. There were ladies all in full dress, wearing all the various national dresses of their country—

some with veils of great size and richest texture thrown over their heads, and falling down in graceful ample folds, and enveloping the entire figure. There were the Knights of Malta. In olden days, there were there also the Knights Templars. There were military and naval officers from many countries. There was the pilgrim with his cockle shell and staff, and the poor Franciscan with his shaven head, coarse habit, bare feet, and hempen girdle. There was the superb costume of Morocco, and picturesque costumes from Dalmatia and the isles of Greece—Indian-looking magnates, with bold brown faces, and with white, gorgeously embroidered silk turbans, belts, and scimitars, and cloaks like Conté de Luna, or an Andalusian cavalier. Amidst the general bustle and excitement, were heard the measured tread of the military pickets and Swiss Guards on duty, with the trumpet flourish and roll of drums. All these seen by the bright gleams of the morning sun, and from the extreme end of the lengthened gallery ascending that noble stairs—the lustrous trains of the cardinals, and the Senator and his pages, and the diplomatic corps—the moving groups dressed in satin, and ermine, and cloth of gold, decorated with gold lace and embroidery, with sparkling diamonds and jewels—the cocked hats and waving ostrich feathers, the glistening scimitars, sabretasches, helmets, and tossing plumes—all culminating as they ascended in a tapering pyramid of the most varied and brilliant colours, presented an unrivalled perspective, that enchanted the eye, and more than realized the creation of the poet's fancy, or all that we read of in Eastern story!

From the castle to the basilica the route lay through a lengthened strait street, and here the crowds were dense, and the carriages rolled on in continuous streaming lines, till they reached the entrance to the vast piazza, where the rush ceased, and, like a streamlet running into a large lake, was calmly dispersed over the extensive surface. The equipages looked most diminutive; and as they disappeared in driving under the colonnade, or under the arches that led to the private entry of the Vatican Palace, they seemed like tiny vari-coloured little ants, running into the crevices of a stupendous mountain! The brilliant corps of the Swiss Guards was, as usual, on duty at the foot of the

Scala Regia. The Swiss Guards wore their full dress uniform. Their tunics were composed of detached stripes, of red, yellow, and scarlet cloth, fastened at the neck, shoulders, and wrists—small-clothes of the same character, fastened at the knees with bands and buckles, and stockings woven of texture of similar colours. Over their military tunics of blue, yellow, and scarlet, they wore polished steel armour, with overlapping steel scales over their shoulders and arms, such as you see preserved in our museums, as interesting curiosities of olden days. The armour of the officers, was richly inlaid with ornamental devices in brass. The officers also wore purple velvet small-clothes, with a gold lace band round the knee, fastened with golden cords, and pendent tassels tied under a large silk rosette. They wore purple silk stockings, the clocks of which were richly embroidered with gold tissue, and there was a silk rosette over the shoe on the instep. All wore burnished steel helmets, of a conical shape, with a scarlet plume pendent from the top. The officers wore kilts, some of silk velvet, others of netted chain work, broad belts, and long swords, and both officers and men wore round their necks a double row of neatly plaited ruffles, and the whole uniform presented a brilliant and exquisitely finished appearance; and when the detachment was seen on duty in St. Peter's, where the daylight was totally excluded, and their vari-coloured uniform, their burnished steel armour, helmets, and halberds glittered in the light of tens of thousands of wax lights, with which the cornices, arches, and dome were festooned, it presented what the world could exhibit nowhere else, and transported you in idea to past ages of religion and chivalry, to the olden days of Cœur de Lion, Peter the Hermit, and the Crusaders, or what you might expect to meet in the state saloons of Caernarvon, Walmer, Raglan, or Kenilworth Castles, in Chillon, Heidelberg, or in the castles on the Rhine, on a noble's festive day! The things of Holy Church belong to no time, or to every time—she is the same yesterday, to-day, and for ever! The costume of the Swiss Guards was designed by Michael Angelo, not merely with a view of introducing a beautiful regimental costume, but still more with an artistic view. Michael Angelo viewed everything in the light of an artist. Observing that the garments usually worn by congregations are of a dark colour, and that they impart a dull aspect to the general appearance, Michael Angelo designed that the costume of the Swiss Guards, who were to be dispersed amongst them, should be composed of a harmonious union of the most brilliant primary colours, blue, yellow, and red, and that those warm and lively tints might relieve the cold and sombre tone, and thereby give a picturesque effect to the general appearance of the congregation. And how effectually he succeeded, a glance at the congregations in the Sistine Chapel, or in St. Peter's, is sufficient to convince an artist.

The great entrance gate, leading to the vestibule, was decorated with immense wreaths, festoons, and crowns of platted green leaves. Here I met the Spanish Marquis Mariano Conrado, who cordially greeted me; but, strange to say, he was the only fellow-passenger, of the two hundred with whom I was so familiar, during my three days' voyage from Marseilles to Civita Vecchia, whom I recognized during these twenty days' festivities, so great was the concourse of visitors in Rome. I entered the church, it was now six o'clock; but though many thousands had arrived, it was as yet not at all crowded, and they seemed but sparsely scattered over the basilica. The floors of the vast spaces of the transepts at either side of the shrines, were converted into inclined planes, gently rising to the rere, and furnished with draped benches—"palchi"—to accommodate ladies and gentlemen in full dress, who secured tickets, and obtained admission through gates for privileged persons. They were crowded to their utmost capacity, and many thousands were disappointed, who made application after all the tickets had been distributed. The colossal marble columns, pillars, and pilasters, were all covered with crimson damask, fluted with lengthened lines of gold lace, throughout the entire extent of the nave, aisles, transepts, and tribune. The great arches of the intercolumniations were draped with vast sheets of crimson silk, fringed with gold lace half-a-foot in width, tied into graceful festoons by gold cords and pendent tassels of astonishing size. Some estimate may be formed of the quantity and the value of the gold lace employed for these decorations, when I tell, if all were connected in one continuous band, they would extend to a distance of fifty miles! Beneath every arch was a painting, suspended from a gilded pole and tassels, representing some heroic passages in the martyr's agony—some miraculous interposition of Divine Providence at the saint's intercession, or the exercise of some characteristic virtue. They terminated in mitred ends, from the angles of which hung golden ropes, supporting tassels of great size. The interior of the basilica is always illuminated on the occasion of the solemnity of a canonization, and the necessary preparations were now made as usual. Every leading feature of the interior architecture of the vast fabric, the lengthened lines of cornices, architraves, capitals of pillars, entablature, and wonderful arches, were all delineated as far as the eye could reach, by myriads of wax candles, in candelabra and crystal chandeliers, most artistically disposed. I say as far as the eye could reach, for though each candle was four feet in length, and of proportionate thickness, as they were not yet lighted, they became totally lost to view, in the extreme distance, as well as on the lofty cornices of the towering dome, the interior apex of which is 400 feet in height, from the plane of the floor upon which we stood. From the centre arch of the nave, was suspended an immense tiara, with cross keys of equal proportion, all composed of crystal pendants, inserted with burnished mineral jets, of purple, blue, vermilion, and azure, and other glowing colours, interspersed with brackets for wax candles, which, when sparkling in the reflected light, produced a most dazzling prismatic effect, and presented the appearance of a large accumulation of jewellery, composed of gold and silver, inlaid with amethysts and sapphires, rubies and pearls, and precious diamonds of the purest water. From the tiara and keys in the centre of the nave, was suspended a great inverted cross, representing that of St. Peter's, all composed of crystal "coronæ," interspersed with festoons and clusters of wax lights. Above this inverted cross, was inscribed in letters of gold, the text, *Respondens Simon Petrus, dixit: Tu es Christus, Filius Dei vivi. Respondens autem Jesus, dixit ei: Beatus es Simon.*—"Simon Peter answered and said: Thou art Christ, the Son of the living God. And Jesus, answering, said to him: Blessed art thou, Simon." (Matt. xvi. 16, 17.) The total number of candles employed in the illumination, amounted to 30,000 ! The pedestals of the large statues of the founders of religious orders, were surrounded by semicircles of gilded candelabra, supporting very massive candles; and the marble panels beneath the interstices of the walls between the statues and niches, were covered with cloth of golden tissue, and festoons and bouquets of gigantic artificial flowers, most tastefully composed and grouped. Over the bronze gates of the great door entering from the vestibule, a great painting was erected, representing the crucifixion of St. Peter. At the extreme end of the tribune, above the bronze ornaments, which surround the chair of St. Peter, was erected an extensive triangular painting on wood, representing the adorable Trinity, all gilded and coloured, from which emanated, to a great extent on all sides, numberless scintillating pencils, or coruscations of golden rays, which, when lit up by hundreds of wax lights, were reflected to extreme distances, with glowing and dazzling effect. In the centre was inserted an entablature, upon which was emblazoned the inscription: *Cathedra Petri, magisterium veritatis, centrum unitatis.* Underneath was suspended a superior painting, representing the apotheosis of the newly-canonized saints, which was screened by a crimson veil, till the termination of the ceremonies, when it was suddenly drawn aside, and exposed to the view of the multitudes during the singing of the *Te Deum.* The marble floor of the great space enclosed within the tribune, was laid down with green cloth, and during the ceremonials it was surrounded by a "cordon" or close line of Noble Guards. Here was erected the Papal throne, draped in crimson velvet and gold lace, and decorated with the Papal arms; and all around were arranged the benches, draped in tapestries, for the cardinals, the bishops, and the many officials and princes, assisting at the august ceremonies and holy sacrifice. Here the ceremonies of the canonization take place, and it is then called the place of the canonization. Here, also, which we shall regard as the back of the altar, the Pope always celebrates, and thus says Mass with his face looking towards the congregation. Around the walls of the tribune were erected the state boxes, draped in scarlet and gold lace, for the accommodation of the royal families, princes, ambassadors, and nobles, and their ladies and other distinguished personages, whose exalted rank entitled them to these privileged positions. Beyond them, was erected the gallery, enclosed in brass rails, for the accommodation of the ordinary papal choir; a second gallery was erected over the great bronze doors, at the entrance to the nave, for another choir; and there was a third stationed high up in the dome. The music was exclusively vocal, as is always the case when the Pope celebrates, and the vocalists in all, on this occasion, numbered 600.

THE GREGORIAN CHANT.

PSALLITE SAPIENTER.—*Ps.* xlvi. 8.
"*Sing ye wisely.*"

The music or song of the Church's liturgy, derives its title from Pope St. Gregory, who, if not the originator, was certainly the great reformer of the plain chant, or "*canto fermo.*" It is very probable that the science of church music has been derived from the Eastern Church, and was introduced into the West by St. Ambrose. The peculiar characteristics of the Gregorian Chant, are its extreme simplicity, combined with beauty and sublimity; it is rich, harmonious, and pathetic, and eminently adapted to choral exercises. I deem it censurable to introduce operatic music, into the functions of the Church. The original object of the introduction of music, into the Church, was that the words of the sacred text, might be conveyed more distinctly to the ear, and the sentiment more impressively, and devotionally conveyed to the heart. But that object is defeated by the frivolous, meretricious character, and complicated variations of operatic music, by which the words become unintelligible, and thus a luxurious music is substituted, for the holy Word of God. Such was the corruption of church music, in the days of Nicholas V., that he was about to exclude music from the Church for ever, as incompatible with devotional, and distinct articulation of the words. Palestrina, however, during a subsequent pontificate, by his simple, plaintive style, convinced his Holiness of their compatibility, and thereby rescued church music from its impending doom. Suppose not that I mean to censure the cultivation of operatic music, in its own sphere, or that I do not appreciate its exquisite and fascinating character, or that Rome and its rulers, are insensible to the refinement, and elegancies of operatic music. So far from that being the case, that many fashionable opera lovers, may be surprised to learn, that the opera, like every other artistic, scientific, and elegant refinement, originated in Rome, and was fostered and patronized by popes, cardinals, and ecclesiastical dignitaries. The first drama that was ever produced in music, was presented to the public, on the Roman theatre, in the year 1440, and the subject was that most interesting, and exciting passage in Sacred History, which records the miraculous conversion of St. Paul. From Rome it emanated, and was soon after introduced into Florence, Venice, and the principal cities of Italy. It was Cardinal Mazarin who introduced operatic performances into France, and they had been entirely unknown in England, until introduced by that great musical genius, Handel, and that at a comparatively late period.

To resume our narrative—a continuous tide of people was now flowing in through every portal, and the congregated masses were continually increasing. At a quarter before seven o'clock, a regiment of soldiers of the line, bearing rifles, and fixed bayonets, and in " review order," marched in double line from the bronze doors to the shrines, then halted, took open order five paces apart, moving the people at either side before them, and then faced each other. An open space was thus instantly cleared from the entrance to the tribune, and through this space the procession and the Holy Father were to pass. No other than official privileged persons were allowed to walk through this passage. See! here is a monsignor, in his purple robes, slight shoes, and buckles, flitting past—now a cardinal's servant, in gorgeous livery, with his Eminence's robes! There is a general, going his rounds of inspection, to see that the troops are all in position. This is a young man, borne out by the soldiers, pale and fainting, from the excessive heat; how languid, debilitated, wan, and deathlike he looks! These are ladies, in the full dress of the Roman court, black silk, without bonnets, no jewels or ornaments, but a black lace veil, thrown over their heads, falls down, and envelops the entire figure, in ample graceful folds; they have mistaken their entrance door, and are led this way through the regimental lines by a gallant officer, a friend of theirs, to the reserved seats. Next passes a "cameriere segreta," a gentleman-at-arms, dressed in black silk, black silk stockings, gold kneebuckles, with a silk apron, and black silk mantle, gold chain, state sword, and ruffles round his neck—such as might have been seen in the court of Louis XIV.—or in the pictures of Vandyke. There is one of the Noble Guard—how elegant and graceful his figure!— he wears a full dress scarlet coat—with embroidered gold belt across his breast, indicative of his nobility, and his entire uniform resembles that of a colonel of the British Life Guards. This is a Chinese bishop, seeking for his chaplain. Now passes a general of one of the Franciscan orders, a small wasted figure, his countenance pale, wrinkled, and emaciated, but beaming with divine love, and with the hopes of heaven; he is bent with the weight of years, the burden of the cross, and lengthened macerations. Clothed in his coarse habit, with hempen rope, and shorn head, and bare feet, he moves noiselessly along. He is accompanied by an "aide-de-camp." The "aide-de-camp" is a colonel of dragoons, in his scarlet regimentals, gold aigulets, and tassels, a steel helmet, and tossing plume, white leather small-clothes, with long glistening boots, which rise above his knees—see he is tall, bearded, and burly, walks erect as an arrow, and soldierlike, his tinkling spurs, swinging sabretasche, and clanking sword, displaying all "the pride, pomp, and circumstance of glorious war." What a contrast between the two figures!—they are perfect personifications of the pride of life and the abjection of the cross,—the wisdom of this world, and the madness of the saints. But this is their day,—the canonization day! *Nos insensati, estimabamus vitam eorum insaniam, et finem illorum sine honore,—ecce quomodo computati sunt, inter filios Dei, et inter sanctos sors illorum est!*—" We fools esteemed their life madness, and their end without honour. Behold, how they are numbered among the children of God, and their lot is among the saints." (Sap. v. 4, 5.)

The daylight having been almost entirely excluded by pendent tinted draperies over the windows, the little that did enter was dyed, and imparted a peculiarly mysterious, sombre, and reverential air, to the spacious structure. An awful solemnity, which insensibly induced a religious dread, and nervousness, obliged the visitor to walk gently on the mosaic pavement, and advance with timidity, imagining he heard an angelic voice whispering into his ear—*Ecce tabernaculum Dei cum hominibus—hæc est porta cœli!* Truly it is the gate of heaven—I thought I could discover here the mysterious contact between natural and supernatural—the visible with the invisible!

Sometimes the Italian sun, watchful of an opportunity to enter, discovered an interstice in the draperies, or an aperture caused by a passing breeze, when instantly he darted in in a refulgent ray, so substantial in its appearance, and so sharp and defined in its outline, that it seemed like an immense bar of gold or silver, thrown transversely across the nave—and when it fell upon the columns, and great festoons of crimson silk, it lit them up into dazzling flames of vermilion, and, as it passed round with the revolving sun, it developed in glowing colours, and deep shadows, the colossal statues, the projecting cornices, the incrusted marbles, the vivid mosaics, or the glaring dyes of some eastern costume, and all the grandeurs of that glorious fabric, in the highest relief. It seemed as if that radiant orb, which had lit up St. Peter's, and displayed its beauties for centuries, to so many wondering eyes, and stood by on this day eighteen hundred years ago, and witnessed on yonder Janiculum, the agonizing pang that won Peter's victory and crown, were disposed to force an entrance, indignant at

LIGHTING THE CANDLES.

being excluded from the universal jubilee on this anniversary day—and excluded, lest his glowing effulgence should eclipse or undermine the dominion of those flickering tapers. Too like the ungenerous and jealous one, who envies the superior brilliancy of his neighbour's virtues, and by disparaging them, screens them, lest they eclipse his own, and denies the world the light of his neighbour's edification, that his own feeble glimmerings may be seen!

It was now 7 o'clock, and the continually increasing concourse of people, became very dense—and I observed little moving atoms, creeping in and through the interstices, and decorations of the statuary, and capitals of the pillars, and along the cornices, and these proved to be the many men employed, at a preconcerted signal, to light simultaneously the candles, in the various regions of the lofty and extensive basilica. The same workmen are always employed, on this and on similar occasions, in the decorations of St. Peter's. They are called "San Pietrini," and number 120 principals, with a large body of assistants, who are guided by their directions. They are intimately acquainted with all the passages around the dome, along the cornices, capitals, and galleries, many of which are of the most intricate character. Their positions are often most critical, in their operations on the dizzy eminences to which they ascend—nevertheless, a fatal accident is of very rare occurrence. Little flames appeared moving in all directions—these proved to be the taper lights, held by the men at the end of long wands, with which they were lighting the candles within their range; but as the wands were entirely invisible in the distances, the little flames, seemed like meteors, or wandering comets, touching the candles, and creating a general conflagration, as they revolved in the eccentric gyrations of their orbits. The flame of each candle appeared about the size of a planet of the third magnitude in the firmament, and glittered like a spangle accidentally dropped on the ethereal blue, and shone as a jewel, set in one of the crowns of the mosaic representations of the saints, with which the arches of the dome are decorated. As the candles were lit, in quick succession, those radiant specks, were continually increasing in number, on this side and on that, in the wondrous attitudes above, and lower down; and all around the spacious concaves, it seemed as if a cloud at night, which had shrouded the horizon, were gradually moving off, and displaying to our astonished vision, the thousands, and the tens of thousands, of resplendent luminaries, which stud the azure, ethereal arch of the firmament. The light of day was dimmed, as it passed through the tinted draperies. A mysterious haze, or visional indistinctness, clothed the various scenes in the expansive aisles. But as the sight became better accommodated to the mysterious light, and haze of the basilica, and as I gazed more intently with wondering eyes, new sparkling lights revealed themselves, more and more numerously. The tiny flames became less vivid, as they receded in the distance, till, without the vision being bounded by any defined termination to the building, they were either entirely lost to view, or so blended their gleamings, as to resemble the galaxy, or milky way buried in the depths of ether, and so lost in the profundity, as to convey the vivid, awful, and sublime idea, of the interminable extent of infinite space, and the astounding myriads of shining orbs, poised therein by the will of the Omnipotent. The more deeply the eye penetrated the haze—the farther it dived into this apparently interminable profundity,—the greater the number of flickering lights, which were revealed upon the vision. At each advance, the eye anxiously descried others previously undiscovered, till they conveyed to the astonished mind, the idea of space illimitable, and light beyond light, numbers beyond numbers innumerable. The vastness of the space, and the number of the lights, reminded me of the wisdom of God, and the ways of His providence—oh! its depth—their inscrutable character!—the more we ponder, the deeper the profundity of that wisdom! the greater the number of His unsearchable ways! Those minute lights, unobserved at a superficial glance, but increasing in number in proportion to the distance the eye penetrated, seemed to resemble those orbs of light poised in the depths of ether, which the unassisted eye could never discern, but which are interminably revealed, in proportion to the power of the astronomer's lenses, till their magnifying power too is lost, in the distance of the journey.

> "Come forth, O man, yon azure round survey,
> And view those lamps which yield eternal day:
> Bring forth thy glasses; clear thy wond'ring eyes;
> Millions beyond the former millions rise:
> Look farther: millions more blaze from remoter skies."

I thought of God's mercy to me! Expansive, indeed, is St. Peter's, and numberless those lights, but God's bounties to me, are more numerous still, yea, more numerous than the grains of sand on the seashore, and His mercies more expansive than St. Peter's, yea, "greater than the heavens!" The circling radiance round the cornices, one above another, of the great dome, of such wonderful circumference, seemed particularly beautiful, and captivating, and were like gigantic crowns of gems, suspended by links of light, over the relics, and shrines, and confession of the triumphant martyrs, whose centenary the congregated world had assembled to commemorate. Very soon the arched aisles, towering dome, transepts, and tribune, as far as the limited vision could reach, were all lit up by those sparkling myriads, each streaming a rivulet of light, till, combining like so many tributaries, they overwhelmed the fabric, with a flood of radiant glory, to which all creation could present no parallel, outside the portals of the heavenly Jerusalem! There it is, the gigantic effort of Angelo's genius, constructed of colossal piles of masonry, and masterpieces of art, and the richest productions in marbles—there it is now, an aerial fabric of light; and as its foundations have remained unshaken for centuries, and generations have entered and passed beneath its dome and arches, it constitutes a lively emblem of the stability and glory of Christ's holy Church. The spacious surface of the dome, and its almost measureless concaves, seemed like one vast, curved, illuminated scroll—every light a glowing letter—every cornice a radiant line—proclaiming, in luminous characters, the virtues and Christian heroism of the twenty-five saints who were to be canonized, and the triumphs and glories of the Princes of the Apostles. Oh! may my faith be immovably grounded on similar adamantine rocks—my hopes cheered by similar glowing prospects—my perseverance exhibit similar constancy—and my future destinies be crowned by similar glories!

There it is, an emblem of the Church!—glorious dome—how majestic, how venerable it looks! How great the strength of the props that sustain the pondrous mole!—there it stands, unshaken, immovable for centuries, whilst palaces have crumbled into dust, whilst dynasties have tottered enfeebled with age, and generations have passed on to eternity, as evanescent as the bubbles of the purling rivulet, streaming on to the ocean!

> "Looking tranquilly, while falls or nods
> Arch, empire, each thing round thee,
>   And man plods
> His way through thorns to ashes—glorious dome
>   Shalt thou not last?"

The Procession.

ECCE REX TUUS VENIT TIBI MANSUETUS . . . . ET CUM INTRASSET JERUSALEM, COMMOTA EST UNIVERSA CIVITAS, DICENS: QUIS EST HIC? TURBÆ AUTEM QUÆ PRÆCEDEBANT, ET QUÆ SEQUEBANTUR, CLAMABANT DICENTES: HOSANNA FILIO DAVID; BENEDICTUS QUI VENIT IN NOMINE DOMINI.—MAT. xxi. 9, 10.

"*Behold thy King cometh to thee meek. . . . . And when he was come into Jerusalem, the whole city was moved, saying: Who is this? And the multitudes that went before, and that followed, cried, saying: Hosanna to the Son of David: Blessed is he that cometh in the name of the Lord: Hosanna in the highest!*"

RELIGIOUS processions are of very ancient origin. In early Christian times, it was usual for the bishops, priests, and the entire congregation, to proceed in public procession to the cathedral, for the celebration of all solemn functions, or to supplicate the divine clemency on the occasion of all public calamities, as well as to express their thanksgiving for any signal favours. Tertullian mentions the existence of this usage in the year 250—it is also mentioned by St. Augustine, St. Ambrose, and St. Leo.

In order to convey orderly, systematic, and adequate ideas of the procession and ceremonies of this memorable day, which were the most august ever celebrated by the Christian Church—the grandest and most sublime ever witnessed by human eye—I shall invite my readers to accompany me in idea, and allow me to introduce them, at six o'clock, into the "Sala Regia," and "Sala Ducale," two extensive and sumptuous halls, in the Vatican Palace, there to witness the assembling of the cardinals, princes, dignitaries, and various officials, privileged to take a place in that most imposing of earthly processions—all waited on by their respective suites, and all wearing their most gorgeous ecclesiastical, military, and court costumes and decorations—to meet, and conduct the Father of the Faithful from the Vatican to the shrines of the Apostles. I shall then conduct my readers to the pedestal of the equestrian statue of Constantine, which stands in a lofty alcove, on one of the great landings of the "Scala Regia," or royal staircase, directly opposite the vestibule of the Basilica of St. Peter's. Here we have before us a commanding view of the magnificent arched vestibule, 65 feet in height, 47 in width, and 439 feet in length ; at either side we have a full view of the "Scala Regia," the grandest staircase ever constructed, and displaying the most captivating perspective—of astonishing length, and terminating beneath in a covered gallery, which is 23 feet wide, and 360 feet long, and which unites with the curved colonnade. What a passage for a procession !—and such a procession ! On other festivals the Papal procession, on descending from the palace, here turns into the vestibule—but the extraordinary length of this day's procession required a longer circuit to extend its serpentine coils, and it passed down to the covered gallery, crossed the piazza, through double files of military in full dress uniforms, to the corresponding covered gallery at the opposite side, ascended to the equestrian statue of Charlemagne, entered the vestibule, and thence, through the bronze gates, into the nave of St. Peter's. On the procession entering the basilica, I shall ask my readers to come with me, and take up a position in the nave, opposite the gates of the "Capella del Coro," the chapel of the choir, whence we shall have a fine view of the lengthened procession moving up the vast nave, passing the "Chapel of the Blessed Sacrament," the "Confession," the "Baldochino," the "Papal altar," and "Shrines," the "place of the canonization," to the extreme end of the "Tribune," and to the "Papal throne," near the "chair of St. Peter." Come, and I shall direct your atten-

ORDER OF THE PROCESSION.

tion to the various official characters—civil, legal, military, and ecclesiastical—and the different representative bodies, as they pass—shall observe their order of precedence, and the various styles and colours of the superb and glittering costumes which they wear.

All the cardinals, princes, bishops, dignitaries, and officials, after awaiting the coming of the Holy Father, from the interior of the palace, and having been marshalled into their order of precedence, at seven o'clock, this most transcendently grand procession issued from the interior of the Vatican Palace, from the Sistine Chapel, from the royal and ducal halls, and after passing the gate of the Paoline Chapel, descended the royal staircase. The procession was headed by a drum-major, holding a grand staff, and dressed in gorgeously embroidered regimentals. He was followed by ten drummers, and trumpeters, in costumes of red trowsers, and blue coats with yellow facings. Next to these marched a company of pioneers, with aprons, axes, and other implements and accoutrements, all in heavy marching order. Then came a battalion of the "Gendarmi," a noble race of fellows, all very tall, athletic, and chosen men, dressed in dark blue state coats, white leather belts, white corded lace, and pendent aigulets and tassels, high bear-skin caps, with festoons of white cords, and tassels falling at the sides, and white plumes, white doeskin small clothes, long boots which rose high above the knees, similar to those of our Life Guards in London. They bore swords, muskets, and fixed bayonets, marched well, and were an exceedingly fine soldier-like corps. Then came several companies of the line, in review order, with sprigs of green boxwood stuck in the white rosettes of their shakos. Then came the pupils of San Michaele, and the orphan boys, all dressed in white cassocks, with white mantles, two and two, each carrying a lighted wax candle. Then came, walking two and two, and bearing candles, hundreds of the members of all the religious orders, in every variety of religious habit : the Franciscans, in coarse brown habits, with hempen ropes round their waists, shaven heads, bare feet, emaciated countenances, with features of heavenly expression ; the Augustinians, in black, with white cinctures ; the Capuchins, with long flowing beards ; the

Redemptorists of Captives, in white, decorated with crosses of crimson and blue; the brothers of Blessed Peter of Pisa, and of St. Francis de Paul; the Minor Observants, the Carmelites, the Dominicans, the Monks of St. Jerome, the Olivetines, the Camaldolesi, the Benedictines, and the Canons Regular of St. John Lateran. The processional cross of the secular clergy was borne next, and was followed by the students of the Roman College, the parish priests of the city of Rome, and the perpetual curates wearing surplices and white stoles. These were followed by the collegiate churches of the minor basilicas and patriarchates. Squadrons of mounted dragoons and detachments of infantry, and military bands of music, marched at intervals between the religious bodies, and the varieties of characters and costumes presented the most charming contrasts. The music, in slow time, was powerful, solemn, and grand. After those came the clergy of St. Jerome of Captives, of St. Athanasius, of SS. Celsus and Julian, of San Angelo in "Pescheria," San Eustachio, Santa Maria in Via Lata, San Nicholas in Carcere, San Marco, Santa Maria "ad Martyres." After these came the Camerlengoes of the Roman clergy: and then the canons of the minor basilicas, of Santa Maria Cosmedini, Santa Maria in Trastevere, St. Laurence and Damasus. Next came the canons of the patriarchal basilicas of St. Mary Major's, St. Peter's in the Vatican, and of St. John Lateran. Next to these follow the ministers of the tribunal of the Cardinal Vicar, and his two lieutenants, who preside over the civil and criminal courts, and the Prelate Vicegerent. At the heads of the various bodies were occasionally borne banners formed like lofty marquees, supported by a large pole in the centre, and composed of alternate pieces of crimson and gold cloth, with a large bell attached, which tolled from time to time. Now come the members of the Congregation of Sacred Rites, and the banners of the beatified who were to-day to be canonized preceded them. These banners were of great size, representing the apotheosis of the saints, and were borne aloft by two gilded poles, and supported by four officials by gold cords, and were followed by members of the religious orders to which the saint belonged, persons from the localities where the saints resided, confraternities or distant relatives, or others who were more especially associated with the saint's history. Next in order follow the officers of the Papal chapel, in all the distinctive habiliments of their various offices.

As we looked up or down the royal staircase—the varying shades of light—the pilasters and rows of Ionic columns, lined at either side with lines of military, who diminished in appearance in the distance, and whose bright uniforms seeming like brilliant fringes with which the skirting was draped for this joyous festival, presented a perspective of the most enchanting beauty. The procession assumed the most graceful serpentine curves, and as neither front nor rear could be seen, it appeared interminable. This line of countless dignitaries, draped in purple, violet, red, blue, and scarlet, in gold lace and bullion, looking like a moving pyramid, displayed all the vivid colours of heaven's bow; and the apex or crest above was continually changing as other officials issued forth. It was, as it were, a moving panorama or a turning kaleidoscope, and elicited astonishment, delight, and a nervous anxiety as to what was to come next. It was now a quarter past seven o'clock, and the sun was just rising over the dome of St. Peter's, and one brilliant solitary ray was beaming in obliquely through a distant window to the royal staircase, which had been previously entirely in the shade. As each of the officials in the procession passed beneath this ray of light, it threw forth in brilliant relief, at one time the mitre of an eastern bishop, at another the gold lace and waving ostrich feathers of the cocked hat of a Noble Guard, at another the flowing beard of a Capuchin, or the emaciated features, the shorn head, and coarse garment of a Franciscan friar; sometimes it lit on the bullion and gorgeous chasubles and lustrous scarlet trains of the cardinals; again it was reflected from the pointed lance and tassels of a Swiss halberd, from the brilliant armour of a mailed warrior, from the burnished helmet and tossing scarlet plume of a stalwart colonel of dragoons, resembling the Black Prince of old, or Reginald Front-de-Bœuf, or an officer of Hugh Raymond's crusaders; at another time reflected from the ornamental hilts of the swords of the Grand Esquire or the Grand Marshal, or from the jewels of the pendent crosses and decorations on the breast of the Prince Assistant at the Throne, till eventually it shone with dazzling brilliancy from the glittering diamonds of the tiara of the Pope, who now issued from the royal hall, and capped the crest of the procession in the distance, and imparted the most captivating pageantry and religious sublimity to the scene. As each personage was illuminated in passing through this brilliant ray, and again enveloped in the shade, it gave a phantom-like flitting appearance to the entire procession. The Vicar of Christ was seated on a throne called the "sedia gestatoria," or portable chair. It was covered with crimson silk velvet, richly embroidered with gold, with gold lace, gold fringes and tassels; it was supported by two long poles like the poles of a sedan chair; they were covered with crimson velvet, and borne high on the shoulders of twelve assistants called "sediari." They were dressed in crimson damask small-clothes, with rosettes at the knees, crimson vests, crimson stockings, with buckles in the shoes, and in flowing crimson damask tunics, white gloves, and heads uncovered. The Holy Father wore a white "lama" cope, and his most precious tiara. The instant he appeared the Papal colours were lowered to the dust, all the military presented arms, and fell on one knee, the officers "grounding" their swords, and, amidst swelling strains of martial music, booming bells, and a prostrate multitude, he slowly descended the staircase; on his approaching near, however, the bells seemed muffled, the loud strains of the military bands ceased, and, after a moment's silence, so profound that it seemed broken by the gleaming rays reflected from the glittering pageantry, the music was resumed by the slender, gentle notes of a soft melodious lute, that seemed to breathe timidly its reverential strains as the Vicar of Jesus Christ was passing by. The Holy Father was followed by a great number of dignitaries; also by six of the Swiss Guards, bearing immense drawn swords, representing the six Catholic cantons of Switzerland. The lengthened and gracefully coiling curves of this serpentine and gorgeously-coloured procession, as it wound from the Vatican, descended the Scala Regia, passed through the sombre light of the covered gallery, crossed the piazza lit up under a cloudless sky by the brilliant rays of a midsummer's Italian sun, flitted under the broken lights of the colonnade, penetrated the darksome shades of the opposite passages, entered the vestibule, and thence through the vast nave of the basilica — sometimes descending, sometimes ascending—sometimes direct, and sometimes circuitous in its route, threw out, in succession, every variety of tint ; and ever varying from the highest lights, softened down into neutral and middle tints, to the darkest shades, which captivated the eye, and presented examples which Turner would have been delighted to study before the execution of some of his glowing pictures! What a school for a colourist!

I shall now invite my readers to take our position in the nave, opposite the gates of the "Capella del Coro." The basilica was now thronged with multitudes to its utmost capacity. More than an hour had elapsed, since the procession commenced to move, but the lines were only now sufficiently extended to enable the Pope and his immediate "entourage" of exalted dignitaries and officials, and general officers, to join the procession. The instant his Holiness commenced moving, it was signalled to the fortress, and the large guns fired many volleys—they were responded to by the guns of another fortress, at the rear of St. Peter's—the reports were thundering—the concussions shook the very ground on which we stood!—it was grand—it was awe-striking! All eyes were now anxiously turned towards the bronze doors of colossal dimensions, at the grand entrance from the vestibule to the lofty aisles, through which this august procession was to enter, and which, when opened, indicated that the procession was near. Those ponderous doors are opened only on the entrance of the Pope, and on some other very rare and solemn occasions. Soon we heard the loud report of the clanking bolts thrown back—a moment's vibration, and I saw a slender thread of light between the dividing portals. It cheered us as indicating that after our anxious waitings, our most sanguine expectations were immediately to be realized. It seemed to me like the gleaming ray of hope, which beams on and cheers the weary expectant in these earthly aisles, who, after a life of fortitude, and heroic, patient endurance, under every trial in the ways of

God, is dazzled by the first gleaming ray of the heavenly Jerusalem, when those "eternal portals" are thrown open through which he is to enter into his everlasting tabernacles!—and see God, face to face!

Soon we heard the faint and distant notes of flourishing clarions, military bands, and rumbling drums—and the whisper ran round—"they are coming"—"they are coming!" Here they are! The procession was headed by a tall drum-major, in a grand state uniform, with a high bearskin cap, and tossing ostrich plumes, and waving a lengthened staff with a great gold head. He was followed by ten drummers of the line—then came a company of pioneers, with aprons, axes, and other implements, all in heavy marching order—then a battalion of the stately "Gendarmes." The rumbling drums as they approached swelled louder and louder, till the decade of drummers entered, and marched under the arches of the vestibule, when the reverberations through the extensive basilica became actually deafening and thrilling, and produced an effect, martial, majestic, and sublime. When they wheeled round in front of the wide marble steps which ascend to the bronze gates, the drum-major signalled by raising his staff, and then the rolling drums ceased instantaneously. They entered the church in solemn silence, and filed off to the right, and stood in position of close order. The effect of this sudden transition from the deafening din of booming guns and clattering drums, to undisturbed silence and quietude, was most impressive, and induced a feeling of nervousness and reverential awe—no whisper invaded the domain of stillness—the vibrations of sound seemed to have lost their elasticity—the very echo of the temple seemed paralysed with awe, on hearing the whisper—"The Vicar of Christ is coming!"

Drummers, cease your rumbling—hush!—observe a reverential silence! here are the "limina apostolorum!" There stands the Vicar of Christ!—in yonder gorgeous confession; surrounded by the hundred ever-burning lamps, are enshrined the sacred relics of the princes of the apostles! Silence—here error was confounded, and truth was confirmed—here the penitent sought forgiveness, and the persecuted and the innocent protection—here mighty

CATHOLIC ORIGIN OF ENGLAND'S CONSTITUTION. 121

potentates bowed in humble submission, and rolled their royal robes in the dust beneath the Vicar's footstool—here landless princes, an O'Neill and an O'Donel, found a refuge, a palace for their residence, and a grave to stretch their bones—here a Stuart found a home—here an O'Connell's heart found a resting-place, after palpitating for five and seventy years for Ireland's liberties. England! from this threshold were despatched, in the year 596, by Pope Gregory, St. Augustin and his companions, to announce to you the faith of Christ, and unfold to you your title-deed to your everlasting inheritances! Our most gracious Queen, in modern days, on presenting a copy of the Bible to an African chieftain, attributed England's glory to the possession of the sacred volume. England! who gave you possession of it?— A Pope gave it you, and popish monks preserved it for you! England! here was educated an Alfred, who laid the foundation of the stately structure of the British constitution—sanctioned and perfected parliamentary representation, instituted by King Ethelbert, Augustin's pupil—and granted to every one arraigned in a criminal court, the noble right of trial by jury. England! from this threshold were sent the bishops, who, in the days of the Heptarchy, established those laws which were subsequently comprised in a uniform digest by King Edgar and Edward the Confessor, and which are now known as the "traditional law," the "lex non scripta," or the common law of England, which is venerated by our modern justices, by their continual appeal to precedent, and which guides all the judgments of the court of Queen's Bench, and by which all the ordinary courts of judicature are guided, controlled, and directed. The common law to-day, is the popish-bishop-made-law of old. It is a law superior even to Parliament, for Parliament is rather the interpreter than the legislator of the common law of England. Popish disciples of those sent from this threshold, won for England the great bulwark of her liberties, "Magna Charta." England! Popery is indelibly stamped upon every office, and institution of your realm and constitution—it is stamped on every coin that issues from your mint—nay, it is stamped on the very forehead of your kings and queens! Who impressed upon them the glorious motto—" Defender of the Faith"—*Fidei Defensor?* It was stamped upon them, on this spot, by Pope Leo X., on the 11th of October, 1521, and subsequently confirmed by Pope Clement VII., and stamped so indelibly, that all the anti-titles acts passed by the parliaments of three centuries, have never been able to obliterate it! England, then, no longer cry "No Popery!"— the pillars that support your constitution are of popish materials, and of popish erection!—beware, then, if you pull them down, you may, like Samson of old, crush yourself, and thousands of others, by the overwhelming mass of the tumbling debris of that towering structure—Britain's constitution!

The "coup d'œil" was now transcendently magnificent and sublime, and shall ever remain indelibly impressed on the memories of those who were present on that memorable morning—comprising, in one glance, all that was astonishing in extent and perspective—all that was noble and majestic in architecture—all that was charming, brilliant, and harmonious in colouring, blending in amity—all that was symmetrical in disposition—all that was grand and lovely in nature, and all that was picturesque in art—all combining to display the most sumptuous and appropriate decorations. The scintillations of the myriads of wax lights, in their towering altitudes, were momentarily increasing in number and brilliancy, lighting up the glowing colours of frescoes, mosaics, and gildings of celestial hosts; and it seemed as if the screen by which mortality clouded my corporeal eyes were gradually withdrawn, and that I was about to see no longer "darkly, and as through a glass, but face to face," the transcendent glories of the beatific vision, and the heavenly Jerusalem, in comparison with which, the illuminations of St. Peter's, and all the glories of this world, are but as the flickering of a taper light or the play-toys of childhood! But how feeble are my most strenuous efforts at description to convey an idea of that dazzling vista!

> " Who hath not felt how feebly words essay,
> To fix one spark of heavenly beauty's ray!"

Let the restless eye, bewildered with amazement,

wander where it would, it was unable to escape, and was inclosed in a labyrinth of wonders, and of beauties—ascending at one time to the heights of the wondrous dome, or resting on pavements of the richest marbles, disposed with the greatest ingenuity—on mosaics, the life-long labours of the most exquisite manipulators—or on a statue, the "chef d'œuvre" of a sculptor unrivalled by the most artistic chisels of the greatest masters,—all reflected by those thousands of glittering lights—gazed upon by thronging multitudes from the utmost limits of the earth, and all consecrated by religion to commemorate the glorious triumphs of the cross, in comparison to which all other miracles, or the phenomena of nature, are but as the insignificant events of yesterday! That basilica on that morning presented a sublime aspect indeed!

> "But thou of temples old, or altars new,
>   Standest alone—with nothing like to thee—
> Worthiest of God, the holy and the true.
>   Since Zion's desolation, when that He
>   Forsook his former city, what could be
> Of earthly structures, in his honour piled,
>   Of a sublimer aspect? Majesty,
> Power, glory, strength, and beauty—all are aisled
> In this eternal ark of worship undefiled.

> "Enter! it's grandeur overwhelms thee not;
>   And why? it is not lessened; but thy mind,
> Expanded by the genius of the spot,
>   Has grown colossal, and can only find
>   A fit abode, wherein appear enshrined
> Thy hopes of immortality; and thou
>   Shalt one day, if found worthy, so defined,
> See thy God face to face, as thou dost now
> His Holy of Holies, nor be blasted by His brow."

After the military, entered the pupils of San Michaele, and the orphans, dressed in white, and then the members of the various religious orders, two and two, bearing wax lights, and in the order I have described, and their numbers seemed numberless, and their lengthened lines seemed interminable; and after passing up between the lines of military, what became of them I could not tell, for though the church appeared thronged to repletion, they were lost to view beyond, in some unexplored labyrinth! Nearly two hours had now elapsed since the procession had commenced to move, and the time was now approaching to nine o'clock. Here come the officers of the Papal chapel, and that portion of the procession immediately attached to His Holiness' person—if that can be called an immediate attachment which extended nearly half a mile in length! They entered the bronze gates—and slowly passed up the great nave, between the lines of soldiery, in the following order—

ESQUIRES,
Two and two, in red serge cappas, with hoods over the shoulders.

PROCTORS OF THE COLLEGE,
Two and two, in black stuff cappas, with silk hoods.

PROCURATORS OF RELIGIOUS ORDERS,
Two and two, in habits of their respective orders.

ECCLESIASTICAL CHAMBERLAINS OUTSIDE THE CITY,
Two and two, in red.

CHAPLAINS IN ORDINARY,
In red cappas, with hoods of ermine: of which there are—
First Mitre Bearer,
Second Mitre Bearer,
Third Mitre Bearer,
One Bearer of Tiara.

PRIVATE CHAPLAINS,
Two and two, in red cappas, and hoods of ermine.

CONSISTORIAL ADVOCATES,
Two and two, in black or violet cassocks and hoods.

ECCLESIASTICAL CHAMBERLAINS,
Private and Honorary, two and two, in red cassocks and hoods.

CHORISTERS OF THE CHAPEL,
Two and two, in violet silk cassocks, over which are surplices.

ABBREVIATORS OF THE PARK.

CLERKS OF THE CHAMBER,
In surplices over rochets, two and two.

MASTER OF THE SACRED PALACE,
In his habit of a Dominican Friar.

AUDITORS OF THE ROTA,
In surplices over rochets, two and two.

DIGNITARIES OF THE PAPAL CHAPEL. 125

THREE ACOLYTES, in surplices over rochets, carrying large candlesticks, with lights. GREEK SUB-DEACON.	INCENSE BEARER. CROSS BEARER, In tunic. TWO PORTERS OF THE RED ROD. LATIN SUB-DEACON, In tunic.	THREE ACOLYTES, in surplices over rochets, carrying large candlesticks, with lights. GREEK DEACON.

PENITENTIARIES OF ST. PETER'S,
Two and two, in albs and chasubles.

Swiss Guards.	**Mitred Abbots,** Of whom only a few are entitled to a place. **Bishops, Archbishops, and Patriarchs,** Two and two, the Latins wearing copes and mitres. THE EASTERNS, In their proper costumes. In all, including the Cardinal Bishops, numbering **506.**	Swiss Guards.

Cardinal Deacons,
In dalmatics and mitres, each accompanied by his chamberlain, carrying his square cap, and followed by his train-bearer.

Cardinal Priests,
In chasubles and mitres, similarly attended.

Cardinal Bishops,
In copes and mitres, similarly attended.

GENERAL STAFF, AND OFFICERS OF GUARD OF NOBLES.

GRAND HERALD AND GRAND ESQUIRE,
In court dresses.

LAY CHAMBERLAINS.

CONSERVATORS OF ROME, AND PRIOR MAGISTRATES OF WARDS,
In vestures ornamented with cloth of gold.

SENATOR.
In scarlet silk robes, and over them a mantle of cloth of gold with a lengthened train, supported by four little pages, in court dresses.

Swiss Guards. Mace-Bearer. Guard of Nobles.	PRINCE-ASSISTANT AT THE THRONE, In a splendid court-dress. GOVERNOR OF ROME, In rochet and cappa. TWO AUDITORS OF THE ROTA, To serve as train-bearers. TWO PRINCIPAL MASTERS OF CEREMONY. **Cardinal Deacon,** For Latin Gospel of Mass.	Swiss Guards. Mace-Bearer. Guard of Nobles.

HIS HOLINESS.

<table>
<tr><td>Second Assistant at Throne.</td><td>Fan borne by a Private Chamberlain.</td><td align="center">**The Pope,**
Wearing a white cope and tiara, Holding in his left hand a wax light, and with his right hand blessing the prostrate people, Borne in his chair by twelve supporters in red damask, under a canopy sustained by eight Referendaries of the Signature, in short violet mantles, over rochets. His Holiness is surrounded by his household. Six of the Swiss Guards, representing the Catholic cantons, carry large drawn swords on their shoulders.</td><td>Fan borne by a Private Chamberlain.</td><td>First Assistant at Throne.</td></tr>
<tr><td></td><td>Private Chamberlain.</td><td align="center">DEAN OF THE ROTA,
In rochet and cappa.

CHORISTERS OF THE CHAPEL,
Singing stanzas of the *Ave Maris Stella.*</td><td>Private Chamberlain.</td><td></td></tr>
<tr><td colspan="2">Majordomo.</td><td align="center">AUDITORS OF THE APOSTOLIC CAMERA,
In rochets and cappas.</td><td colspan="2">Treasurer.</td></tr>
</table>

PROTHONOTARIES APOSTOLIC.

REGENT OF THE CHANCERY, AND AUDITORS OF CONTRADICTIONS,
All in rochets and cappas, two and two.

GENERALS OF RELIGIOUS ORDERS,
Two and two, in their religious habits,
While the Pope was passing, the lines of military presented arms, kneeling on one knee, and the ensigns drooping the colours, and officers grounding swords.

As several of the bishops had only recently arrived, and as very many had never previously seen St. Peter's, I was much interested in observing the evident manifestations of astonishment they evinced, as each turned from the vestibule through the bronze gates into the nave, where suddenly its vast expanse, its costly marbles, mosaics, and gorgeous decorations, and brilliant illuminations, and all its radiant glories, were instantly displayed to their view. They seemed electrified with amazement—some raised their hands in silent expressions of wonder, or opened wide their eyes, to drink in at one draught all its glowing splendours. There was an evident struggle between the yearnings of curiosity to survey the dazzling spectacle displayed, and a desire to observe that exterior gravity of deportment, indicative of interior recollection of spirit, and that custody of the eyes, so edifying in all, but more especially in the ministers and dignitaries engaged in the Church, in celebrating the august functions and mysteries of holy religion.

The sunbeams, in their passage through the crimson silk, gold lace, and embroideries in the draperies of the windows, were dyed ruby or azure colour, or in the glowing tints of the sapphire, and the amethyst, and the jasper; and thus, reflected on the marble pavement, seemed as if strewn before the footsteps of the pontiffs, to welcome their arrival at the shrines, like the gems that were strewn in the pathway of princes we read of in eastern story! But why should I attempt by such similes to add brilliancy to the radiant splendours which dazzled the eyes of every beholder of the scenes in that basilica on that glorious day! —vain attempt!—as futile—to employ the words of our great poet—as to attempt—

> "To guard a title that was rich before,
> To gild refined gold, to paint the lily,
> To throw a perfume on the violet,
> To smooth the ice, or add another hue
> Unto the rainbow, or with taper-light
> To seek the beauteous eye of heaven to garnish."

After all its tortuous coilings through the Scala Regia, the piazza, covered galleries, and vestibule, the procession now advances through the centre of the vast nave in all its majesty—those mitred pontiffs two and two—they are the great captains of the Church's army. They walk two and two, to signify the fraternal charity, the mutual support and edification, with which all Christians should aid each other in their pilgrimage through life. They move forward, to signify that all virtue is progressive—and they chant the praises of the Almighty as they advance, to signify that we should commence here the happy occupation in which we hope to be engaged for eternity. In their left hands, in their own dioceses, they carry a crozier, to signify that they are the shepherds commissioned to tend the flock throughout the various portions of the world assigned them, and to feed the "lambs and the sheep." On their heads they wear a helmet, but it is the "galea salutis," the helmet of salvation. On their lips is "Pax," for of their empire indeed it may be said, "l'empire est paix!" In their right hands they carry not a sword, but a lighted candle, for darkness is the only enemy against which they war, and light is the only weapon they require to extend the kingdom of Christ!—their watch-cry is "Let there be light!"—and on that day indeed "there was light!"—"circumspice!" look around! not merely at the 30,000 flickering lights of wax, for how dim and insignificant are these material lights when contrasted with the 506 burning lamps of the sanctuary, and 100,000 faithful souls from the four quarters of the globe, reflecting the light of Christian faith, and every Christian virtue, and evangelical counsel!—look at those, and say was there light!—there was light, and "God saw it was good!"

When the Pope arrived opposite the gates of the first chapel, called the "Pieta," the entire procession halted—and the Dean and Chapter of St. Peter's here advanced, and, when approaching the Holy Father high on his throne, and led by their conductor, the canons sung forth in harmonious strains, which were lost in the distance of the vast fabric : *Tu es Petrus, et super hanc petram edificabo ecclesiam meam, et portæ inferi non prevalebunt adversus eam. Et tibi dabo claves regni cœlorum*—"Thou art Peter, and upon this rock I will build my Church, and the gates of hell shall not prevail against it. And I will give to thee the keys of the kingdom of heaven." Behold the fulfilment of that promise!—behold your Sovereign Pontiff!--ye princes of Holy Church!—ye pontiffs!—ye cedars of Lebanon!—ye hundred thousand souls from every clime on the habitable globe!—raise your eyes reverentially, and look at him. There he is, Peter's successor!—the 253rd link of that unbroken chain of Popes, that connects you and me with Peter, and through him with Christ Himself! *Mihi adhærere Deo bonum est*—"It is good for me to adhere to Peter!" How many years and centuries have elapsed since Christ made that promise of building that Church upon that rock! Yet there it stands! How many summers have unfolded their blossoms—how many autumns have shed their numberless leaves—how many spring-time rain-drops have moistened the soil—how many winter's storms have tossed the ocean into undulating mountains—and how many earthquakes have convulsed the globe to its very bowels, since that promise was made—yet, there upon that rock that holy Church stands—its foundations unshaken, its most delicate and loftiest pinnacles uninjured, even by the most virulent and oppressive efforts of all the gates of hell! How many momentous events have occurred since then!—appalling wars have upturned the very foundations of society—armadas have been wrecked, and whole empires have been emancipated from slavery—new kingdoms and dynasties have started into existence, have lived their age, and have sunk into dissolution, and are forgotten—diplomatists have conceived mighty projects and important speculations—legislatures have been changed, and congested masses of humanity have moved towards Eastern Europe, under the Crusaders' floating banners, to the relief of Palestine! Since Christ made that promise, the extensive dominions and the stately fabric of the Roman Empire have been dissolved, and we know nothing of it, save what we read in the records of history, or what we see of its once mighty monuments, in the mouldering stones which still surround St. Peter's towering dome, or the Quirinal, or the Vatican, the gorgeous palace of the Fisherman's successor! Since then, how many changes have occurred!—has Holy Church undergone any change? No, there it is standing on that rock, as unchangeable as its founder, Christ Himself—the same yesterday, to-day, and for ever. The stately bark, steered by that blessed pilot, steadily advances, each swelling surge only tending to elevate the ship still higher, as she floats buoyantly over the undulating wave, which is lost in the ocean behind her—or dashes to spray every presumptuous billow that attempts to oppose her voyage with her precious freight, to the heavenly port for which she is bound! Since then, Holy Church has undergone no change—neither shall she—but shall continue equally unchangeable to the very last moment of time, when this world, writhing in the agonies of fire, shall suffer her expiring pang. Then the last Pontiff, when the things of time shall be no more, and shall be rolled up like a parchment scroll that has been read and cast aside, will return the keys of the kingdom of heaven, that had been transmitted to him, into the hands of St. Peter; St. Peter will hand them to Christ; Vicars will be superseded—Christ Himself will evermore govern as supreme and visible head of His Church triumphant! And, as all the obedient children of Peter's flock will then have passed those "eternal portals," you, and I, and all of us, shall dwell, may we humbly hope, with him all the days of our eternal lives in the house of the Lord; and our joy shall be full—so full that a thousand years shall be but as yesterday!

After those solemn salutations of the Dean and Chapter of St. Peter's, they then joined the procession, and all proceeded, amidst the dense multitude, through an open passage, closely lined, shoulder to shoulder, by the Swiss Guards and the Grenadier Guards. The procession again halted opposite the Blessed Sacrament Chapel. The Pope's chair was lowered, he descended, the cardinal took the tiara from his head, removed his white cope, and replaced it with one of silk crimson velvet and gold, and knelt, surrounded by the cardinals, on benches covered with tapestry, and all adored the Blessed Sacrament, which was exposed. Formerly the Blessed Sacrament was carried before the Pope during the entire procession; it is not so at present. The Pope was raised again on the shoulders of the "sediari," and all proceeded to the high altar, where the Pope again descended, and knelt for some time before the "shrines." All moved slowly on by the shrines, the "baldaccino," the high altar, and the "confession," and the lamps unceasingly burning around it, and the procession passing them, arrived at the grand Papal throne erected in the tribune. An extensive area of the marble pavement was here covered over with green cloth, as fine and smooth as that of a billiard table, and the vast space was closely surrounded by lines of the Swiss and Noble Guards, in their state uniforms of blue, red, yellow, and scarlet; and it actually looked like a charming lawn dyed in all the verdure of summer, and bordered with violets, tulips, carnations, and moss roses. The scarlet stockings, gold buckles, and scarlet silk trains of the cardinals, and the gorgeous embroidered vestments of the Pope, bishops, princes, and many officials, as they moved in the ceremonies, presented a beautiful contrast, and appeared in vivid relief on this green ground of fine cloth. When the Pope ascended the throne, a prolonged, gracefully waving flourish of trumpets, from a company of trumpeters inside the bronze gates, undulated to the extreme limits of the spacious fabric, and threw up their swelling notes to the highest curves of the dome—they hovered long in the arched altitudes, before the vibrations calmed into stillness! On tables which stood at intervals all round, and covered with green cloth, were displayed all the valuables in gold and silver plate, from the treasury of St. Peter's, consisting of gold chalices and altar plate, elaborately chased, and studded with diamonds and precious gems—gold salvers of vast size, remonstrances, cruets, large vases, basins, and very many other articles of altar plate in gold, silver, and silver gilt, in great numbers, and of enormous value. When the sun in its revolution shone upon each, the brilliancy of the reflected gleamings, became overpowering to the dazzled eye.

When the Pope is seated on his throne, the cardinals, princes, bishops, and dignitaries commence the ceremony of paying the "homage." After moving in a circuitous line, each in his order of dignity and seniority ascends the throne at one side, and descends by the other, and in passing the Pope, bowing profoundly, the cardinals kiss his hand, the bishops his knee, and the abbots, the Governor of San Spirito, and the penitentiaries of the basilica, and other dignitaries to whom the honour is conceded, kiss his foot. This being completed, the function of the canonization commenced.

The Canonization.

UT GLORIETUR SUPER TE JERUSALEM, ET SIT NOMEN TUUM IN NUMERO SANCTORUM ET JUSTORUM.—JUDITH, X. 8.

"*That Jerusalem may glory in thee, and thy name may be in the number of the holy and just.*"

THE Cardinal Procurator, accompanied by a consistorial advocate, advanced, and profoundly bowing, and on bended knees, read aloud the following form of petition:—
"Most Holy Father, the Most Reverend Cardinal Procurator here present,"—*instanter*—"earnestly begs that the venerable and blessed Josephat Kuncevich, bishop; Peter d'Arbues; Nicholas Pichi, with his companions, namely, Jerome, Theodoric, Nicasius, John, Willehad, Godefrid de Mervall, Antonius de Werde, Antonius of Horn, Francis, John, Adrian, James, John, Osterwich, Leonard, Nicholas, Godefred Dunes, Andrew, priests, and Peter and Cornelius, laymen, martyrs; Paul of the Cross and Leonard of Port Maurice, confessors; Maria Frances, and Germaine Cousin, virgins; may be inscribed by your Holiness in the catalogue of the saints of Jesus Christ our Lord, and be honoured as saints by all the faithful of Christ."

The Secretary of Briefs, Monsignor Pacifici, after a moment's hesitation, announced, in the name of the Pope, that although his Holiness was perfectly convinced of the virtues and merits of the beatified, he hesitated to exercise so important a function of his jurisdiction, without previously supplicating the guidance of the Most Holy, through the intercession of Blessed Mary, and of Saints Peter and Paul, and all the saints of God. The Cardinal Procurator and his advocate retiring, yielded to the delay, and consented to await so pious a condition to the accomplishment of their anxieties. The Pope descended from his throne, and kneeling before the faldstool, and surrounded by the prostrate multitudes of pontiffs, each holding a lighted candle in his hand, the Litanies of the Saints were entoned, and sang as far as the last "Agnus Dei." Here all arose, and the Sovereign Pontiff again ascended his throne, and again the Cardinal Procurator and his advocate knelt, approaching still nearer to the foot of the throne, before his Holiness, and again supplicated his Holiness still more earnestly to concede the prayer of their petition, employing the words *instanter* and *instantius* earnestly and very earnestly. Still the Holy Father hesitated, and the Secretary of Briefs again announced that before his Holiness could yield in a matter of such momentous importance, he should still further delay, until he had invoked the inspiration of the Holy Ghost Himself to guide his decision. The Cardinal Procurator and the consistorial advocate seeming confident of their cause, and that as heaven was witness to the merits of their clients, and that the Holy Ghost Himself would secure the ultimate triumph of their petition, again consented to wait, and retired. The Pope again descended from his throne, and requested all the cardinals and bishops to unite with him in supplicating the guidance of the Holy Spirit; and in his name the first Cardinal Deacon called out in a loud voice, *Orate!* All knelt, and, with the Vicar of Christ, joined in mental prayer—the most profound silence and deathlike stillness reigned throughout the vast fabric, and over the tens of thousands therein congregated. The silence was awful—it induced a species of nervousness—a religious dread, a sinking of the heart—a depressing feeling of solitude insensibly overwhelmed the soul. Silence and solitude under the same roof with the Vicar of Christ, surrounded by the forty-six cardinals, 506 bishops, and 100,000 people ! Yet it was so; that solitude and silence were profound! Every soul was in converse with God!—their bodies were there, but all their souls were around God's throne in heaven! Oh! the stillness and solitude!—tick—tick—tick-a-tick—you fancied you heard the tiny ticking of your watch; your very breath seemed an intrusion on the still domain!—the solitude seemed thick about you—you fancied you could feel it! To feel alone on the distant beach when the sea is still, and whilst surveying the vast expanse of waters, is not unnatural—to feel alone in the fastnesses of some extensive forest, is not unnatural—but silence and solitude in that mighty basilica, in presence of the Holy Father, attended by his numerous dignitaries, and surrounded by so many princes of the Church, so many royal personages with their courtiers—by knights, military officers, ambassadors, and so vast a congregation assembled from all quarters of Christendom, seemed indeed mysterious and supernatural! The anxious interval was still protracted—all was hushed—the only sound that reached the ear was an occasional rustle of the silk robes of the cardinals, as they moved their positions, and it seemed like the rustle of a falling leaf, as it fell from branch to branch in the solitude of a forest! The choir, after this interval, sang the *Miserere*. The second Cardinal Deacon, at its termination, called out, *Levate!*

All arose, and two of the bishops, assisting at the throne, presented a book to the Holy Father, from which he entoned the *Veni Creator Spiritus*, which the choir sang to the conclusion, when the Pope sang the prayer *Deus qui corda Fidelium*, &c. Once more the Holy Father ascended his throne, and the persevering cardinal and advocate reiterated their demand, with increased earnestness, urging that they begged it might be granted without any further delay, not only *instanter* and *instantius*, but *instantissime*. The Secretary of Briefs said that his Holiness could hesitate no longer, but would concede a prayer which he believed to be the will of heaven. The august assembly arose, and the Pope, as the Vicar of Jesus Christ, the great doctor and visible head of the Church, pronounced the decree of canonization in the following terms:—

"In honour of the holy and undivided Trinity, for the exaltation of the Catholic faith, and the increase of the Christian religion, by the authority of our Lord Jesus Christ, of the blessed apostles Peter and Paul, and by our own authority, upon mature deliberation, and after having often implored the divine assistance, and having taken counsel with our venerable brethren the cardinals, patriarchs, archbishops, and bishops, who are in the city, we do decree and declare the blessed Josaphat Kuncevich, bishop; Peter d'Arbues; Nicholas Pichi, with his companions, namely, Jerome, Theodore, Nicasius, John, Willehad, Godefrid de Mervall, Antonius de Werde, Antonius of Horn, Francis, John, Adrian, James, John, Osterwick, Leonard, Nicholas, Godefrid Dunes, Andrew, priests, and Peter and Cornelius, laymen, martyrs; Paul of the Cross, and Leonard of Port Maurice, confessors; Frances, and Germaine, virgins, to be saints: and do appoint that memory shall be made of them, with pious devotion, in the Universal Church, on their birthday in each year, to wit, the memory of Josaphat, on the 12th November; of Peter, on the 17th September; of Nicholas and his companions, on the 9th July, as holy martyrs; of Paul, on the 28th April; of Leonard, on the 26th November, as confessors and bishops; and of Mary Frances, on the 6th October; and of Germaine, on the 15th June, as holy virgins. In the name of the Father, and of the Son, and of the Holy Ghost. Amen."

When the great sentence of canonization had been pronounced by the Vicar of Christ, the consistorial advocate, in the name of the Cardinal Procurator, expressed his most thankful acknowledgments to his Holiness, accepted it, and still further solicited its publication by the execution of the necessary apostolic letters, addressing the Holy Father in these terms:

"Most Holy Father, the same Most Reverend Cardinal here present accepts the sentence pronounced by your Holiness, and for it he returns immortal thanks, and earnestly supplicates that your Holiness be pleased to decree the apostolic letters regarding this same canonization."

The Pope replied, "We decree it." His Holiness then presented his hand, which was kissed by the Cardinal, and the advocate kissed his knee, and on rising addressed the prothonotaries, saying:

"All the prothonotaries and notaries here present, are requested to execute the public documents relating to this canonization, that the record thereof may be for ever perpetuated."

The prothonotaries reply, "We shall execute them," and turning to the chamberlains who surround the throne, they said, "You are witnesses."

The Pope's mitre was then removed, and in thanksgiving to the great God, eternal and invisible, for so singular a cause of exultation to Holy Church, his Holiness intoned the *Te Deum*. The instant these words were intoned, a lengthened tremulous flourish of trumpets resounded through the entire fabric—the great bells of the basilica tolled out their booming notes, they were responded to by the large bell of the Capitol, and all the bells of the four hundred churches of Rome and the environs, and thus continued tolling merrily for an hour. The guns of the fortress of San Angelo fired thundering volleys, till they completed a salute of 101 guns, in honour of God's fellow-citizens!

The incipient words of this august hymn of joyfulness had scarcely been intoned by the Vicar of Christ, when the notes of the anthem were swollen into a mighty volume by the collective outpourings of expressions of adoration, thanksgiving, and divine love, from 506 bishops, 25,000 priests, and 100,000 faithful souls. The rumbling notes were as those of an approaching tornado, or of pealing thunder—they agitated the air as the raging tempest maddens the ocean into such resistless fury, that it tosses ponderous navies on its surging crests as though they were but cockle shells! The undulating tide surged to the concave altitudes of that stupendous dome, and finding no egress, receded—flowed in rapids and circling eddies round and round the spacious basilica. Oh! sublime prayer of tens of thousands, from every clime gathered together in God's name, and Christ and His Vicar in the midst of them! Who that heard it can ever forget its awful grandeur and sublimity! There was no discordant note—no sigh from this valley of tears—the children of sorrow dried their tears, and attuned their voices into dulcet notes of jubilee, and love, in one universal chorus of harmonious symphony. The hoary, and those bent with years, sung the song of joy, and the "lips of the young perfected praise." It was an universal jubilee!—and it was meet it should be so!—for the Vicar announced that twenty-five members of the family had left the territories of strife—had thrown off corruption and mortality, and put on incorruption and immortality—had passed the "eternal gates," and climbed to the "eternal hills"—had attained the object of creation, of redemption, of Christ's resurrection—had grasped the treasure which cost the blood of a God—had entered into the enjoyment of the beatific vision, and of those eternal inheritances which they should now possess from everlasting to everlasting! *Te æternum Patrem omnis terra veneratur!*

In singing the versicles after the *Te Deum*, the Cardinal Deacon, for the first time, introduced into the public liturgy of the Church the names of the newly canonized saints, singing, *Orate pro nobis sancti Josaphat, Peter, &c.* The chanters answered, *Ut digni efficiamur promissionibus Christi.* After which the Pope chanted the prayer supplicating the intercession of the saints now canonized. The Auditor of the Rota then elevated the Papal cross before the throne. The Cardinal Deacon then sung the *Confiteor*, and the Pope gave the absolution, again introducing the names of the saints after those of SS. Peter and Paul. The Cardinal Deacon proclaimed the indulgences conceded by the Holy Father, being a plenary indulgence for all the faithful present at these solemnities, and seven years and seven quarantines to all the faithful, who should, on their festival day, visit the shrines of those saints. Finally, the Holy Father conferred the apostolic benediction.

Soon after the day of canonization, the promoters of each cause present a fine painting of the saints whose cause they advocated, to each of the cardinals members of the Congregation of Rites. His Eminence of Dublin being a member of that sacred congregation, received these pictures, with the exception of that of St. Frances, the community of which she was a member, pleading inability to bear the expense, being exempted.

The Solemn Papal Mass.

VINCENTI DABO MANNA ABSCONDITUM, ET NOMEN NOVUM.
—Apoc. ii. 17.

"*To him, that overcometh, I will give the hidden manna, and a new name.*"

WHEN the function of the canonization had terminated, tierce was chanted, and the Pope, assisted by Cardinal Patrizi, Cardinal Bishop assisting, by Cardinal Mertel as Assistant Deacon, and by Monsignor Negroni, Auditor of the Rota, as Subdeacon Apostolic, and by other dignitaries, commenced vesting. The vestments were grand indeed, most sumptuous, of the greatest beauty of texture, and richness of embroidery. The Pope wears many vestments and ornaments which are different from those worn by other bishops, and are peculiar to himself. He wears the "Orale," or what is also called the "Fannon," which signifies a veil or banner. The first mention of its use, made by history, occurs in the year 1200, during the pontificate of Innocent III. It is a species of tippet, made of silk, striped with four colours, and double—one side is laid on his Holiness' shoulders, and the other thrown over his head till he is vested, when that is again turned back over the chasuble. It is believed to be the ancient amice, which, though worn inside, according to present usage, was in early ages worn outside all the vestments. He wears the "Succinctorium," which is like a long maniple, falling at the side, and supported by the cincture, and bearing a richly embroidered lamb and cross. He wears also the "Balteum pudicitiæ," and during the Mass he uses the "Golden Star." He uses the "Fistula," or golden syphon or tube, at the consumption of the sacred species from the chalice, and it is also used at the purification of the chalice. The "Flabelli," or fans, borne by deacons at either side of the Holy Father, at processions, and on other solemn occasions, are of very ancient, and probably of eastern origin. They are made of the feathers of that vain bird, the peacock, and are intended to symbolize the evanescent character, and vanity of all temporal things—and as there are eyes in each of the many feathers, they remind the Pope, that the eyes of the world are fixed upon his Holiness, as the model whom the people are to imitate, and as the bright lamp that is to illuminate the darkness, and show them the way in which they are to walk. St. Basil and St. Chrysostom, mention the "Flabelli," as having been used in the ceremonies of the Greek and Syrian churches. The "Vexillum Crucis" is carried before him as the "Labarum" of old was carried before the emperors. The "Sedia Gestatoria," or portable chair, is believed to have been first introduced by the people, who, through respect for Christ's Vicar, carried him on their shoulders, on the occasions of public processions. Its use is continued, as significant of the Pope's authority over the people, and also of his superiority over other prelates, and of his primacy of honour and jurisdiction. On the occasion of the Pope's inauguration in former years, his Holiness was presented with the "Ferula," which was a kind of staff: whether it was bent like the end of a crozier or not, it is now difficult to ascertain. The Pope now never uses a crozier, except when he officiates in the diocese of Treves. Other bishops use a crozier, significant of jurisdiction, but it is bent or crooked at the top, to signify that their jurisdiction is limited, and restricted, whereas the Pope's jurisdiction is universal. The Pope wears the tiara, which combines the twofold character of an ecclesiastical, and royal ornament. In shape it resembles a mitre encircled by three crowns. Innocent III. says the Church first presented the Pope the crown, together with the mitre, in the year 1200.

Boniface VIII., in the year 1300, added a second coronet, to signify the Pope's spiritual and temporal power, and John XXII., or Urban V., added the third, to signify the pontifical, the imperial, and royal authority. The tiaras are of great value, of the purest gold, of exquisite manipulation, and studded with the most precious jewels, gems, and diamonds of the purest water.

When the Pope is vested he blesses the incense; and then the cardinals, high ecclesiastical dignitaries, and other officers, assistants at the Mass, form a procession, which takes a circuit from the throne to the end of the tribune, and thence proceeds up the centre, to the Papal altar over the shrines, and advances slowly in the following order:—

THE THURIFER—WITH INCENSE.
THE CROSS-BEARER—SUB-DEACON,
With four Acolytes on his right and three on his left.
GREEK SUB-DEACON.   GREEK DEACON.
THE LATIN SUB-DEACON,
Carrying Book of the Gospels with the Pope's maniple.
THE CARDINAL-DEACON OF THE GOSPEL.
THE CARDINAL-BISHOP ASSISTANT.
TWO CARDINAL-DEACONS ASSISTANTS.
TWO AUDITORS OF THE ROTA.
FOUR MASTERS OF CEREMONIES.

𝔗𝔥𝔢 𝔓𝔬𝔭𝔢.

TWO PRIVATE CHAMBERLAINS ASSISTANTS.
AUDITOR OF THE ROTA,
In charge of the mitre.
PATRIARCHS, ARCHBISHOPS, AND BISHOPS,
Assistants at the throne.

On the procession reaching the altar, formerly all the cardinals and bishops assisting came forward to meet the Pope, each kissing his Holiness on the cheek, and on the breast, as significant of their faith in the humanity, and divinity of Christ, the one being openly apparent, the other concealed within. Now, however, this ceremony is confined to the three junior cardinals, as, when many assisted, the ceremony became too protracted ; as well as to signify the three wise men who journeyed from the East, to visit Christ on His first appearance clothed with humanity. Then the Pope ascended the altar, and being incensed, and having intoned the *Gloria in excelsis*, again descended, and went to his throne. The Gospel was sung by the Latin and Greek deacons, in the Latin and Greek version of the sacred text. After the Gospel the Holy Father delivered a homily. The Pope again ascended and intoned the Credo. His Holiness' voice is full, sonorous, very plaintive, and devotional—his musical talents are very superior—and he sings the notes with the utmost precision of key, volume of tone, and accurate observance of time.

THE PRESENTATION OF THE OFFERINGS.

The presentation of the offerings, which is a very ancient usage, was observed at the Offertory of the Mass. They were offered by the seven postulators, of the seven causes, and presented by the Cardinal Procurator, and the Cardinals of Sacred Rites. An entire suite or set was presented for each cause. Each set consisted of five wax candles, two of them weighing sixty Roman pounds each, and three twelve Roman pounds each, decorated with exquisite taste, in painting and gilding—two loaves, one richly gilded, the other silvered—two gilded barrels, one containing wine, the other water—two doves, two pigeons, three cages of beautiful design and richly decorated, each containing several small birds. Each cage and offering was borne separately by ecclesiastics, all of whom formed a very lengthened line, and advanced processionally two and two—and amongst the ecclesiastics upon whom that honour was conferred, were Monsignor Moran, and also Rev. Professor Verdon, of the Seminary of Holy Cross. The little songster birds, imprisoned tenants of the groves, draped in their vari-coloured enamelled plumage, rivalled the chromatic effect of the gorgeous vestments of the officiating dignitaries. They warbled sweetly ; and without a score or a conductor, they rivalled, in their artless lays, the most scientific compositions, and most elaborate motettes, even of Mustapha, Capocci, or Meluzzi themselves !

This presentation of offerings at religious ceremonials, is a usage which derives its origin from the most remote antiquity ; it was even prescribed in the ceremonials under the old dispensation, and is employed by Holy Church as a means, by this offering of material things, to signify that interior worship of the heart which is due by every creature to the Sovereign Lord of all creation, and the Giver of every good gift. The candles are emblematical of the light of faith, the brilliant virtues, and burning lamp of edifying example, the flame of divine charity, and the vigilance with which the saints watched, and seized every opportunity of exercising good works, and by which they have illuminated the house of God, and all the members of the holy Christian family. The bread represents that food of the strong, that bread which they eat when hungry, lest they faint by the way—on the strength of which they journeyed through the wilderness of this world, unto the mountain of God, Horeb, and by which they secured the possession of a blessed immortality : " He that eateth this bread shall live for ever." The wine is typical of the sanctifying grace which invigorated their souls whilst walking in the ways of God. *Introduxit me in cellam vinariam* (Cant. ii. 4). "He brought me into the cellar of wine." It is also typical of that wine of compunction which fed them " with the food of tears, and gave them drink of tears in measure," during their holy lives, melted down their souls to the most tender sentiments of piety and divine love, and also of that torrent of delights which now inebriates their souls in the heavenly Jerusalem. *Flumine voluptatis tuæ potasti eas.* The water represents the virtue of temperance, and the sufferings of this life—that draught of vinegar and gall, which those children of the cross quaffed for Christ's sake, which they endured for love of Him who expired in agonies for them, and the pains of martyrdom, which have wrought in them an eternal weight of glory—an inexhaustible fountain for ever springing up to eternal life. The doves and pigeons are emblematical of their meekness of spirit, their fidelity to all their holy obligations, and their love of retirement, by which they withdrew from the dissipating occupations of secular cares, turned aside from the crowd, entered into "the desert to rest a little," and by which they preserved the interior life, and the intimate communion of their souls with God. The dove has been ever regarded as an emblem of peace, and is now typical of that peace of God which exceedeth all understanding. As the dove of old, which was liberated from the ark by Noah, flitted back with the olive branch, indicating that the waters of the deluge were subsiding, and that dry land had appeared, even so the dove presented in these ceremonials indicates that the cross by which they had been drenched with a deluge of trials, by which these saints had been inundated, was subsiding—that the ark of religion floated buoyant over the swelling tide, and that they are landed in safety on the heavenly mountain of Ararat—that the winter has passed, the summer has come, that they already hear the early notes of the springtime, which promises a summer that is never to end. *Vox turturis audita est in terra nostra!*—" The voice of the turtle is heard in our land." As little birds love to soar above the earth, they, too, are introduced into these oblations, to signify that the souls of the saints yearned for God, and, by continued contemplation of the things of heaven, continually soared above all sublunary things; and as those birds, when fatigued, seek their rest beneath the leaves and extended branches of the shady tree, and screen themselves from the parching heats of the meridian sun, so the weary souls of the saints fled for repose beneath the shady branches of that tree that bore the precious fruit of life from which their blessed Jesus was suspended. *Sub umbra illius quem discaraveram sedi*— "Under the shadow of Him whom I have desired, there have I sat."

The Music at the Offertory.

At the Offertory, the "motette," composed by the celebrated soprano Mustapha, to the words *Tu es Petrus, et super hance petram edificabo ecclesiam meam, et portæ inferi non prevalebunt adversus eam*, was sung by three choirs—and for originality of composition—for the harmonious captivating character of the music—for the number of vocalists, and choirs, and the artistic ingenuity of their disposal—and the sublimity of the effect produced, it has, perhaps, never been equalled by any effort of musical genius in modern times. For those who enjoyed the happy fortune of having heard it, the mere reminiscence, shall ever soften their souls to compunction, and veneration, and cause every fibre of their hearts to vibrate in harmony. The number of vocalists amounted to six hundred—divided into three choirs. One was placed within the tribune, opposite the Pope's throne, in the position in the brass-wired gallery usually occupied by the Papal choir, and this choir represented the especial Church of Rome, or that of "urbis," the city. The second, composed of two hundred tenors and basses, was placed over the portico of the grand entrance door far away beyond the sea of foreign heads in the vast nave, representing the Universal Church, to the utmost bounds of the earth, or that of the "orbis." Lost to sight in the altitudes of the dome, was placed a third choir, consisting of four hundred trebles and sopranos, selected from the juvenile choirs of Rome, representing the choirs of the heavenly Jerusalem, which join their joyous accents of jubilee with the churches militant on this memorable anniversary, and proclaim the triumphs of those blessed members of the family, who "fought the good fight," and won the palm of victory.

After a period of stillness, quietude, and silence, a slender thread-like tremulous octave note was heard singing *Tu es Petrus*—the voice seemed as it were timidly advancing from a place of modest retirement, and awe-stricken at the presence of the august majesty of the personage it was saluting. Soon it assumed a little confidence, and gradually swelled its tones into a louder, fuller, and more decisive melody. Immediately it was joined by another; and many former companions of its retirement, approaching nearer to the throne, swelled the volume into the most dulcet and heavenly chords that ever fell upon terrestrial ears, chanting *Tu es Petrus*. Was there ever so explicit, so solemn, so sublime an act of faith, in the perpetuity, supreme jurisdiction, and apostolic succession of the Sovereign Pontiff, Peter's successor! There he is, Pius IX., the two hundred and fifty-third link of the unbroken chain of succession to Peter's chair! A hundred thousand of his faithful subjects congregated within that temple, from the ends of the earth—forty-six princes of the Church—and five hundred and six bishops, representing two hundred millions of people, raise their eyes reverentially, and look on his Holiness seated on that throne: their heads bowing in submission to the sentiment, and their hearts beating in unison to the faith expressed by the choir, in the words, *Tu es Petrus*. There they are, with their hands outstretched, clinging to that rock for support—and amidst all the fluctuating vicissitudes of temporal events—amidst the tossings by "every wind of doctrine;" hurried along by the rapid current, or sinking in the waters, they grasp at that rock, crying, *Tu es Petrus, salva nos, perimus*—"Save us, or we perish."

When the Papal choir within the tribune representing the Church of Rome, or the "urbis," had terminated the last softened cadences of this song of faith to Peter's enduring supremacy, the other choir, situated in the high balcony over the threshold on the *limina Apostolorum*, at the extreme end of the lengthened basilica, and beyond the vast congregation—that undulating ocean of congested Christianity from the uttermost ends of the earth—and representing the Universal Church, or the "orbis," commenced singing, in firm, decisive, and virile bass notes, which seemed to rumble to the very foundations of the church building, *Et super hance petram edificabo ecclesiam meam*, dwelling in prolonged strains on *hance petram*, and *ecclesiam meam*, for the two were there, *diffusa et cathedra*. Occasionally they swelled into the most overwhelming burst of enchanting harmony, wafted towards us from the distant region beyond that expansive sea of God's people, and again the cadences softly and gently died away over the multitudes. The varied intonations seemed like the soft notes of an exquisitely-strung Æolean harp, which the gentle breeze of a summer's zephyr, swelled into the most harmonious and dulcet tones, or again softened down to the gentlest breath, as the declining breeze died away into the languid stillness. At length these captivating notes were thus prolonged, and attenuated, till only one melodious slender octave voice preserved the gentle echo it received from below, gradually dying away till it stole our senses towards heaven, and made us doubt if it were not a celestial note, that had made a brief visit to our earthly functions, and was returning to the halls of the heavenly Jerusalem, from which it emanated.

It seemed echoed back again, by the softest, and sweetest soprano voice that ever captivated human ear, from amongst the four hundred children choristers, lost to view in the expansive spaces which arched the distances of the wondrous dome! The theme of its strains, was, *Et tibi dabo claves regni cœlorum.* At first the thread-like note was so thin and flitting, that it required that every nerve of the ear should be strained to its utmost expansion, to decide if it were reality, or the mere creation of some enthusiastic imagination. Gradually it increased in volume, in sweetness, and distinctness, and was soon joined by another, and another, and a multitude of voices. Oh! the song was joyous and thrilling, and it echoed again and again—*Et tibi—et tibi —et tibi—dabo claves regni cœlorum!* Every breast heaved with emotion—every heart thrilled with exultation—and every eye trickled a tear of devotion!

Thus they commenced to sing—the inflexions of the various notes wound through each other in intricate mazes, without entangling the coil, twining in the most graceful curves round the words of the sacred text, to sip the honey of devotion as they flitted by, and moistened in the unctious melody, eventually they united again. Those devotional notes caused all the faculties of the soul to harmonize with the faculties of the Deity, and to blend with the waters of that eternal fountain and source from which they emanated!

The fourth part of this wonderful musical composition, was commenced by the choir in the distance over the vestibule, representing the Universal Church militant, by many deep, sonorous bass voices, rumbling as if they issued from the bowels of the earth—*Et portæ inferi non prevalebunt adversus eam!* They sang deeper and louder, more and more defiantly, *Non prevalebunt—non—non prevalebunt*, in strains replete with awe, impressiveness, and determination. Soon the Papal choir in the tribune joined in the defiant strains—nay, the powers of heaven seemed moved, and the four hundred trebles, sopranos, and octaves in the dome chimed in most enthusiastically in their highest notes, combining in the most charming musical chords : thus heaven and earth uniting in one overwhelming chorus, proclaimed their confidence in the Church's perpetuity against the united efforts of her most powerful enemies, and in the midst of the most fearful convulsions—*Portæ inferi non prevalebunt adversus eam*. The heart of the Sovereign Pontiff, of the princes, of the bishops, of the twenty-five thousand priests, and the hundred thousand in the congregation, beat responsive to the confident defiant notes—*non prevalebunt—non—non prevalebunt*—the octaves resounded through the subterranean crypt—encircled the sacred shrines of the relics of the Apostles, blessed Peter and Paul—they reverberated from the tribune to the vestibule, through the arches of the nave and aisles, and long after the voices had ceased, rumbled round and round the dome, unwilling to leave—*non—non prevalebunt!* Neither shall they!—Christ has said it—ye timid ones, why do you quail?—ye of little faith, why are ye afraid? Tis He whom the winds and the waves obey—He has only to speak, and there cometh a great calm—*non prevalebunt*—no ! when God is for us, who shall be against us?

The Mass proceeded, and the numerous retinue, as they moved to and from the throne to the altar, over the fine green cloth, produced a superb effect. The Pope was always followed by twelve bishops assistant at the throne, of whom six were patriarchs, and six were archbishops, one of whom, on this occasion, was his Grace of Westminster, Henry Edward, Most Reverend Dr. Manning. During the celebration of the august mysteries, the Pope was surrounded by sixty assistants of every ecclesiastical grade, dignity, and costume; and when their varied and superb vestments—their glittering embroidery of gold and silver—and the sparkling diamonds and jewels, were dimly seen through the folding volumes of fragrant incense that ascended to the lofty dome, the effect was surpassingly grand and mysterious looking!

At the Offertory, the sacristan presented three hosts, two of which the Cardinal Deacon pointed out, and which the sacristan then immediately took and eat. The Cardinal Deacon then took the other for the consecration at the Mass. The keeper of the wine-cellar in like manner presented a vessel of wine, with a portion of which the sacred vessels were washed, and which he himself then drank, and out of the remainder the cruet for the Mass was then supplied. This usage is very ancient, and seems to be a precaution against poison; but as to the time when it first originated, or whether any occasion of suspicion caused its introduction, it is difficult to ascertain.

From the Preface of the Papal Mass to the Communion, two deacons stand at either side of the altar, in profound recollection, and as immovable as statues; and they are intended to represent the angels whom Mary saw at the head and feet of our blessed Lord, in the sepulchre at Easter, as recorded in the twentieth chapter of St. John, verse the twelfth—"And she saw two angels in white, sitting, one at the head, and one at the feet, where the body of Jesus had been laid."

At the Consecration, the Papal choristers ceased singing, and a breathless silence prevailed throughout the prostrate multitude; and, after an awful nervous pause, the Sacred Host and Chalice were elevated; and at that instant, by one simultaneous movement, the Noble Guards, and the military of the various regiments of the line, that were on duty in the church, fell on their knees. Every sword was lowered, every musket was presented, and from a distant balcony over the grand entrance, twelve trumpeters, from twelve silver trumpets, breathed forth a flourish of as soft, harmonious, silvery chords, as ever struck the human ear, entrancing all the feelings of the soul, and captivating them up to heavenly things. They echoed again and again through the lofty walls of the vast basilica, and hovered round the dome, as if reluctant to part so prepossessing and sublime a scene. At the same moment several thundering volleys of artillery were fired from the Castle of San Angelo, and rumbled through the fabric. Every one was electrified—some looked at each other with amazement; others struck their breasts, bent low in sentiments of adoration, and tears of devotion trickled down the cheeks of many! A profound sense of awe pervaded the entire congregation, forcibly expressive of their faith, in the presence of the Divine Majesty.

The Pope consecrates in secret, in the usual manner, but before the Communion he descends from the altar, and accompanied by his numerous dignitaries and assistants, ascends his throne, and there he consumes. This is significant of the life of Christ, hidden in the early part of His ministry, but public and exalted on the cross, before the eyes of the world, when He consummated the sacrifice. This was the ancient usage—to descend from the altar after the Canon—the Pope dividing the Sacred Host amongst the bishops and priests who assisted at the sacrifice—the deacon dispensing what remained after the Pope had distributed communion. The Pope, after the *Agnus Dei*, gave the *Pax*, and then left the altar. The Cardinal Deacon then exhibited the Most Holy over the patena, and under the "Golden Star," and turning to one side and the other, all prostrated themselves and adored—he then gives the Host to the other deacon, who conveys it to the Pope, and he himself conveys the Chalice. The Pope breaks the Host, consumes one portion himself, and divides the other for the deacons. The Cardinal Bishop assistant then presents the golden tube, or "fistula," to the Pope, through which he consumes a portion of the Sacred Species out of the chalice. The deacons return to the altar, and purify the chalice through the same "fistula." The Pope takes the ablution from another chalice, presented to his Holiness by the Cardinal Bishop. In early Christian ages, when the communion was administered to all the faithful under both kinds, this "fistula" was introduced to obviate the unseemliness of presenting the same chalice to the lips of all—but still more to preclude the possibility of the irreverence, so liable amongst many communicants, of one drop of the sacred blood of Christ falling to the ground. Since the discipline of the Church was changed, by administering communion to the faithful under one kind only, the "fistula" has fallen into general disuse; but the Pope still employs it on these solemn occasions, as a relic of early Christian times, and through veneration for ancient usages. After his own communion, the Pope gives communion to some of the bishops and princes, and he again ascends the high altar, and proceeds with the concluding portions of the Mass. The proper prayer of the saints newly canonized, is sung after those of the Mass of the day, under one conclusion.

During the canonization, and not far from where I stood, one of the large chandeliers fell with a great crash, but it was providential indeed, that, though dense the mass of people beneath, no person was hurt. During the Mass, the silk draperies of one of the windows of the transept caught fire, from one of the wax lights—it was soon extinguished by the admirably disciplined corps of the fire brigade, who, with their engines, were on duty all day around the basilica. The withering thought of the disaster at St. Iago occurred to my mind—for though the basilica, which is not only built, but roofed with stone, could not be burned, the effect of a sudden panic amidst such a multitude of human beings, might have eventuated in the death of thousands—but "the Lord guarded the city!"

During the ceremonies, and about the time of the Offertory, a poor weak-minded and enthusiastic man, named Achilli Rossi, a native of Cremona, whilst kneeling before the Blessed Sacrament altar, was so enraptured at the transcendent earthly glories by which he was surrounded, that he cried out he should see the greater glories of heaven!—and to effect his fancied conveyance there, he stabbed himself three times in his neck, and from the wounds flowed copious streams of blood, which saturated the marble pavements around. Under such circumstances, of blood being maliciously shed, a church is desecrated, and requires a lengthened interval, and a solemn ceremony, before it is "reconciled," and before the Holy Sacrifice is again allowed to be celebrated therein. On the occasion of the martyrdom of St. Thomas à Becket, Canterbury Cathedral remained desecrated, and deserted for an entire year. A similar lengthened interval elapsed, before the reconciliation of the church in which the Archbishop of Paris was assassinated. On this occasion, however, when the event was whispered to the Pope, his Holiness, in order to avert any interruption to the august functions, blessed the church himself immediately. The ceremony was unobserved by the general congregation, and was only noticed by those who surrounded the throne, and who formed his Holiness' immediate *entourage*. Poor Achilli Rossi died in the hospital, on that night, from his self-inflicted wounds.

The reserved boxes, or arched galleries, which surrounded the tribune, were occupied by numerous distinguished personages, in every variety of gorgeous costume, and military uniform ; and the ambassadors, and all the diplomatic corps, representing almost every royal court in the world, were all in their court dresses, with the insignia of their various orders, ribbons, crosses, and stars, glittering with jewels and brilliants. Lord Northesk, a British nobleman, was there. His Majesty the ex-King of the Two Sicilies, with the princes, and other members of the royal family, occupied one of the royal galleries—they all appeared in grand full court costume, attended by a numerous courtly retinue of staff officials, " aides-de-camp," and general officers, who stood behind the royal personages during the entire ceremony. Her Majesty the Queen Dowager of Naples was present. There was present also her Royal Highness the Princess Isabella, the Infanta of Portugal. Her Royal Highness wore no feathers in her hair, no lappets, diamonds, jewels, or other ornaments ; but a black silk veil, suspended from her hair, fell behind with great simplicity and grace. She wore a full dress of black silk. Her lady-like placidity of expression, her easy gentleness of manner, and dignified deportment, invested her with the *air distingué*, and quite accorded with her Royal Highness' exalted rank. Every heart thrilled with joy—it was a universal jubilee—yet no ! the jubilant expression of joyous countenances is not universal—there is one exception—see the venerable father yonder—his countenance seems clouded ; and sorrow, to-day banished elsewhere, seems to have found a refuge, and to have settled on his brow ! He represents the most aristocratic Catholic family in England—the purest blood of the Howards circulates in a crimson flood through his veins— he is Philip Henry Howard, Esq., of Corby Castle, in Cumberland. Every eye that witnesses his depression, and every ear that hears of his tale of sorrow, causes every string of sympathy to vibrate in the hearts of the nobles of Rome, the peasant, and the stranger. But a few days ago, and his eldest daughter, who had scarcely counted her twentieth summer, endeared to her acquaintances, of prepossessing appearance, gifted with every engaging accomplishment, and adorned with every virtue, bound to his heart by a thousand ties of affection, and reflecting all his own goodness and graces, was rudely torn from his arms by remorseless death. She returned from viewing the picturesque scenery of Naples, to witness the grandeurs of the Centenary, flushed with the sanguine hopes of a lengthened life of temporal happiness, and behold her sparkling eye has lost its lustre, is now as a dim ball of clay, and she dwells in the darksome recesses of the tomb! Her name was Mary Frances—her mother's name, Eliza Minto Howard, *née* Minto Canning, of Foxcote, Warwickshire. Her illness was a virulent fever, to which she succumbed after a few days, on the evening of St. John the Baptist's day. Her obsequies were presided over by Right Rev. Dr. Strain, Bishop of Edinburgh, and were attended by the Rector, and Vice-Rector of the English College, Dr. Neve, and Dr. Giles, and by a large number of the most distinguished residents in Rome, on the 26th of June, in the church of Santa Maria del Popolo. The English prelates were unable to attend, in consequence of being obliged to wait on the Holy Father at the Consistory, which occurred at the same time, in the Vatican. Yet, fond father, "be not sad, like others who have no hope." Let resignation to God's providence dry your tears—the blow was not a random one—it was aimed, with unerring accuracy, by the invisible hand of God! Did you think her light was to be permanent here?—she was here but as an evanescent meteor—God wished for the jewel, and broke the casket to pick it out, and fix it with the saints in heaven—where her light shall be permanent, and where she shall shine as a fixed star for all eternity. She died in the odour of sanctity, at the "Limina Apostolorum," and from which, may we piously hope, she has stepped to the threshold of heaven, and is now associated with the saints, whose triumphs we celebrate to-day. She died young—others have had a lengthened voyage, and only through many tribulations have entered into the kingdom of God—she had scarcely embarked, when she arrived at the destined port! Perhaps a solicitous providence removed the delicate flower from the tempestuous wintry blasts of the world, to shelter its delicate tendrils and secure her virtues in the preserves of heaven, under the genial ray of His countenance, where she "shall see God face to face!" Then, mourning father, be cheerful—unite in the general joy of St. Peter's to-day—God knows what is best for you and for her. When He gave her to you, He was good; when He took her from you, He was good—He is equally good when He sends joys, and when He sends crosses—

> "Good when He gives, supremely good,
> Nor less when He denies;
> Ev'n crosses from His sov'reign hand,
> Are blessings in disguise!"

After the Post-Communion and *Ite Missa est*, the Holy Father gave the Benediction. After Mass is over, the Pope leaves the altar, lays aside the pallium, mitre, and vestments—makes his thanksgiving, with two acolytes holding wax lights, kneeling at either side. He then resumes his tiara and cope—ascends the "Sedia Gestatoria," till he reaches the relics which are exposed, and which he venerates with uncovered head. After the Mass had terminated, the Cardinal Archpriest of St. Peter's, Cardinal Matthei, accompanied by the canons of the basilica, took from a grand purse, an offering, which, in the name of the chapter, he presented to the Pope on the occasion of his singing the Mass—and this is called the offering of the "presbyterium." The Pope gave it to the Cardinal Deacon, the Cardinal Deacon gave it to his train-bearer, who retained it as his perquisite. The Apostolic Chamberlain then demanded a return of the revenues, and tributes due to the Roman Church—and the Holy Father reiterated his protestations against all those who had been deficient in their bounden obligations, and against all the usurpations prejudicial to the rights of the Holy See, and to the temporal power of the Sovereign

Pontiff. The Cardinal Dean then offers his felicitations—and amidst thrilling music, pealing bells, and thundering artillery, the procession returns through the basilica as it entered.

The choir or venerable assemblage within the tribune, during the ceremonies, consisted of 506 patriarchs, archbishops, and bishops—and very many other dignitaries, princes, and officers of the ceremonies. The number of people who assisted at the functions within the basilica, was calculated to have approximated to 100,000. The expenses of the functions, decorations, and offerings, were contributed partly by the Pontifical Government, partly by the governments and people of the countries in which the saints had resided, and principally by the religious communities with which the canonized saints had been associated, and which they had honoured and illustrated by their virtues. The ceremonies occupied a period of six hours—commencing at seven o'clock, and terminating at one o'clock.

The ceremonies of that memorable event form a compendious volume, the theme of which is the Church—of which the spacious basilica of St. Peter's is an illuminated page—the vast dome, the margin—the cornices, so many gilded borders—the lengthened processions, so many glowing lines—and every bishop a period, at which to pause and ponder—all proclaiming, in eloquent language, the august character of that divine institution—and that volume shall be deposited in her archives, and may ever be adduced as a conclusive argument of the unity, sanctity, catholicity, and apostolicity of Holy Church, and as such must ever remain irrefutable.

THE PAPAL BENEDICTION FROM THE "LOGGIA."

In consequence of the very protracted period occupied by the ceremonies, the Papal Benediction from the "Loggia" was not given to-day, which many of those who should never again have the opportunity of witnessing it, deeply lamented. But as it usually follows the celebration of the Papal Mass on Easter day, and on other great festivals, I deem it will prove interesting to my readers to describe it, as I witnessed it on a former festival. It is justly regarded as the grandest, the most impressive, and the most sublime spectacle which the world can present to the human eye—how gratifying, too, and how salutary to the Christian's heart!

I shall now invite my readers to ascend the staircase which leads to the roof of the covered gallery, from which we shall obtain a commanding view of that grandest of ceremonials. The "Loggia" is an arched balcony in the very centre of the façade of the basilica, commanding an extensive view of the piazza, the city, and environs. A great awning was stretched above it, to screen the Pope from the glaring rays, and excessive heat of the sun. Beneath us was the "piazza," presenting the most transportingly beautiful appearance, where 10,000 men, of various regiments, in their state uniforms, were drawn up in lines, describing beautiful figures, with their bands, drums, and colours, and all facing the façade, and preserving an open space, in the centre of which the Generalissimo, in state uniform, was seated on horseback. There were the "Grenattieri"—the "Caribinieri"—the "Dragoni Pontefici"—the "Gendarmi"—the "Cacciatori"—the "Guardia del Senato"—the "Svizeri"—the "Antibes Legion"—and there was that distinguished corps, the "Papal Zouaves," so loyal to their Pontiff-King—so exemplary as Christians—so brave in the field—and so heroic in works of self-sacrificing charity. The Pope's Guard of Zouaves number 4,593 members, amongst whom are 1,910 Dutch, 1,301 French, 686 Belgians, 157 Romans and other Pontifical subjects, 135 Canadians, 101 Irish, 87 Prussians, 50 English, 32 Spaniards, 22 Germans, 19 Swiss, 14 Americans, 14 Neapolitans, 12 Modenese, 12 Poles, 10 Scotch, 6 Tuscans, 5 Portuguese, 3 Maltese, 2 Russians, and a South Sea Islander, an Indian, an African, a Peruvian, a Mexican, and a Circassian. This gallant corps of Christian heroes, is now commanded by Lieutenant-Colonel Baron Athenasius de Charette.

Very many, even of the privates of the Zouaves, are personages of the highest social position, who regard it an honour to be allowed to serve the Holy Father in any military capacity. Many youths of the most noble blood of

Italy, have joined the ranks of the Zouaves. Within the last few months, the young Prince Don Alfonso, Infanta of Spain, son of the Archduchess Beatrice D'Austria—Este, and of the Infanta Don Juan, has enlisted as a private in the Zouaves. Around the military stood at least 100,000 people, all awaiting the appearance of the Holy Father on the lofty balcony of the " Loggia." The " Loggia " was gorgeously draped with crimson and gold, its pillars festooned, and from the balustrade hung rich tapestry, and purple velvet, and embroidered "lama d'oro," above was suspended a crimson velvet "baldocino," or canopy, and over all was the vast awning to screen off the rays of the sun. In the midst of the multitudes in the piazza, the Egyptian obelisk reared the glorious ensign of the cross, and at either side the two playing fountains, unrivalled for beauty, threw up their showers of crystal waters. When the Pope appeared, surrounded by the dignitaries, the great bells pealed, the bands played, the guns boomed, the multitudes prostrated, and the general waved his sword, and a rumbling roll of drums ran along the lines, and the flickering sheen of ten thousand swords, and bayonets, seemed like a peal of thunder, and a flash of lightning that gleamed through the piazza. The Pope then appeared on the lofty "Loggia." Other mighty kings, and emperors, and earthly potentates, may, on festive anniversaries, stand on high places, and survey their extensive dominions, and present themselves wearing their sceptres, and diadems, and flowing robes of crimson drapery, tinctured with the most brilliant dyes, and surrounded by all their courtiers, and glittering pageantry. Contrast those mighty ones, with the overwhelming majesty of the Pontiff-King, on Easter Day—how do they hang their diminished heads, and dwindle into atoms of despicable insignificance! Contrast his boundless domain, which is not circumscribed even by the circumference of this little earthly sphere, with their most extensive empires, and they become but as little spots in a valley viewed from a lofty mountain! Their numberless subjects are but as units, when compared with the hundreds of millions who bow to his supremacy!—and all their power is but as the impotence of an infant's grasp, when contrasted with his power who is the Vicar of Him whom "the winds, and the waves, and all things obey," and who can "bind and loose," not only on earth, but also in heaven! On such occasions kings are received with rapturous plaudits, with waving of handkerchiefs and hats, and vociferous cheering—and those demonstrations are esteemed as tokens and pledges of affection, respect, and loyalty. But, in the august presence of the Holy Father of the faithful, no such demonstrations dare intrude. There the only demonstration manifested was the bended knee, the downcast look, the prostrate figure, the reverential silence of tens of thousands, who assembled to receive that benediction, and when they received it, retired, as Pope said, with—

"What nothing earthly gives or can destroy,
The soul's calm sunshine and the heartful joy."

The Vicar of Christ arose, lifted up the light of his countenance, raised his aged hands to heaven, and appeared clothed with more than earthly majesty. His right hand, after unbarring the treasury of God's graces, descends laden with the benediction of heaven, and, with the triple sign of salvation, he imparts it to his people. Instantly that benediction springs forth from the "Loggia" on its flight, like a winged courier, and is borne on strong pinions, that convey it with more rapidity even than the measureless wire does the electric spark. Contrast the progress of a telegram despatched to a distant country, with the rapidity with which that benediction speeds its way to the ends of the earth, and the progress of the telegram when contrasted with it will be regarded as a tardy gait indeed. Away it goes on mercy's errand—its copious diffusiveness envelops the whole world as a speck! and its language is intelligible in every tongue! Standing on that "Loggia," the Pontiff-King, greater than Moses—looking towards the Eternal City, towards the extended Campagna, and the everlasting hills in the distance—he directs that benediction to go *Urbi et orbi*—to the city and to the universe. Instantly it flies, obedient to the command—no lane in that city so narrow—no staircase or garret so tortuous or inaccessible—no cellar so deep—no palace so gorgeous and extensive, into which that blessing does not enter, and offer its sacred salutation! That blessed gleam of the Sun of Righteousness radiates to every clime, and country, and people to which the compass points—it travels to where the east is reddened by the rising sun, and thence to the back of the western hills, and from the oppressive heats of the tropics, to where the blood becomes gelid iu the freezing regions of the north, vivifying, consoling, strengthening all beneath the influence of its genial ray. It conveys a balsam to cure the wounded heart—it refreshes the weary and the heavy laden—it dries up the trickling tears of the afflicted, and administers a cordial to invigorate the sick and the languishing—it penetrates the darksome dungeon, and imparts a cheering ray to the desponding captive—it is a staff to support the tottering pilgrim, and the labours of the distant missionary—it is a genial ray, that unfolds the blossoms of all our hopes of God's mercies, and a blessed immortality, and is received as a welcome guest into the hearts of 200,000,000 of Catholics dispersed into every quarter of the habitable globe !

> "Thou, of all consolers best,
> Visiting the troubled breast,
> Dost refreshing peace bestow :
> Thou, in toil our comfort sweet,
> Pleasant coolness in the heat,
> Solace in the midst of woe !"

The Cardinal Dean presented his felicitations to the Pope, and let fly two paper documents, commemorative of this memorable event, and all retired amidst a deafening chorus of music, bells, and artillery. An hour elapsed before the dissolving, streaming multitudes enabled me to wade through the piazza.

The Girandola, or Grand Display of Fireworks.

Aspectus eorum quasi lampades, quasi fulgura discurrentia.—Nahum, ii. 4.

"*Their looks are like torches, like lightning running to and fro.*"

THE "Girandola" is the term employed to signify the grand display of fireworks at Rome, and the word is derived from the revolutions of the fire-wheel, which originally constituted one of the principal entertainments; but the word "Girandola" is now employed to signify the entire pyrotechnic display. This pyrotechnic entertainment was displayed with unusual splendour on this great commemorative Centenary—and many were the expectants who yearned for the anticipated enjoyment. The "Girandola" at Rome, whether for the number of rockets engaged, the ingeniousness of the devices, the variety of combinations, and glowing colours, the general brilliancy and charming character of effect, has long been regarded as the most unrivalled display of pyrotechnic art which the world can exhibit. The display took place at the Piazza del Popolo, a circular space, which occupies a very extensive area, immediately inside the Porta del Popolo, one of the principal gates by which the city is entered, and situated near the site of the great Flaminian gate of ancient Rome. On one side a temporary gallery was erected, covered and draped; and to this all visitors presenting an introduction were politely admitted, and entertained, at the expense of the municipality, with coffee, confectionery, and ices. In the centre of the piazza stands the fine ancient obelisk, erected some thousands of years ago, in Egypt, by King Rameses I. In front rises abruptly the lofty and almost perpendicular hill of Monte Pincio. On the sides and summit of this hill the pyrotechnic display was exhibited. Tens of thousands streamed into this piazza from every leading avenue from the city and environs, and after sunset the dense mass of congregated humanity was so closely packed, that each individual had merely standing room ; and when the countenances of all were upturned, and their complexions were dyed by the various colours of pink, and vermilion, crimson, yellow, blue, and azure, it seemed as if the piazza were paved with rubies, and amethysts, sapphires, and topaz, all sculptured into human faces !

The darkness became dense—impenetrable—nature seemed to have taken a sponge, and wiped out buildings and obelisk, hills, groves, and figures from the picture, and left nothing depicted on the black ground of the canvas. The atmosphere was still—lulled into quietude—all nature was at rest—the evening, apparently exhausted after the excessive heats of the meridian sun, seemed immersed in the refreshing balm of tranquil repose. A lengthened interval elapsed, during which hundreds of thousands of eyes were penetrating the gloom, in nervous expectation of the radiant lights which were soon to display their glowing splendours, relieved on the curtain of the dark sky behind. At length there was a thundering discharge from a piece of artillery of heavy calibre. The concussion was terrific—it shook the surrounding buildings, and the very ground on which we stood. The flashing sheet of flame in the darkness, and the rumbling report, produced an awful, sublime effect. Terror seemed to have employed it as the trumpet, to announce that the fiery entertainments had commenced. Another and another, and several such booming reports reverberated on all sides. There was then a continued discharge of crackling grenades from either side of the hill, resembling a general fusilade from compact masses of infantry. A sky-rocket then ascended to an immense height. The night, scared by these strange convulsions, seemed to have started from her repose, and become distracted. Rocket pursued rocket in quick succession. Sometimes one ascended to a great height, and exhausted itself, and vanished—this one seemed like the man, who, after a long and unprofitable life, disappeared without effecting any permanent good. Another ascended, and the little tiny spark was scarcely observable, till it reached its highest altitude, when it bent its head, burst, and displayed glowing clusters of red, blue, scarlet, pink, and vari-coloured balls floating around—this one seemed like the good Christian, who treasured up many good works—concealed them from the gaze of the world, but, after an unostentatious life, bent his head in death, when all his good works were proclaimed by the poor, and the objects of his benevolence, and many charities, and thereby edified the community by his many brilliant and glowing virtues. Many beautiful rockets were fired up simultaneously from opposite sides of the hill, and crossing each other in parabolical, or semicircular lines, seemed like the graceful curves of ripples over the surface of a lake, crossing each other from opposite shores. Then ascended a rocket gracefully bending its head, and burst in white bell-shaped lights, resembling the chaste blossoms of the snowdrop, that welcome spring-time harbinger, of the troops of the flowery family, which are coming to embroider our parterres, and meadows, and fringe our rivulets. A rose-tree in full blow appeared next—and succeeded by a vase, bearing a vast bouquet of clustered flowers, exquisitely disposed, and of every graceful shape, tinted with every glowing dye, and the leaves and tendrils sparkling with the pendent pearly drops of the morning dew! Another shot up, and represented, in emerald lights, the drooping willow, conveying a sense of melancholy, as it were, to remind us, amidst this cheering scene, that there was no temporal happiness without some alloy of sorrow. There now is a cluster of glittering fire-flies, pursued through the gloom by hissing, coiling, fiery snakes! Again another rocket burst, and the sable sky seems studded over with myriads of bright glow-worms. Now volleys of rockets ascend again and again, and in quick succession, and reveal hundreds of constellations, eclipsing in splendour even those suns of various colours, fixed in distant ether, which we learn that Rosse's telescope displays to the astronomer's eye. Oh! there is a vine-tree, its leaves of emerald colour, and its drooping branches weighed down by clusters of grapes, of glowing auburn, red, amber, ruby-colour, and purple, apparently enclosing bulbs of sparkling juices, deliciously ascidulous, matured in the vintages of Herez and Bourdeaux, or under the sunny climes of Spain or Sicily. There goes a rocket with a luminous tail, like one of those truant meteors, which, after wandering for centuries through infinite space, again returns periodically to visit our planet with unerring precision. These pyrotechnic wonders were succeeded by wheels of vast circumference, enclosing many of lesser radius, eccentric, and concentric, revolving with great rapidity, throwing out glowing balls, coloured red, scarlet, vermilion, pink, yellow, emerald, and ever changing their gyrations and colours, and dispensing ever-varied fiery favours. There were magnesium balloons, tourbillions, fanfaronades, and pots d'aigrettes, Italian mines, neud d'or—there were grenades, asteroid rockets, ostrich plumes, Roman candles, pots de saucissons, and salamanders, silver streamers, and the golden fuschia, and numberless other devices, with clusters of brilliants, and spangles, and all reflected on the playing waters beneath, gave the "barcaccia" the appearance of a fairy fountain of playing gems! Now succeeded a lengthened interval of profound silence and impenetrable darkness—the nerve of every eye was strained to its utmost tension, to catch a glimpse of the next display. At length the cannons again thundered forth their terrifying volleys, with sheets of flame, like flashes of lightning from the electric fluid, during a thunderstorm at night. See! Oh, astonishing spectacle! an extensive gothic church appears on the dark sky—its nave and aisles, towers, spires, pinnacles, pointed arches, lancet and rose windows, and crotcheted ornaments, all minutely delineated in myriads of flickering lights, of every glowing colour—the windows all furnished with stained glass, and the interior seems all illuminated for the first vespers, or the vigil of a great festive day! It burned for a considerable time—the lights gradually grew dim—it eluded our vision's grasp—it faded away! Soon after, the framework which supported the lights, and which was itself a perfect skeleton of the cathedral, was illuminated by Bengal lights, of different colours, which were concealed from the spectators, but thrown on the structure by reflectors, and displayed it tinted in a delicate tinge of crimson, and again of sienna, or blue, or azure, and it actually appeared like the spectre of the visionary minster which had just dissolved from our view! After another interval, a vast palace of Italian structure, and of exquisite architectural design, appeared in similar brilliant jets, its windows illuminated as if for a prince's banquet, and under its colonnades, and through its receding arches beyond arches of various hues, the bewildered eye was lost in inextricable mazes. There were beautiful vases all round the pleasure-grounds, communicating with each other by trains of fireworks, which, as they successively exploded, blew off the covers, when out of one flew off a flock of liberated pigeons, out of another larks, out of another canaries and goldfinches, till eventually the train exploded a large and more beautiful vase in front, when a charming little boy, dressed in scarlet silk, stood up and bowed most gracefully to the thousands of enraptured spectators. Cheer after cheer, enthusiastically proclaimed the people's amazement, and delight. The extensive plantations and picturesque groves, which clad the Pincian Hill, all round this visionary palace, were then lit up by similar Bengal lights, and the trunks of the trees, the extended branches, and the pendent delicate spray of the leaves, were tinged in amber and yellow, blue and vermilion, and seemed groves of emerald and gold, and realized the ideas formed by astronomers of the charming combination of lights displayed in those distant planets, which they tell us are illumined by many revolving suns of varied colours. Then reservoirs of rockets were opened, and torrents, and cascades, and floods of golden rain, of jessamine fire, fell down in copious showers, and inundated that palace, like that which flowed on the house of Danae of old!—and more than realized the descriptive creations of the poet's fancy, portrayed in the Eastern stories. Then came the grand explosion of 500 rockets at one volley, blowing up into ether, fiery minsters, and palaces, and hills, and golden groves, by one terrifying Vesuvian eruption! Would I could convey a feeble idea of the grandeur and sublimity of the effect! All again became a darksome void—when, after a short interval, the Pope's arms, the tiara and keys, and the words, "Pio IX.," appeared in lustrous jets. Then, in compliment to the strangers congregated from the four quarters of the world, the words Europe—Asia—Africa—America—appeared in the sky, in large glowing letters. Cheer followed cheer, expressive of the multitudes' thankful acknowledgments. There seemed then a disposition to move away, as all thought the entertainment had terminated. But it had not. The venerable Egyptian obelisk, of old King Rameses, which stood in the centre of the piazza, and rose up amidst the surrounding multitudes, and which, during the evening, was illuminated by every variety of reflected hue, seemed too majestic, too magnanimous, and too proud to receive even light without repaying it, and returning it with interest. A rocket started from the base of the obelisk, and guided by an invisible wire over the heads of the people, shot off, hissing, to the extreme end of the piazza, and there lit a glowing ball of magnesium light, so intensely brilliant, that the eye could not gaze on it—having discharged its errand, it returned to the obelisk, and darted to the opposite extreme of the piazza, and there lit another, returned again, and traversed another of the various radii of the great circle, lighting a ball at every extreme, which illuminated the entire piazza brighter than day. The rocket then ran up the massive column of Egyptian granite, in a spiral circuit, lighting, as it ascended, myriads of flickering lights, which seemed like studs of pearls, or of diamonds, from Coromandel or Golconda, till it reached the top, where it illumined a cross of great size, and most lustrous brilliancy, brighter than that which appeared to Constantine and his army, with the words, "By this sign shalt thou conquer," ensuring the triumph of the cross! Oh! glorious termination of the spectacle—climax of beauty—culminating point of the Christian's delight, ambition, and of all his ardent aspirations! The triumph of the cross! Oh, glorious cross! on it Christ with His blood signed my title-deeds to my everlasting inheritances!—by it, to-day, the Princes of the Apostles subjected the entire world to the reign of Christ's kingdom!—

on the day of terrible assize, it will be borne before the Omnipotent One, coming in the clouds of heaven, with great power and majesty, to judge the world—oh ! may I cling to the cross now, it will then be the door which will open to me the mansions of blessedness ! *In cruce salus !*

Observe the multitudes who have congregated on this evening, to enjoy this display of fireworks—they may be counted by tens of thousands—many of them have travelled from the uttermost ends of the earth—they have assembled long before the appointed hour in anxious expectation— and have patiently stood at great inconvenience for a lengthened period—and all that they may see some flickering lights, vari-coloured, and ingeniously disposed, and the ascent of some fireballs, which burst, descended in sparks, and in a few seconds were reduced, and burned to ashes ! Yet how few rise above these amusing earthly trifles, and expand their ideas with true magnanimity of soul, to contemplate the stupendous fireworks of nature, the planets, the fixed stars, and those wandering truants, the comets, those stupendous rolling globes of fire, which travel round their measureless orbits through the trackless regions of ether, with such unerring precision ! See ! nature veils the sun, that their radiant brilliancy may be more strikingly displayed, on the sable ground of the vast azure concave, within which they whirl with such astonishing velocity. Hundreds of years may have elapsed since they last passed us by, yet astronomers can calculate, to the precision of a second, when again we may expect another visit ! How great their dazzling lustre !—the glowing sapphire, the amethyst, and ruby, and sparkling diamond of the Pope's tiara, hide their bashful blushes, if contrasted with their radiant glories ! Their beauteous beamings are not confined to the sightseers in the Piazza del Popolo, but are equally displayed to the eye of the savage on the Rocky Mountains, as to the refined votary of fashion in the Parisian capital !— and they are not lit up as an illumination of one gala evening, but our forefathers saw them, and they are burning since, and so shall they be seen by future generations, and yet their wick is not consumed, nor their oil extinguished ! See ! star beyond star as far as the eye can reach, and many others behind them, perhaps, whose ray, though travelling since creation, has not yet reached us!—all set like spangles to beautify that mighty dome—but if we look at the other side of that dome—if we could find some fissure through which we might catch a glimpse of the regions of blessedness beyond, and of the eternal luminary that illuminates them all, and that bliss which heart cannot conceive, then indeed we should regard even Rome herself, with all her imposing ceremonies, and gorgeous costumes, and thrilling music, and fascinating illuminations, as a cheerless region and a desert waste! Glorious things are said of thee, O city of God! If the contrast should stimulate our souls to yearn after those captivating delights, then indeed shall we have derived profit from our visit to Rome—our assisting at her ceremonies—and our enjoyment of her entertaining festivities.

St. Paul's Day.

VAS ELECTIONIS EST MIHI ISTE.—ACTS, ix. 15.
"*This man is to me a vessel of election.*"

ON this day the Church made solemn commemoration of St. Paul, the Prince-companion in the Apostleship, the fellow-labourer and associate in martyrdom with St. Peter. The cardinals, princes, bishops, and an overwhelming tide of people, poured out from six o'clock in the morning, in one continuous flood, to the Basilica of St. Paul, outside the walls, which is situate about four miles from Rome, on the Ostian Way. The road lay between the banks of the Tiber, on the one side, and the wooded sides of the Aventine Mount, and Monte Testaccio on the other, and continued through hedge-rows, groves, and plantations. The road was watered and sanded over, as the Pope's cortege was to pass that way. Equipages rolled past in endless lines, vehicles of every description, omnibuses crowded to repletion; and steam-boats plied on the river. The Ostiensian Basilica dates its origin from the earliest epoch of Christianity. Near this spot, at the "Three Fountains," the blessed Paul was martyred, and here his relics were laid. St. Anacletus, soon after the days of Peter, here consecrated an oratory, and cemetery; and Constantine, at the suggestion of St. Sylvester, erected a basilica, which was consecrated in the year 324. It was still further enlarged by the Emperor Valentinian, in the year 386. It was completed by Theodosius and Honorius—and was restored by Leo III., in the eighth century. In every age it has been a sacred shrine, to which pious pilgrims have journeyed, from the most distant regions, and shall ever be venerated as one of the most venerable, as well as the most magnificent temples of the earliest ages of faith. It is committed to the care of the Benedictines; and as the Emperor of Austria is the protector of St. Peter's; the kings and emperors of France the protectors of St. John Lateran's; and the Queen of Spain of St. Mary Major's; so, in the good old days of Catholic England, the sovereigns of England enjoyed the honour of being protectors of St. Paul's church. A portion of the bodies of St. Peter and St. Paul are enshrined under the high altar of this basilica, another portion of their bodies under the high altar of St. Peter's, and the heads of the blessed martyrs are preserved in St. John Lateran's. Platina, in his "History of the Popes," asserts that the body of St. Paul lay for some time in the Vatican, and that portion which now reposes in Paul's, was removed to that basilica in the year 251, during the pontificate of Pope Cornelius. In this basilica the Princes of the Apostles were venerated, and God worshipped, and the Holy Sacrifice uninterruptedly offered, for a period of fifteen hundred years, when—disastrous event!—on the 15th of July, 1823, the temple took fire, and its colonnades of marble columns, its gorgeous windows, its bronze gates from Constantinople, its elaborate carvings in cedar wood from Lebanon, its invaluable relics of antiquity, its costly shrines, marbles, monuments, paintings, altars, and the mosaic portraits of all the popes from St. Peter himself, were all reduced to one indiscriminate heap of smouldering ashes! The venerable Pontiff Pius VII. was then fast approaching the termination of his lengthened pontificate. His Holiness was much attached to this basilica—he made his religious profession in the adjoining monastery—the disaster was concealed from him, and his heart spared a bitter pang—he died soon after. But there is a vitality in everything belonging to Holy Church, to which the motto may well be applied: *Rescissa vegetior assurgit*—"Cut down, it buds forth more luxuriantly!" Pope Leo XII. courageously undertook to repair the disaster—and subsequent pontiffs energetically advanced the works, under the guidance of the Academy of St. Luke, and of the architects Pasquale Belli, Professors Poletti, Bisio, and Camporese. Though all the venerable relics of antiquity are irreparably lost, the Basilica of St. Paul is to-day a more magnificent temple than it ever before had been! The nave is flanked by double aisles, divided by eighty monolithic columns, of great beauty, the Corinthian bases and capitals being of carved white Carrara marble. The high altar and shrines are of inestimable value—the baldachino over the confession, is supported by four columns of golden-hued oriental alabaster, the most valuable in the world, and were presented to Pope Gregory XVI. by Mahomed Ali. The plinths are of lapis lazuli, and brilliant malachite, the gifts of the late Emperor of Russia, Nicholas. The wonderfully-chased gates of the confession, as well as the eighty pomegranite shaped branches which support the lamps, ever burning round the shrine, are all composed of ormolu and silver. The walls all round are encrusted with valuable marbles, and the floor laid down in mosaic pavements, so highly polished, that all the pillars, portraits of the popes, and your own figure, are reflected in them, as though walking on, and surrounded by so many brilliant mirrors! Fancy that basilica illuminated by tens of thousands of wax lights, and every light multiplied tenfold by the reflecting marbles! The lights, under the judicious directions of Commendatore Poletti, were so disposed, as to preserve all the architectural features of the structure—they ran along the lines of the cornices, over the arches, round the mosaic portraits of the popes, clustered over the capitals of the pillars, rose on the walls in lines above lines, encircled the tribune, and over the Pope's throne displayed a tiara and cross keys in glittering jets—and they were reflected again and again from the polished marbles all around. The illuminations, in beauty and brilliancy, fully rivalled those of St. Peter's itself on yesterday. The Pope presided at the Solemn Mass, which commenced at ten o'clock, and was celebrated by Monsignor Ballerini, the Patriarch of Antioch.

Address of the Patriarchs, Archbishops, and Bishops to the Pope.

INTUEMINI IN RUPEM UNDE EXCISI ESTIS.—ISAIAS, li. 1.

"*Look unto the rock whence you are hewn.*"

ALL the bishops in Rome assembled on this day, July 1st, at the Vatican, to present their address to the Pope, in reply to his Holiness' allocution. The trains of carriages that rolled into the piazza seemed endless, and many of the equipages and suites were glittering and gorgeous. I was personally acquainted with many of the prelates who passed in, and others of their lordships were indicated to me. There is Monsignor Ledochowski, Archbishop of Posen—he brought 100,000 thalers as Peter's Pence. This is His Eminence Cardinal Sterckx, Archbishop of Mechlin—he presented 400,000 francs. This next prelate is Monsignor Gainza, Bishop of Nueva-Cáceres—his offering amounted to 500,000 francs. There are the English bishops —in number they amounted to eight. See, amongst them are Most Reverend Thomas Grant, D.D., Bishop of Southwark, and His Grace of Westminster, Dr. Manning—they were the two prelates elected to represent the English hierarchy in drawing up the address.

The original draft of the address consisted of fifteen points, which was read to the assembled bishops on the 22nd inst., by Cardinal de Angles, and they were agreed to as the basis. It was first written in Italian, and then in Latin, and was twice read in the Latin version, first by the Cardinal Bishop of Besançon, and afterwards by the Archbishop of Colocza, in Hungary. The sub-commission requested the Archbishop of Colocza, and the Archbishop of Thessalonica, to draw up the address, grounded on the fifteen points—they did so, and it was ultimately adopted and engrossed, and signed on the 27th and 28th days of June. The Bishop of Granvaradino occupied a very prominent position in the commission, as one of the representatives of the bishops of the oriental rite.

The address was presented in the "Hall of Consistories." All the bishops assembled at eleven o'clock, and were dressed in their scarlet, and purple, and lace pontifical robes. At half-past eleven the Holy Father entered, accompanied by his ministers of state, and the august assembly received the Holy Father standing, and with every demonstration of respect, veneration, and homage. The Pope ascended his throne, and his Eminence Cardinal Patrizi, Bishop of Porto and St. Rufina, in the name of the assembled prelates, read the address. During those most important proceedings, an event occurred which edified the entire Christian world, and is eminently calculated to excite the zeal of the faithful in the exercise of a most salutary devotion. During the reading of the address, the clock struck the mid-day hour, and the great bell of the basilica tolled for the *Angelus Domini* —instantly the Pope stood up, and commenced to recite the *Angelus*, and it was responded to by the 506 bishops. Christians, what an example! Instantly the Pope forgot all else, in the recollection of the august mystery—the momentous event of the incarnation of Jesus Christ, of whom he was the representative and the vicar! Oh, mystery of mysteries! that He, who was clothed with light from eternity, should put on the lowly garment of our humanity!—that He, whose presence fills infinite space, should be enclosed within the narrow limits of a virgin's womb!—that He, who was from the beginning, should be born in time, and become one day old!—that, for the love of me, He should become "despised and abject"—He, the Omnipotent Fabricator, so exalted that He looks down on the most culminating point of creation as on a flat!—in whose sight all worlds are but as an imperceptible speck—and whole oceans are but as a drop of morning dew, pendent from a rush's point! Mystery! sufficient to engross a Christian's memory, not merely during his entire life, but to elicit expressions of adoration, thanksgiving, and divine love, during an endless eternity!—from everlasting to everlasting! Taught, then, by our Holy Father's impressive example, Christians should never forget to recite the devotion of the *Angelus*, morning, noon, and eve, in commemoration of this profound mystery of divine love! Oh! if an archangel, or a seraphim thus humbled himself, and humbled himself for a saint, it would still be mysterious—but that the Son of God should thus humble Himself, and humble Himself for a rebellious creeping clod of clay!

Oh! how weighty the debt I owed!—how rigid the satisfaction justice required!—how infinite the love that paid the ransom! "And the Word was made flesh!"

"He, with his whole posterity, must die.
Die he, or justice must; unless for him
Some other able, and as willing, pay
The rigid satisfaction, death for death.

"Say, heav'nly pow'rs, where shall we find such love?
Which of you will be mortal, to redeem
Man's mortal crime, and die, the dead to save?
He ask'd; but all the heav'nly choir stood mute,
And silence was in heaven."——

After the recitation of the *Angelus Domini*, Cardinal Patrizi continued to read the address, of which the following is an English version:

Most Holy Father,

Your apostolic voice has again resounded in our ears, announcing a new triumph of eternal truth, refulgent with the glory of the saints, and the ancient honour of the Eternal City, consecrated by the blood of the blessed Apostles Peter, and Paul, the universal commemoration of whose martyrdom fills this day all Christendom with joy, and raises the minds of the faithful to the salutary thought of the loftiest subjects. We could not hear the delightful words of your apostolic mouth, lovingly inviting us to these festivals, without immediately thinking of those solemnities which, five years ago, we celebrated in this city standing at your side, nor without recalling the grateful memory of the kindness, and courtesy with which in your paternal charity you received us on that happy day. This pleasing recollection, these words of a fond father, who entreats rather than commands, have induced us to retread the way to Rome with an alacrity which is sufficiently demonstrated to you, Most Holy Father, by this most numerous assemblage of bishops, who have come to you for the third time, and by the piety and faithful veneration of all. This great number of bishops, the like of which is scarcely to be found in the annals of past ages, is only equalled by the amount of your charity and benevolence to us, only equalled by our love and obedience to you. These things strongly impel us this day to pay new homage to your excelling virtues, which adorn the Holy See with new splendour, and to console, with renewed testimonies of affection and admiration, the grave afflictions by which your noble soul is tried, though not subdued.

But, in carrying out your wish, we had another most desired object in view—viz., to comfort, by the sight of your paternal countenance, our hearts, which the many sufferings of the Church have wounded, to strengthen fraternal charity in us, and to find a common subject of rejoicing for yourself and us.

This cause of joy you afford to us largely, when, by inscribing in the calendar of the Church the names of so many saints, you teach men how great, and how inexhaustible is the fecundity of the Church, our mother. She is adorned by the glorious blood of triumphant martyrs; she is clothed in the spotless virginity of inviolate confession—neither rose, nor lily is absent from her wreath. Showing men the heavenly rewards of virtue, you teach them to raise their eyes from the contemplation of vanity, to the joyous glory of heaven. While men are exulting in the wondrous works of their own genius, and industry, you, raising the triumphal standard of the saints of God, admonish them to turn their eyes away from the pomp and show of visible things, and of human joys, unto God, the fountain of all wisdom and beauty, lest they, to whom was said, "Make the earth subject, and be ye lords over it," should ever forget that supreme command : "The Lord thy God shalt thou adore, and Him only shalt thou serve."

And now that, gazing upon the heavenly Jerusalem, exulting in the glory of new saints, we acknowledge and profess, with humble hearts, the marvels of the Lord, we feel ourselves still more inflamed to celebrate them when, on the universal solemnity of this day, we contemplate the unmoved steadfastness of that rock, on which our Lord and Redeemer built the edifice, and the perpetuity of His Church. For we see how, by the divine virtue, the chair of Peter, the organ of truth, the centre of unity, the foundation and bulwark of the liberty of the Church, amid such adversities and uninterrupted machinations of its enemies, after eighteen hundred years have passed away, stands safe and fast ; and while kingdoms and empires, in their vicissitudes, rise and fall, stands like a safe lighthouse in the stormy sea of life, directing the way of men, and showing them by its light a secure station and port of safety.

In this faith, and with these feelings, Most Holy Father, standing before your throne five years ago, we bore due testimony to your sublime ministry, and openly offered our prayers for you, for your temporal sovereignty, for the cause of justice and of religion. In this faith we then professed verbally, and by writing, that nothing was more desirable and more habitual to us, than that we should believe, and teach what you believe and teach, that we should reject whatever errors you reject, that under your leadership we should walk of one mind, in the paths of the Lord, that we should follow you, and that we should combat with you for the Lord, prepared for every danger, and for every vicissitude. All these things which we then declared, we now confirm with most dutiful hearts, and wish the whole world to know it, remembering with pleasure, and praising with full assent, the things which you have done since that time, for the good of the faithful, and for the glory of the Church.

For you have made, and clearly show that you always make, a sacred and constant duty of what Peter said of old,

"We cannot but speak what we have seen and heard." Your mouth has never been silent. You have deemed it the duty of your supreme ministry, to announce eternal truths, to smite with the sword of the apostolic word the errors of the age, which threaten to subvert both the natural, and the supernatural order of things, and the very foundations of ecclesiastical, and civil authority. You have deemed it your duty to dispel the mists which the depravity of new doctrines spreads over men's minds, and intrepidly to declare, to counsel, and to commend, all things necessary and salutary for individuals, for Christendom, and for civil society, in order that all may know what a Catholic ought to hold, to observe, and to profess. For this distinguished zeal we offer thanks to your Holiness, and will always thank you; and believing that Peter has spoken by the mouth of Pius, whatever things have been said, confirmed, published by you, in order to guard the deposit, we, too, say, confirm, and proclaim, and with one mouth, and one mind, we reject all things which you yourself have judged ought to be reprobated, and rejected as adverse to divine faith, to the salvation of souls, and to the welfare of society. For that which the Florentine fathers, in their decree of Union, unanimously defined, is firm and deeply enfixed in our minds, that the Roman Pontiff "is the Vicar of Christ, and the Head of the whole Church, and the Father and Teacher of all Christians, and that to Him, in blessed Peter, was delivered by our Lord Jesus Christ, full power of feeding, ruling, and governing the Universal Church."

But there are other things which call forth our affection, and gratitude towards you. For with great delight we admire that heroic virtue, which, resisting the pernicious machinations of the age, endeavours to keep the Lord's flock in the way of safety, to fortify it against the seductions of error, to guard it against the violence of the mighty, and the craft of the falsely wise. We admire that indefatigable zeal, with which, embracing, in your apostolic providence, the nations of the East, and of the West, you have never ceased to promote the good of the Universal Church. We admire that magnificent spectacle of a good shepherd, which you exhibit to the race of man, which is daily deteriorating, impressing the minds of the very enemies of the truth, and attracting their eyes even against their will towards you by the excellence, and dignity of your deeds.

Continue, therefore, in the exercise of your vicarial authority of Pastor of pastors, to defend with confidence in God, all that belongs to your divine office. Continue to feed with the helps of eternal life, the sheep committed to you. Continue to heal the bruises of Israel, and to seek the lambs of Christ who are in danger of perishing. May Almighty God grant that those who, unmindful of your love and care, still resist your voice, may follow better counsels, and, returning to you, may change your sorrow into joy. May the fruits of your pastoral cares increase daily, under the blessing of the divine benignity. May the happy conversion of souls, which God is daily effecting by your ministry, be amplified more and more. And may you, by the power of your virtues, and the glorious success of your labours, winning souls to Christ, and extending the boundaries of His kingdom, be able to exclaim truly with your Lord, and Master, "All that the Father giveth to me shall come unto me."

Yes, Blessed Father, signs of a good and happier time are visible. Witness that love which the faithful of all nations show, ready as they are to suffer all things for you, while they long to spend, and dedicate their strength of body and mind, and very life for the rights of the Church, and in asserting all that adds to the glory of the Apostolic See. Witness that prone reverence of Catholic minds, which eagerly gazes towards you, the Supreme Pastor, which joyfully accepts the oracles of the apostolic chair, and glories in adhering to them with firm assent, and obedience. Witness that filial disposition with which the Christian people, following the footsteps of the faithful, who formerly brought of their own accord their property to the feet of the Apostles, up to this day relieve your wants, and cease not continuously to relieve them. These proofs of filial piety we see with heartfelt emotion, and will always strive, that this sacred fire, kindled in the hearts of the faithful, may be cherished and strengthened, and that, animated by our example, and that of the whole clergy, all may carry on that excellent disposition and liberality, and more amply supply you with temporal assistance to aid you in procuring their own eternal salvation.

And deeply as we are affected, Most Holy Father, by the piety of all the faithful towards you, we derive a peculiar happiness from the faith, love, and obedience with which the worthy citizens of the Eternal City, feel towards you, their Father, and most indulgent Sovereign. Happy people, and truly wise, who know what nobility and glory accrues to it, from the Chair of Peter being fixed in Rome, and who understand, that no other limits are set to the divine benignity towards them, than those which they set for themselves in their veneration for the Vicar of Christ, and their love for their most sacred Sovereign. Be this your desire—be this your pursuit—O city of Rome! Be your piety constant and unshaken. May the city of Rome, which the Christian world willingly recognises as its own head, and as the chief of cities, outshine all others by its example—may it flourish in heavenly gifts, and graces—may it be blessed both with virtue, and with prosperity. Such, Most Holy Father, have been the results of the splendour of your pontificate, which illustrates not only your city, but the whole world; and our admiration of it is so strong, that we believe that we have to take example from it, for our own sacred ministry.

But our inmost hearts are not less penetrated by the mild accents of your voice, than our minds are struck, by the portrait of your pontifical piety. Therefore, our souls are filled with the greatest joy, when we learn from your sacred mouth, that you have come to a resolution, amid the many dangers of the present time, of convoking an Œcumenical Council, as "the greatest remedy in the greatest peril of Christianity," according to the words of your renowned predecessor Paul III.

May God favour this resolve which He has Himself inspired you with, and may the men of the world, who, infirm in faith, always learning, and never arriving at the knowledge of the truth, are blown about by every wind of doctrine, have, in this sacred Synod, a new, and most opportune occasion, of coming to our Holy Church, the pillar and foundation of truth, of knowing saving faith, of rejecting pernicious errors; and, by the help of God, and the intercession of the

Immaculate Mother of God, may this Synod be a great work of unity, sanctification, and peace, whence the Church may derive new splendour, and a new triumph of the kingdom of God be obtained.

And, again, may the effects of your providence, show the world the immense benefits conferred on human society, by the Roman pontificate. May it be clear to all, that the Church, because she is built on a very solid rock, has power to drive away errors, to correct morals, to assuage barbarism, and to be called, and be, the mother of civil society. May it be clear to the world, that by this manifest example of divine authority, and of the obedience due to it, which is afforded by the divine institution of the pontificate, all those things are established, and consecrated, which consolidate the foundations, and stability of society.

When sovereigns and nations have learned this, they will not allow your august rights, the most certain security of all authority, and of all rights, to be trampled on with impunity. They will themselves take steps to secure to you, both the liberty of power, and the power of liberty, and to provide means for the efficacious exercise of your sublime ministry, which is of the greatest benefit to themselves. They will not suffer that your words should be kept from the flocks of Holy Church, lest they perish miserably for want of the food of eternal truths, and lest, from the relaxation of the bonds of obedience, and reverence towards the divine authority, residing in you, there should follow, to the certain injury of the State, a collapse of that authority, by which kings reign, and lawgivers decree just things.

This is the hope which we cherish in our hearts. This is, and ever will be, the constant theme of our prayers.

Be of good courage, therefore, Most Holy Father. Continue, as hitherto, to steer the vessel of the Church, through the tempest, to the port, with a firm hand. The Mother of Divine Grace, whom you have saluted with her fairest title of honour, will guard your course by the help of her intercession. She will be to you the Star of the Sea, gazing upon which, with your wonted invincible confidence, you will steer your course to Him, who has willed through her, to come to us. You will have the help of the heavenly

ADDRESS TO THE POPE. 179

hosts, of saints whose blessed glory, inquired into with great zeal, and continual apostolic efforts, you have announced to an exulting world, both in these days and in days gone by. You will be assisted by Peter and Paul, the Princes of the Apostles, who will second your solicitude with their powerful prayers. On the poop where you sit Peter sat of yore. He will intercede with the Lord, that the ship which, helped by his prayers, traversed safe the deep sea of human life for eighteen hundred years, may enter the heavenly harbour with swelling sails, laden with a treasure of immortal souls. For this end, we will be the faithful and devoted associates of your cares, prayers, and toils, and we now implore the divine clemency, that every blessing of heaven may be heaped upon you, that your strength may be preserved and increased, that your life may be enriched with ever new conquests of souls, that it may be long on earth, and that it may one day be happy in heaven!

Marius Cardinalis Mattei, Episc. Ostien. et Veliternen., et S. Collegii Decanus.
Constantinus Card. Patrizi, Episc. Portuen. et S. Ruphinæ.
Aloisius Card. Amat, Episc. Prænestin.
Ludovicus Card. Altieri, Episc. Albanen.
Nicolaus Card. Clarelli Paracciani, Episc. Tusculan.
Philippus Card. De Angelis, Archiep. Firmam.
Engelbertus Card. Sterchx, Archiep. Meclinien.
Aloisius Card. Vannicelli Casoni, Archiep. Ferrarien.
Cosmas Card. Corsi, Archiep. Pisan.
Dominicus Card. Carrafa de Traetto, Archiep. Beneventan.
Xistus Card. Riario Sforza, Archiep. Neapolitan.
Jacobus Maria Card. Mathieu, Archiep. Bisuntin.
Franciscus Augustus Card. Donnet, Archiep. Burdigalen.
Carolus Aloisius Card. Morichini, Episc. Æsinus.
Joachim Card. Pecci, Episc. Perusin.
Antonius Benedictus Card. Antonucci, Episc. Anconitan.
Enricus Card. Orfei, Archiep. Ravennaten. et Administrator Diœcesis Cæsanen.
Joseph Maria Card. Milesi, Abbas Trium Fontium.
Michael Card. Garcia Cuesta, Archiep. Compostellan.
Joseph Aloisius Card. Trevisanato, Patr. Venetiarum.

Ludovicus Card. De La Lastra-y-Cuesta, Archiep. Hispaleu.
Philippus Maria Card. Guidi, Archiep. Bononien.
Henricus Maria Card. de Bonnechose, Archiep. Rothomagen.
Paulus Card. Cullen, Archiep. Dublinen.
Rogerius Aloisius Antici Mattei, Patriarcha Constantinop.
Paulus Ballerini, Patriarcha Alexandrin.
Paulus Petrus Mashad, Patriarcha Antiochen. Maronitar.
Gregorius Joseff, Patr. Antiochen. Græc. rit. Melchitar.
Joseph Valerga, Patr. Hyerosolimitan.
Thomas Iglesias y Barcones, Patriarcha Indiar. Occiden.
Antonius Hassun, Primas Constantinop. Arm. rit.
Joannes Simor, Primas Regni Hungariæ, Archiep. Strigon.
Aloisius Maria Cardelli, Archiep. Acriden.
Laurentius Trioche, Archiep. Babilonen.
Meletius, Archiep. Dramaten. Græc. rit.
Petrus Apelian, Archiep. Marascen, Arm. rit.
Ignatius Kalybgian, Archiep. Amasien. Arm. rit.
Petrus Ricardus Kenrick, Archiep. S. Ludovici.
Petrus Cilento, Archiep. Rossanen.
Alexander Asinari de Sanmarzano, Archiep. Ephesin.
Alexander Angeloni, Archiep. Urbinaten.
Georgius Hurmuz, Archiep. Siunien. Arm. rit.
Aloisius Clementi, Archiep. Episc. Ariminen.
Felicissimus Salvini, Archiep. Camerinen.
Eduardus Hurmuz, Archiep. Siracen. Arm. rit.
Raphael d'Ambrosio, Archiep. Dyrechien.
Julius Arrigoni, Archiep. Lucanus.
Joseph De Bianchi Dottula, Archiep. Tranen. Nazaren. et Barolen.
Eustachius Gonella, Archiep. Epis. Viterbien. et Tuscanien.
Joseph Rotundo, Archiep. Tarentin.
Gregorius De Luca, Archiep. Compsanus, Administrator Campanien.
Joannes Hagian, Archiep. Cesarien. Armen. rit.
Joannes Baptista Purcell, Archiep. Cincinnatten.
Renatus Franciscus Regnier, Archiep. Cameracen.
Maximillianus De Tarnoczv, Archiep. Salisburgen.
Beniaminus, Archiep. Neaupolit.
Elias Mellus, Archiep. Acren. et Zibaren. Caldæor.

Fredericus De Furstenberg, Archiep. Olomucen.
Paulus Brunoni, Archiep. Taronen.
Joseph Matar, Archiep. Marouita Aleppensis.
Philippus Cammarota, Archiep. Cajetan.
Franciscus Xaverius Apuzzo, Archiep. Surrentin.
Cajetanus Rossini, Archiep. Epis. Melphiten, Jovenacen. et Terlitien.
Petrus Vilianova Castellacci, Archiep. Petren.
Vincentius Tizzani, Archiep. Nisiben.
Vincentius Spaccapietra, Archiep. Smirnen.
Marianus Ricciardi, Archiep. Reginen.
Carolus Pooten, Archiep. Antibaren. et Scodren.
Franciscus Emilius Cugini, Archiep. Mutinen.
Jacobus Bosagi, Archiep. Cæsarien, Armen. rit.
Raphael Ferrigno, Archiep. Brundusin.
Salvator Nobili Vitelleschi, Archiep. Epis. Auximan. et Cingulan.
Alexander Franchi, Archiep. Thessalonicen.
Petrus Bostani, Archiep. Tyren. et Sydonien. Maronit.
Patritius Leahy, Archiep. Casselien.
Josephus Hippolitus Guibert, Archiep. Turonen.
Marinus Marini, Archiep. Epis. Urbevetan.
Georgius Claudius Chalandon, Archiep. Aquen.
Gregorius Szymonowicz, Archiep. Leopolien. Armen. rit.
Joachim Limberti, Archiep. Florentin.
Antonius Salomone, Archiep. Salernitan.
Philippus Gallo, Archiep. Patrassen.
Petrus Gianelli, Archiep. Sardien.
Joseph S. Alemanny, Archiep. S. Francisci de California.
Franciscus Pedicini, Archiep. Baren.
Emmanuel Garcia Gil, Archiep. Cæsaraugustan.
Arsenius Avav-Varten-Angiarakian, Archiep. Tarsen. Armin. rit.
Julianus Florianus Desprez, Archiep. Tolosan.
Ignatius Akkani, Archiep. Hauranan. Græc. Melchitar.
Franciscus Xaverius Wierzchleyski, Archiep. Leopolitan. rit. Lat.
Spiridion Maddalena, Archiep. Corcyren.
Gregorius Balitian, Archiep. Aleppen. Armen. rit.
Joannes Maria Odin, Archiep. Novæ Aureliæ.

Joannes Martinus Spalding, Archiep. Baltimoren.
Leo Korkoruni, Archiep. Melitenen. Arm. rit.
Carolus De la Tour D'Auvergne-Lauragias, Archiep. Bithuricen.
Joannes Hagg, Archiep. Hæliopolitan. Maron. .
Miecislaus Ledochowski, Archiep. Gnesnen. et Posnanien.
Walter Steins, Archiep. Epis. Bosrensis. Vicar. Apost. Calcut.
Primus Calvus Lopuz, Archiep. S. Jacobi de Cuba.
Benvenutus Monzon y Martin, Archiep. Granaten.
Joseph Berardi, Archiep. Nicen.
Petrus Alexander Doimo Maupas, Archiep. Jadren.
Athanasius Raphael Ciarchi, Archiep. Babilonen. Syror.
Georgius Darby, Archiep. Parisien.
Antonius de Lavastida, Archiep. Mexican.
Clemens Munguia, Archiep. Mecoacan.
Paulus Hatem, Archiep. Aleppen. Græc. rit. et Melchitar.
Petrus Matah, Archiep. Jaziren, in Syria.
Ludovicus Anna Dubreil, Archiep. Avenionem.
Joannes Ignatius Moreno, Archiep, Vallisolitan.
Martialis Guillelmus de Cosquer, Archiep. Portus Principis.
Laurentius Pergeretti, Archiep. Naxiensis.
Ludovicus Gonin, Archiep. Portus Hispaniæ.
Melchoir Nasarien, Archiep. Marden. Armen. rit.
Darius Bucciarelli, Archiep. Scopien.
Franciscus Felix-y-Solans, Archiep. Tarraconen.
Ludovicus Haynald, Archiep. Colocen. et Bacsien.
Basilius Michael Gasparien, Archiep. Cypren. Armen. rit.
Joannes Paulus Franciscus Maria Lyonnet, Archiep. Albien.
Henricus Eduardus Manning, Archiep. Westmonasterien.
Joseph Sembratowicz, Archiep. Nazianz. Græc. rit.
Paulus Melchers, Archiep. Colonien.
Franciscus Xaverius de Merode, Archiep. Melitonen.
Antonius Rossi Vaccari, Archiep. Colossen.
Aloisius Ciurcia, Archiep. Irenopolitan.
Alexander Riccardi, Archiep. Taurinen.
Joseph Benedictus Dusmet, Archiep. Catanien.
Joseph Cardoni, Archiep. Edessen.
Joannes Baptista Landriot, Archiep. Rhemen.
Carolus Martialis Allemand Lavigerie, Archiep. Julia Cæsarien.

Aloisius Puecher Passavalli, Archiep. Iconien.
Aloisius Nazarri di Calabiana, Archiep. Mediolanen.
Joannes Petrus Losanna, Episc. Bugellen.
Ignatius Giustiniani, Episc. Chien.
Raphael Sanctes Casanelli, Episc. Adiacen.
Guillelmus Aretini Sillani, Episc. jam Terracinen.
Modestus Contratto, Episc. Aquen.
Theodosius Kojumgi, Episc. Sidonien, Melchitar.
Joseph Maria Severa, Episc. Interamnen.
Fredericus Gabriel de Marguerye, Episc. Augustodunen.
Meletius Findi, Episc. Heliopolitan. Græc. rit. Melchitar.
Franciscus Victor Rivel, Episc. Divianen.
Julianus Meirieu, Episc. Dinien.
Ludovicus Besi, Episc. Canopen.
Antonius Ranza, Episc. Placentin.
Dionisius Gauthier, Episc. Emausen.
Georgius Antonius Stahl, Episc. Herbipolen.
Andreas Raess, Episc. Argentinen.
Carolus Gigli, Episc. Tiburtin.
Franciscus Maria Vibert, Episc. Maurianen.
Joannes Fenelly, Episc. Castorien.
Stephanus Ludovicus Charbonneaux, Episc. Jassen.
Petrus Paulus Lefevre, Ep. Zetlhan. Adminis. Deroiten.
Joannes Illarius Boset, Episc. Emeriten.
Fredericus Manfredini, Episc. Patavin.
Nicolaus Grispigni, Episc. Fulginaten.
Guillelmus Augebault, Episc. Audegavan.
Joseph Armandus Gignoux, Episc. Bellovacen.
Joannes Baptista Bertaud, Episc. Tutelen.
Eleonorus Aronne, Episc. Montisalti.
Cajetanus Carli, Episc. Almiren.
Joannes Franciscus Wheland, Episc. Aurielopolitanus.
Joannes Thomas Ghilardi, Episc. Montis Regalis.
Paulus Georgius Dupont des Loges, Episc. Meten.
Petrus Severini, Episc. Sappaten.
Petrus Joseph de Preux, Episc. Sedunen.
Joannes Doney, Episc. Montisalbani.
Carolus Fredericus Roussalet, Episc. Sagien.
Jacobus Bailles, Episc. jam Lucionen.
Joannes Williams, Episc. Bostonien.

Cajetanus Carletti, Episc. Raetin.
Joannes Brady, Episc. Perten.
Felix Cantimorri, Episc. Parmen.
Petrus Paulus Trucchi, Episc. Forolivien.
Stephanus Marilley, Episc. Lausanen. et Geneven.
Guillelmus Massaja, Episc. Cassien.
Guillelmus Bernardus Ullathorne, Episc. Birminghamien.
Alexius Canoz, Episc. Tamassen.
Henricus Rossi, Episc. Casertan.
Joannes Baptista Pelei, Episc. Aquæpenden.
Franciscus Mazzuoli, Episc. S. Severini.
Flavianus Abel Hugonin, Episc. Bajocen.
Philippus Mincione, Episc. Mileten.
Amadeus Rappe, Episc. Clevelanden.
Joannes Corti, Episc. Mantuanns.
Aloisius Ricci, Episc. Signin.
Jacobus Alipius Goold, Episc. Melbournen.
Eugenius Bruno Guiques, Episc. Outovien.
Guillelmus De Cany, Episc. Cargianen.
Paulus Dodmassei, Episc. Alexien.
Camillus Bisleti, Episc. Cornetan. et Centumcellar.
Thomas Mullock, Episc. S. Joannis Terræ Novæ.
Maria Julianus, Episc. Diniensis.
Franciscus Gandolfi, Episc. Antipatren.
Joannes Antonius Balma, Episc. Ptolemaid.
Aloisius Kobes, Episc. Methonen.
Laurentius Guillelmus Renaldi, Episc. Pinerolien.
Joannes Maria Foulchier, Episc. Mimaten.
Rudesindus, Episc. Portus Victoriæ in Australia.
Antonius Boscarini, Episc. S. Angeli in Vada et Urbanien.
Januarius Acciardi, Episc. Anglonen. et Tursien.
Antonius De Stefano, Episc. Benden.
Guillelmus Keane, Episc. Cloynensis.
Antonius Felix Philibertus Dupanloup, Episc. Aurelianen.
Ludovicus Franciscus Pie, Episc. Pictavien.
Livius Parlatore, Episc. S. Marci.
Ignatius Maria Siletti, Episc. Melphien. et Rapollen.
Petrus Simon Dreux Brézé, Episc. Moulinen.
Joannes Ranolder, Episc. Visprimien.
Franciscus Petagna, Episc. Castri Maria.

Petrus Cirillus d'Urix y de Labairù, Episc. Bosnien. et Sirmien.
Raphael Bachettoni, Episc. Compsan.
Georgius Strossmayer, Episc. Pampilonen. et Tudelen.
Georgius De Luca, Episc. Nursin.
Alexander Tachè, Episc. S. Bonifacii.
Joannes Mac-Gill, Episc. Richemondien.
Hieronymus Verzeri, Episc. Brixien.
Petrus Lacarriera, Episc. jam Bassæ Terræ.
Ludovicus Theophilus Pallu du Parc, Episc. Blesen.
Philippus Fratellini, Episc. Forosempronien.
Aloisius Margarita, Episc. Oritan.
Joseph Arachiel, Episc. Ancyran. Armen. rit.
Thomas Grant, Episc. Southwarcen.
Vincentius Bisceglia, Episc. Termular.
Mathias Augustinus Mengacci, Episc. Civitatis Castellan. Hortan. et Gallesin.
Joannes Petrus Mabile, Episc. Versalien.
Cajetanus Brinciotti, Episc. Balncoregien.
Colinus Mak Kinnon, Episc. Arichaten.
Bernardus Pinol, Episc. de Nicaragua.
Ludovicus Eugenius Regnault, Episc. Carnuten.
Joannes Jacobus Guerrin, Episc. Lingonen.
Aloisius Sodo, Episc. Thelesin seu Cerretin.
Bartholomacus D'Avanzo, Episc. Calven. et Thænen.
Joannes Joseph Longobardi, Episc. Andrien.
Joannes Petrus Bravard, Episc. Constantien.
Theodorus de Montpellier, Episc. Leodien.
Antonius La Scala, Episc. S. Severi.
Jesualdus Vitali, Episc. Ferentin.
Carolus Maria Dubuis, Episc. Galvestonien.
Jacobus Stepischnegg, Episc. Lavantin.
Aloisius Philippi, Episc. Aquilan.
Jacobus Ginoulhial, Episc. Gratianopolitan.
Joseph Chaixal-y-Estrade, Episc. Urgellen.
Franciscus Joseph Rudiger, Episc. Lincien.
Joannes Loughlin, Episc. Brooklynien.
Thaddeus Amat, Episc. Monteregen.
Jacobus Roosevel Baylley, Episc. Nevarcen.
Ludovicus Goesbriand, Episc. Burlingtonen.

Emigdius Forchini, Episc. Civitatis Plebis.
Vincentius Materozzi, Episc. Ruben. et Bituntin.
Petrus Aloisius Speranza, Episc. Bergomen.
Thomas Michael Salzano, Episc. Tanen.
Felix Romano, Episc. Isclan.
Aloisius Landi Vittori, Episc. Assisien.
Vincentius Zubranich, Episc. Ragusin.
Benedictus Riccabona, Episc. Tridentin.
Ludovicus Forwerk, Episc. Leontopolitan.
Franciscus Antonius Maiorsini, Episc. Lacedonien.
Innocentius Sannibale, Episc. Eugubin.
Nicolaus Renatus Sergent, Episc. Corosopiten.
Joannes Rosati, Episc. Tudertin.
Dominicus Zelo, Episc. Aversan.
Cajetanus Rodilossi, Episc. Alatrin.
Franciscus Gallo, Episc. Abellinen.
Petrus Rota, Episc. Gaustallen.
Joannes Joseph Vitezich, Episc. Viglien.
Franciscus Gianpaolo, Episc. Larinen.
Franciscus Roullat de La Bouillerie, Episc. Carcassonen.
Franciscus Paulus, Episc. S. Agatæ, Gothorum.
Alexius Joseph Wicart, Episc. Vallis Vidonia.
Guillelmus Vaughan, Episc. Plymouth.
Nicolaus Pace, Episc. Amerin.
Joannes Benini, Episc. Piscien.
Joseph Del Prete, Episc. Thyateren.
Joseph Formisano, Episc. Nolan.
Claudius Henricus Plantie, Episc. Nemausen.
Ludovicus Augustus Delalle, Episc. Ruthenen.
Vincentius Moretti, Episc. Imolen.
Antonius Joseph Jordanus, Episc. Foroiulien. et Tolonen.
Joannes Renier, Episc. Feltr. et Bellunensis.
Patritius Moran, Episc. Dardanen.
Laurentius Gilooly, Episc. Elphinensis.
Guillelmus Emanuel, Episc. Moguntinus.
Joannes Farrel, Episc. Hamiltonen.
Elias Ant. Alberani, Episc. Ascul. in Piceno.
Joannes Ghiureghian, Episc. Trapezuntin, Arm. rit.
Andrianus Languillat, Episc. Surgiopolitan.
Stephanus Semeria, Episc. Olympen.

Jacobus Bernardi, Episc. Massan.
Thomas Passero, Episc. Troian.
Claudius Jacobus Boudinet, Episc. Ambianen.
Corradus Martin, Episc. Paterbonen.
Joseph Emanuel Arroyo, Episc. De Guayana.
Joseph Romero, Episc. Dibonen.
Vincentius Cina, Episc. Adramiten.
Enricus, Episc. Casertanus.
Dalmatius Di Andrea, Episc. Boven.
Vincentius Casser, Episc. Brixinen.
Philippus Vespasiani, Episc. Fanen.
Clemens Fares, Episc. Pisuaren.
Franciscus Marinelli, Episc. Porphyrien.
Henricus Iunker, Episc. Altonen.
Joannes Mac-Evilly, Episc. Galvien.
Guillelmus Clifford, Episc. Cliftonien.
Petrus Giraud De Langalerie, Episc. Bellicen.
Petrus Maria Ferré, Episc. Casalen.
Ludovicus Delcusy, Episc. Vivarien.
Petrus Buffetti, Episc. Brictinorien.
Joseph Stephanus Godelle, Episc. Thermopylen.
Jacobus Fredericus Wood, Philadelphien.
Joannes Baptista Scandella, Episc. Antinoen.
Joseph Targioni, Episc. Volaterran.
Aloisius Maria Paoletti, Episc. Montis Politiani.
Joseph De Los Rios, Episc. Lucen.
Micheal O'Hea, Episc. Rossen.
Patritius Lynch, Episc. Carlopolitan.
Joseph Maria Papardo, Episc. Sinopen.
Vitalis Justinus Grandin, Episc. Satalen.
Guillelmus Henricus Elder, Episc. Natchezensis.
Clemens Pagliari, Episc. Anagnin.
Fortunatus Maurizi, Episc. Verulan.
Petrus Sola, Episc. Nicien.
Ferdinandus Blanco, Episc. Abulen.
Paulus Benignus Carrion, Episc. De Porto Rico.
Jacobus Jeancard, Episc. Ceramen.
Carolus Joannes Filion, Episc. Cenomanen.
Joannes Sebastianus Devoucoux, Episc. Ebroicen.
Ignatius Senestry, Episc. Ratisbonen.

Ricardus Roskell, Episc. Nottinghamen.
Pascalis Vuicic, Episc. Antiphellen.
Ludovicus Idèo, Episc. Liparen.
Michael Payày y Rico, Episc. Conchen.
Jacobus Etheridge, Episc. Toronen.
Petrus Cubero y Lopez de Padilla, Episc. Oriolen.
Dominicus Fanelli, Episc. Dianen.
Joachim Lluch, Episc. Canarian. et S. Christophori in Laguna.
Ignatius Papardo, Episc. Minden.
Joannes Antonius Augustus, Episc. Apamien.
Petrus Tilkian, Episc. Brussen. Arm. rit.
Antonius Maria Valenziani, Episc. Fabrianen. et Mathelicen.
Hyacinctus Luzzi, Episc. Narnien.
Thomas Grace, Episc.' S. Pauli, de Minesota.
Antonius Halagi, Episc. Artuinen, Arm. rit.
Joseph Teta, Episc. Oppiden.
Joannes Baptista Siciliani, Episc. Caputaquen. et Vallen.
Franciscus Xaverius D'Ambrosio, Episc. Muran.
Michael Milella, Episc. Aprutin.
Rodesindus Salvado, Episc. Victorien.
Simon Spilotros, Episc. Tricaricen.
Felix Petrus Fruchaud, Episc. Limovicen.
Aloisius Maria Epivent, Episc. Aturen.
Joseph Lopez Crespo, Episc. Santanderien.
Vincentius Arbelaes, Episc. Maximopolitanus.
Joannes Quinlan, Episc. Mobilien.
Petrus Joseph Tardoya, Episc. Tiberipolitan.
Joannes Monetti, Episc. Cervien.
Alexander Paulus Spoglia, Episc. Comaclen.
Aloisius Mariotti, Episc. Feretran.
Valerius Laspro, Episc. Gallipolitan.
Aloisius Lembo, Episc. Cotronen.
Jacobus Rogers, Episc. Chatamen.
Patritius Dorrian, Episc. Dunen. et Connoren.
Andreas Ignatius Schæpman, Episc. Esbonen.
Alexander Bonnaz, Episc. Csanadensis.
Sebastianus Dias Larangeira, Episc. S. Petri Flum. Grandem.
Michael Domenec, Episc. Pittsburgen.
Aloisius Antonius Dos Santos, Episc. Fortalexien.

Antonius de Macedo Costa, Episc. Belem de Para.
Walterius Steins, Episc. Nilopolitan.
Claudius Maria Maguin, Episc. Annecien.
Julius Ravinet, Episc. Trecen.
Antonius de Trinitate de Vasconellos Pereira de Mello, Episc. Lamacen.
Jacobus Donnelly, Episc. Clogheren.
Gerardus Petrus Wilmer, Episc. Herlemen.
Georgius Butler, Episc. Limericen.
Corolus Theodorus Colet, Episc. Luçonen.
Eustachius Zanoli, Episc. Eleutheropolitan.
Fredericus Maria Zinelli, Episc. Tarvisin.
Aloisius de Canossa, Episc. Veronen.
Robertus Cornthwaite, Episc. Beverlacen.
Benedictus Vilamitiana, Episc. Derthusen.
Petrus Maria Lagüera y Menezo, Episc. Oxamen.
Callistus Castrillo y Ornedo, Episc. Legionen.
Silvester Horton Rosecrans, Episc. Pompejopolitan.
Victor Felix Bernardon, Episc. Vapincen.
Augustinian David, Epis. Briocen.
Ludovicus Nogret, Episc. S. Claudi.
Antonius Boutonnet, Episc. Guadalupen.
Pantaleo Monserrat y Navarro, Episc. Barcinonen.
Joseph Fessler, Episc. S. Ippoliti.
Marianus Puigllat-y-Amigo, Epis. Illerden.
Constantinus Bonet, Episc. Gerunden.
Joannes de Franca Castro e Moura, Episc. Portugallien.
Joannes Gray, Hypsopolitan.
Bernardinus Trionfetti, Episc. Terracinen. Privernen. et Setin.
Franciscus Gainza, Episc. de Caceres.
Antonius Alves Martins, Episc. Visen.
Joseph Papp-Szilägyi de Illesfalva, Episc. Magno Varadinen. Græc. Ruth.
Gionnichius Episc. Palmiren. Greco-Cath.
Joannes Petrus, Episc. Constantien.
Joannes Jacovacci, Episc. Erythrensis.
Joannes Baptista Greith, Episc. S. Galli.
Nicolaus Conaty, Episc. Kilmoren.
Nicolaus Adames, Episc. Alicarnassen.

Fidelis Abbati, Episc. Sanctorinen.
Joannes Baptista Gazailhan, Episc. jam Veneten.
Antonius Monastyraki, Episc. Premislien.
Joannes Zaffron, Episc. Sebenicen.
Joseph Nicolaus Dabert, Episc. Petrocoricen.
Petrus Marcus Le Breton, Episc. Anicien.
Joannes Claudius Lachat, Episc. Basileen.
Joseph Pluym, Episc. Nicopolitan.
Felix Maria Arriete, Episc. Gatitan et Septen.
Franciscus Andreoli, Episc. Callien et Pergulan.
Paulus Micaleff, Episc. Civitatis Castelli.
Antonius Maria Pettinari, Episc. Nucerin.
Joannes Petrus Dours, Episcopus Suessionen.
Gregorius Lopez, Episc. Placentin. Compostellen.
Joseph Aloisius Montagut, Episc. Ovoten.
Joachim Hernandez y Herrero, Episc. Segobricen.
Paulus Beriscia, Episc. Pulaten.
Joannes Strain, Episc. Abilen.
Edmundus Franciscus Guierry, Episc. Danaben.
Hyacinthus Vera, Episc. Megaren.
Gasper Mermillod, Episc. Hebronen.
Angelus Kraljevic, Episc. Metellopolitan.
Agapitus Dumani, Episc. Ptolemaiden. Græc. rit. Melchitar.
Thomas Nulty, Episc. Midensis.
Joseph Salandari, Episc. Marcopolitan.
Franciscus Nicolaus Guellette, Episc. Valentinen.
Guillelmus Renatus Meignan, Episc. Cathalaunen.
Stephanus Ramadiè, Episc. Elnen.
Raimundus Gargia y Anton, Episc. Tuden.
Hyacinthus Maria Martinez, Episc. S. Christophori de Havana.
Henricus Franciscus Bracq, Episc. Gandaven.
Nicolaus Power, Episc. Sareptan.
Laurentius Bonaventura Shiel, Episc. Adelaidopolitan.
Aloisius Riccio, Episc. Cajacien.
Ferdinandus Ramirez y Vazquez, Episc. Pacen.
Victor Augustus Dechamps, Episc. Namurcen.
Joannes Joseph Conroy, Episc. Albanen. in America.
Joannes Marangò, Episc. Thinen. et Miconen.
Raphael Popow, Episc. Bulgaror.

Nicolaus Frangipani, Episc. Concordien. *electus*.
Joseph Romeo, Episc. Dibonen.
Joannes Lozano, Episc. Palentin.
Antonius Jordà y Soler, Episc. Vicen.
Agabius Biscia, Episc. Cariopolitan.
Stephanus Melchisedechian, Erzerumien. Armen. rit.
Carolus Philippus Place, Episc. Marsilien.
Joannes Baptista Lequette, Episc. Atrebaten.
Petrus Alfredus Grimardias, Episc. Cadurcen.
Joannes Maria Bécel, Episc. Veneten.
Georgius Dubocowich, Episc. Pharen.
Jacobus Lynch, Arcadiopolitan.
Joseph De la Cuesta y Maroto, Episc. Aurien.
Jacobus Chedwick, Episc. Hagulstadesn. et Novo Castrens.
Angelus Di Pietro, Episc. Nyssen.
Joseph Aggarbati, Episc. Senogallien.
Joseph Bouieri, Episc. Montis Fallisci.
Julius Lenti, Episc. Sutrin. et Nepesin.
Thomas Gallucci, Episc. Recineten. et Lauretan.
Joannes Baptista Cerruti, Episc. Savonen. et Naulen.
Salvator Angelus Demartis, Episc. Galtellein. Noren.
Philippus Manetti, Episc. Tripolitan.
Conceptus Focaccetti, Episc. Lystren.
Anselmus Faùli, Episc. Grossetan.
Joseph Rosati, Episc. Lunen.-Sarzanen.
Josephus Giusti, Episc. Aretinus.
Carolus Macchi, Episc. Regien.
Joannes Zalka, Episc. Jaurinensis.
Cajetanis Franceschini, Episc. Maceraten. et Tolentin.
Antonius Fania, Episc. Marsicen. et Potentien.
Andreas Formica, Episc. Cuneen.
Carolus Savio, Episc. Asten.
Laurentius Gastaldi, Episc. Salutiar.
Eugenius Galletti, Episc. Alba Pompejen.
Antonius Colli, Episc. Alexandria. Pedemontan.
Augustinus Hacquard, Episc. Verdunen.
Joseph Alphredus Faulon, Episc. Nanceyen. et Tullen.
Henricus Bindi, Episc. Pistorien.
Antonius Grech Delicata Testaferrata, Episc. Calydonien. *electus*.

Franciscus Zunnui, Episc. Uxellen. et Terralben.
Petrus Georgius di Natale, Episc. Amiden. Chaldeor.
Leo, Episc. Rupellensis et Santonensia.
Franciscus Gros, Episc. Tarantasiensis.
Joannes Chrisostomus Kruesz, Archiabbas O.S.B.S. Martini.
Guillelmus de Cesare, Abbas Montis Virginis.

To this address his Holiness replied as follows—

VENERABLE BRETHREN,—

Most pleasing to Us, although fully expected from your faith and devotion, was the noble concord with which, when separated and dispersed, you professed to hold and assert the same things which We taught, and to execrate the same errors which We had condemned—errors spread for the destruction of religious, and civil society. But much more pleasing has it been to Us, to learn this from your mouth; and now once more to receive it more explicitly and more solemnly, from you altogether, while you accumulate upon Us those offices of love, and veneration, which reveal your thoughts, and feelings, more clearly than words.

For why have you so willingly seconded Our desire, and, disregarding every inconvenience, have flocked to Us from all parts of the world? The reason is, that the solidity of the rock was known to you, on which the Church has been built—its vivifying virtue has been experienced by you—nor did it escape you, how clear a proof of both is derived, from the canonization of the Christian heroes. You have flocked hither to celebrate this double feast, not only in order to add splendour to these sacred rites, but in order that, representing as it were the whole Christian family, you should testify, not less by your presence, than by a learned profession, that the same faith flourishes now, which flourished eighteen centuries ago—that the same bond of charity still unites us all, that the same virtue always emanates from this Chair of Truth.

You have thought fit to commend our pastoral solicitude, and whatever We do to the best of Our power to spread the light of truth, to disperse the darkness of error, to drive away destruction from Christian souls, in order that, by the

united judgments and words of their own proper teachers,
Christian nations may be confirmed in their obedience, and
love to this Holy See, and may more intently direct towards
it their mental vision. You have come hither, after having
collected subsidies from all quarters, to sustain Our Sovereignty, which is attacked with such perfidy, in order that,
by this conspicuous act, and by the united suffrages of the
Catholic world, you might assert the necessity of that sovereignty for the free government of the Church.

You have thought fit to bestow deserved praise on Our
loved people of Rome, and on their indisputable and conspicuous proofs of love, and obedience to Ourselves, in order
that you might inspire them with a bolder spirit, and might
vindicate them from the calumnies forged against them,
and might brand the foul stigma of sacrilegious treachery
upon those, who, under a pretence of the happiness of the
people, endeavour to depose the Roman Pontiff from his
throne.

And while you have endeavoured, by this assembly, to
bind all the churches of the world by closer bonds of mutual
charity, you have also achieved this—you will depart hence,
filled with a fuller gospel spirit at the tombs of the Blessed
Peter, the Prince of the Apostles, and of Paul, the Doctor
of nations, to break the phalanx of the enemy, to defend
the rights of religion, and to inculcate more efficaciously
upon the flocks committed to you, the love of unity.

This object is still more openly revealed, in your common
wish for an Œcumenical Council, which you all deem not
only useful, but necessary. For human pride, renewing its
old attempts, has long been striving, by its lying progress,
to build up a city, and a tower, whose top is to reach the
heavens, in order that God Himself may be cast down thence.
But He seems to have descended to inspect the work, and so
to confuse the tongues of the builders, that none of them
may hear the words of his neighbour. For this is the object
presented to the mind, by the troubles of the Church, by the
miserable condition of civil society, and by the general confu-
sion in which we live. To this grievous calamity, the divine
virtue of the Church can alone be opposed, and it is chiefly
manifested when the bishops, convoked by the Supreme Pon-

tiff, and presided over by him, meet, in the name of the Lord, to treat of the affairs of the Church. We rejoice greatly that you have anticipated the design concerning this matter, which We have long conceived, of commending this sacred assembly to the patronage of her, whose foot in the beginning was set upon the serpent's head, and who since then hath alone destroyed all heresies. Wherefore, in order to satisfy your common desire, We now announce that the Council which is to be on a future day, will be constituted under the auspices of the Mother of God, the Virgin Immaculate, and will be opened on that day, on which the memory is celebrated of this signal privilege bestowed on her. May God grant, may the Virgin Immaculate grant, that we may derive the greatest benefit from this most salutary design. And, in the meantime, may she, by her most powerful prayers, implore for us the help necessary in present circumstances, and may God, at her entreaty, pour the riches of her mercy upon us, and upon the whole Church.

For Ourselves, impelled by inextinguishable sentiments of love and gratitude, We earnestly implore of God everything that may conduce to your spiritual good, to the advantage of the flocks entrusted to you, to the defence of religion and justice, to the peace of civil society. And since We find that some of you, compelled by the special needs of your flocks, are about forthwith to leave Us, to such, if want of time do not allow Us to embrace each of them, We wish them now every blessing, and pray for them, with cordial affection. And upon all, as an augury of all blessings, and of plenteous divine help, and also as a proof of Our good will and gratitude, We warmly bestow, from the bottom of our heart, our apostolical benediction.

When the Pope had concluded his reply, His Holiness imparted the apostolic benediction—he bade farewell to the prelates, and retired.

Later on the same day, His Holiness received a deputation, numbering 1,500 Italian gentlemen, representing "the Hundred Cities of Italy," who came to present an address, expressive of loyalty, attachment, and veneration to the

THE POPE'S REPLY TO "THE HUNDRED CITIES."

person and throne of the Pontiff-King; together with the offerings of Peter's Pence, collected at the office of the "Unita Catholica," and which amounted to one million of francs, besides a large collection of jewellery, and other most interesting and valuable objects. The address was read by Count Claudio Boschetti.

To this address the Holy Father replied nearly in these words:—

On this ancient wall the archangel is represented putting up the sword in the scabbard. It was in this manner, on this very day, that he announced in former times the cessation of the plague. I seem to see him now put back the sword in the scabbard, in obedience to the divine decrees, for to-day commences the hour of mercy.

At the commencement of this century—on this very day—hostile troops invaded this city, and one of my predecessors had to hide himself, and go in exile, persecuted by enemies like to those who desire now to snatch from our hearts our holy faith, under the pretext of securing the happiness of their country.

Later—again on this day, since the first Vespers of the 2nd of July had commenced—an army of liberation entered this Holy City, to disperse the enemies of God and His Church, who aimed at abolishing in this Holy City—the centre of Catholic Faith—the reign of Jesus Christ. They said that this day was fatal to Rome; but I say that the hour of its triumph has commenced. They have said that I hated Italy. No! I never was its enemy. I have always loved it. I have blessed it. I have desired its happiness. God knows how often I have shed tears—how often I have prayed—how often I pray for it.

Let us pray for this nation, so unhappy at this moment. Let us pray that those who govern it may be enlightened. They have desired to found its unity, but how can unity be begotten of self-love? It is not blessed, this unity, which destroys charity and justice—which tramples under foot the rights of all—of the ministers of God and of the truly faithful.

Their enemies multiply around them; they have as enemies all the world—all are against them. What is far more terrible, their great enemy will always be God. The hour is come—the triumph cannot fail. It would be better if they were spared, but if it be necessary, they will feel the stroke of divine justice. I am touched by these demonstrations of affection—by these sentiments which you have expressed to me in your name, and in the name of the hundred cities of Italy. The majority is truly with you; it is that which fills me with consolation, with love, with gratitude.

I bless the signatories and their families. I grant to you and to your families a special benediction; and if any of yours go astray—if father, son, or brother, seduced by false opinions, is led to the ways of error, may this benediction lead him back into the right path. May this benediction accompany you everywhere; may it follow you in the voyage which you are about to undertake to return to your homes; may it accompany you to the last day; and if, at the end of your life, you be forsaken by all, may this benediction never forsake you. The memory of this day will give you strength, serenity, and peace.

I bless this land—fertile mother of so many saints—which has given to the Church and to Heaven so many heroes of righteousness and of sanctity. I pray God that it may preserve the ancient faith, which constitutes the highest title of its glory. I bless you anew—and your families. May the benediction, which I give you in the name of God, be to you a pledge of happiness, so that we may attain to that blessed eternity in which we may praise and thank God for ever and for ever. *Pax et benedictio Dei.*

During the delivery of this reply, the Pope's feelings were most sensibly affected, and a sympathetic emotion pervaded the entire deputation, and at its conclusion, they burst forth into long and enthusiastic exclamations of " Eviva il Papa Ré !"

The Secular Fetes.

July 1st.—On every day, during the eight days succeeding the great festival, a series of secular fetes was provided, either by the government, the municipality, the princes, or by the boards of public institutions, for the entertainment and amusement of the people, and admission to all those amusements was free of all expense. The first of the series commenced on this evening, and consisted of horse-races, on the flat, and hurdle-races, chariot-races, and a balloon ascent, which were displayed in the Villa Borghese. The Villa Borghese is the great park of Rome, and is situate quite adjacent to the walls, and is approached by the Porta del Popolo, and, though the private property of the Borghese family, is thrown open for the recreation of every grade of the people, at every season, with princely liberality. The circuit of the grounds is three miles in length, and they present the eye with charming vistas, ever-varying, picturesque scenery, verdant meads, undulating hill and dale, lakes, cascades, and groves planted with pines, ilex, laurels, and avenues of cypresses. In the centre of the demesne stands the Casino, rich in antiquities, paintings, and sculpture of the highest class of art, from the pencils and chisels of the first masters. The races took place in the natural amphitheatre, surrounded by tiers of stone seats, and surmounted by slopes, clad in verdant herbage. The congested masses of humanity, of every social grade, from the prince to the peasant, constituted a crowd the most dense my eye had ever beheld;—they must have numbered one hundred thousand persons. As those races are under the censorship, and subjected to the sanction of the ecclesiastical authorities, and carefully secured against the introduction of gambling, improprieties, or disedification of any kind, there is no prohibition against any persons, even clerics, being present, and enjoying the sports. All the riders of the horses entered for the several races, were dressed in brilliant silk jackets, silk helmets and plumes, white small-clothes, and long boots, first formed a procession, two and two, and, headed by a cavalry band, walked round the entire course, and presented a very pretty spectacle. The competing horses for the different races, varying in number from three to nine horses, were then brought to the post, and capital starts were effected by the sound of trumpet. Though the animals seemed in good condition, and well up to their work, they displayed little of the high breeding of our English and Irish racers, and the jockeys were wanting in the game-like mount of one of our own jockeys in training for a Punchestown, Ascot, or Derby day. Still, the heats were interesting, very exciting, and well-contested. In every race two rounds of the course were covered, so that all the spectators got a satisfactory peep at each, as the competing bloods swept past in right sporting style. Sometimes the most intense excitement of the multitudes was elicited by two good ones in the van, flying past, neck and neck, straining every sinew to its utmost tension, and their jockeys getting out of their animals every inch that was in them, when up comes an outsider, steals in between them, jostles them out of their stride, creeps ahead, and drawing away cleverly, comes home a length in advance, and is declared the winner, amidst the thrilling cheers of tens of thousands! Sometimes all sped along, and rounded the course in a compact cluster, when the moving brilliant colours seemed like a charming bouquet whirled along in a storm,—no horse indicating any decided superiority—when a whipper-in in the rear, finding an opening, exhibited a favorable move— soon looked dangerous—shot through a fissure in the whirling column—left them toiling behind—attained an advanced position—and triumphantly came in, leaving his quondam associates nowhere! Sometimes a clever horse had it all his own way, and had soon all his competitors attendants at his heels, and won in a canter. There were then a series of hurdle-races—sometimes the fences were taken in beautiful fashion—sometimes shied and sometimes bolted—there were no falls. After every race, the winner was proclaimed with a flourish of trumpets—he advanced to the throne—Prince Borghese presented him a brilliantly coloured silk banner, which he carried on horseback round the course, amidst the swelling notes of clarions, and the thrilling cheers of thousands. After the horse-races, there were several chariot-races. The chariots presented very graceful outlines, being formed like shells, and open behind in the ancient fashion—supported on two massive, elaborately carved wheels, and were brilliantly painted and gilded, and were drawn each by two horses abreast. The horses were caparisoned in the antique style, the harness studded with brass ornaments, and their heads, manes, and tails decorated with plumes and ribbons. The charioteers were dressed in red, blue, and yellow silk, with silk helmets and red waving feathers, and silk mantles fell from their shoulders. They looked very beautiful—they stood erect in their chariots—and managed their horses with great dexterity; but, as the horses were heavy, the wheels low, and the chariots weighty, the rate of speed attained in the races was not very high. The winners, as before, drove round the course, bearing their triumphant banners to the sounds of cavalry bands of music.

When the horse-races and chariot-races had terminated, there was an interval, during which the military bands executed some exquisite pieces of music. There was then a balloon ascent. It was a fire-balloon, of great height, at least thirty feet. It was brilliantly painted in various devices, and round the centre belt was inscribed in Latin, "In memory of the eighteenth centenary, of the martyrdom of St. Peter, and St. Paul." Underneath there was a pendent car, in which there was an effigy of an aëronaut holding his hat in his hand. It ascended gracefully and majestically, amidst cheers, flourishing trumpets, and rolling drums, and brass band music; and as the evening was still—a breathless calm—it ascended, ascended perpendicularly—and though the atmosphere was so transparent, that the eye seemed capable of penetrating any distance into infinite space, in twenty minutes it was lost to view, and totally engulfed in the ether tinge. The vast tide of people then flowed back to the city: the large city gate being blocked up by the overwhelming flood. All horses and carriages were obliged to take a detour by another route, lest they should incommode the people on foot, returning by the ordinary ingress to Rome. It was a delightful evening's recreation—the people were amused, cheered, and invigorated. Here were no book-makers or gamblers! Here all was gaiety, good faith, integrity, honesty, and innocence. At night the Corso was brilliantly illuminated, and military bands played in the piazzas.

Alarming rumours of cholera having reached the city, created a very nervous sensation about this time. Intelligence of the execution of the Emperor Maximilian, reached Rome, and electrified the city with a thrill of horror, and shrouded the joyous festivities in a temporary gloom. The Pope directed that the Holy Sacrifice of the Mass, should be celebrated for the repose of his soul, in the Sistine Chapel.

The officers of the Pontifical army lately gave a brilliant soiree, at their casino in the Piazza Colonna, in honour of the foreign bishops now assembled at Rome. The bishops and distinguished visitors at Rome invited the officers, in return, to a grand dejeuner at the Minerva Hotel. Monsignor Mermillod, Bishop of Geneva, was introduced by Colonel Count d'Argy, and Colonel de Charette, to the general officers and staff, and General Kanzler requested his lordship to address a few words to the brilliant assembly. His lordship complied; he spoke of the joy and consolation it afforded the bishops of the world, who were labouring in distant regions for the salvation of souls, to find on their arrival at Rome so many gallant soldiers and brave hearts, united by faith, devotion, and loyalty to our Pontiff-King, and heroically battling against the tyranny of anarchists, to secure for him that freedom of action which would enable him to establish over the world the reign of true liberty of soul. His lordship was loudly cheered, and the cries of "Viva il Papa Re" were re-echoed by the crowds in the piazza outside.

Academy at the Roman College.

July 2.—The Roman College issued invitations, for this evening, to a very large and distinguished assemblage of dignitaries, princes, clergy, and lay gentlemen, to a polyglot academy, an "accademia di poesia;" the subject of the poem being "the Triumph of St. Peter in the Church of Christ," or "the Martyrs of the Vatican." The academy was held in the lower portion of the nave of the Church of St. Ignatius, adjoining the college. This church almost rivals the Gesu, in extent, magnificence, and the gorgeous brilliancy of its decorations, and artistic works; and in the costly shrines of St. Aloysius Gonzaga. It is particularly remarkable for fresco paintings on the roof, and tribune, which display the most successful specimens of perspective, and have long acquired universal celebrity for the pencil of the reverend artist who executed them, who was Padre Pozzi, a Father of the Society of Jesus. The church was lined with a company of that fine corps, the "Gendarmes," in their state regimental uniform, and I particularly admired the judicious disposition with which they took up their positions. Every two stood one at either side of a column along the lengthened nave, and their noble majestic figures, standing gracefully at ease, and motionless, with their long military boots, and tall bearskin caps, and long swords, gave them the appearance of stately statues of heroic size, erected to decorate the base of the classic column. It occurred to me, how much the judicious position of our own soldiers, might be made available to the ornament and artistic display of the architectural features of own public buildings, on similar festive occasions. The transept was screened off by volumes of crimson drapery, and the arches between the columns were festooned with scarlet silk, and golden cords and tassels, falling at either side of glittering crystal chandeliers. Ornamental galleries, and tribunes, covered with tapestry, were erected in front for the speakers, and singers ; and benches for the visitors, occupied the space to the extreme end of the nave. The youthful president sat on a throne, covered with crimson velvet, and gold lace, —he was the most distinguished speaker of all the young gentlemen of the schools,—his name was Signor Francesco Conte Messina, del Collegio dei Nobili. He delivered the opening address. The speakers, to the number of fourteen, then presented themselves in succession, each dressed in the costume of the school to which he was attached—the German student in red cassock, others in purple, white, black, scarlet, and others in the full dress of secular gentlemen ; and each delivered an ode in his native language, including Greek, Portuguese, French, Arabic, Spanish, English, Celtic, Latin, Italian, German, and other languages. At various intervals during the recitations, several concerted pieces of music, of the highest character, and entirely original, were executed with exquisite skill, precision, and expressiveness, and charmed the captivated assembly of distinguished personages. The orchestra consisted of a full military band, one hundred vocalists, and many instrumentalists, and were led as conductor by the celebrated musical genius, Meniconi, of the Papal choir. The poem alluded to the glorious pontificate of our present Holy Father, the disastrous persecutions of the present age, and to the Catholic demonstrations of this eighteenth centenary of the Princes' victory. Amongst the very large and august assemblage, there were fourteen cardinals—the Senator of Rome—141 bishops—about 800 priests—very many lay gentlemen—among them several Italian princes, and the elite of the city—there were no ladies present. There were many Jesuits, one of whom was his Paternity the Father-General. The academy commenced at seven o'clock, and terminated at ten o'clock.

ILLUMINATION OF THE ROMAN FORUM.

July 3.—After nightfall on this evening, the Campo Vaccino, or to speak more classically, the Roman Forum, was brilliantly illuminated with Bengal lights. On this spot the eye is presented the most convincing testimony of the dominion of time over human greatness, in the cluster of nodding crumbling ruins which constituted the glories of Ancient Rome. One view circumscribes the site of the ancient Via Sacra, the Lacus Curtius, the ruins of the Colisseum, the Arch of Constantine, the Palace of the Cæsars, the Temple of Antoninus, the Temple of Peace, the Arch of Septimius Severus, the Temple of Antoninus and Faustina, the Capitol, the Comitium, the Arch of Titus, the Palatine, the three beautiful Corinthian columns of the ancient Temple of Jupiter Tonans, the Temple of Fortune, the Mamertine Prison, the Temple of Mars, the Temple of Venus, the Meta Sudans; that gem of architectural perfection, the solitary pillar—

"The nameless column with the buried base."

Look around you, and be convinced of the evanescent character of temporal things, and the vanity even of Roman greatness!

THE CAPITOL ILLUMINATED.

> "Cypress and ivy, weed and wall-flower grown
>   Matted and mass'd together, hillocks heap'd
> On what were chambers, arch crush'd columns strown
>   In fragments, choked up vaults, and frescoes steep'd
>   In subterranean damps, where the owl peep'd,
> Deeming it midnight :—Temples, baths, or halls?
>   Pronounce who can ; for all that learning reap'd
>   From her research hath been, that these are walls.—
> Behold the Imperial Mount! 'tis thus the mighty falls."

Those ruins were this night illuminated with Bengal lights, which dyed their venerable remains in every variety of glowing tinge, and threw out the architectural beauties and the *bassi relievi* with wonderful effect by the contrasts of light and shade. Military bands were stationed in every prominent position, and the concourse of spectators was very great.

July 4th.—On this evening the exterior of the Capitol was illuminated with exquisite skill and brilliancy, and the ancient statues of the museum in the interior were illuminated by torchlight, and thus displayed those unrivalled specimens of antique art, in the highest relief, and boldest contrasts of the "chiaroscuro." Amongst them is the peerless triumph of art, the "Dying Gladiator," who

> "Consents to death, but conquers agony."

The municipality invited all the bishops to their saloons on this evening, that they might enjoy that interesting spectacle, as well as a conversazione with musical and poetical recitations, and during which they were hospitably entertained with delicious refreshments. To defray the expenses of the evening, the municipality voted 50,000 frs.

SAN PIETRO IN MONTORIO.

July 5th.—On this evening, the Pope, ascending by the new road, visited, in state, the Church of San Pietro in Montorio, and there was a brilliant display of fireworks on the Janiculum, which commands the most extensive view of the city, and one of surpassing beauty. On this mount stands the Church of San Pietro in Montorio, originally founded by Constantine, and subsequently rebuilt by Ferdinand, and Isabella of Spain. Adjacent, in the cloister, stands the beautiful temple, erected after the designs of Bramante, consisting of a circular building, supported by sixteen granite columns of the Doric order, and covering the identical spot upon which St. Peter was crucified. In the centre is the hole in which the cross stood, and in it a lamp is continually burning. Raphael's great picture of the "Transfiguration" was originally painted for this church. Besides the all-absorbing interest which this church must ever elicit in every Christian's heart, it possesses for Irishmen the additional interest of being the resting-place where repose the ashes of the exiled princes of the North, O'Neill and O'Donel, and also of Eugene Matthews, formerly Archbishop of Dublin, and, in addition, it is the church which gives title to Ireland's only cardinal, his Eminence the Cardinal Archbishop of Dublin.

July 6th.—The Corso was again brilliantly illuminated this evening, and military bands of music played for the entertainment of the people, in many of the piazzas. Very many soldiers of the different regiments mingled with the crowds. The Pontifical army, counting all grades and arms, at present musters 12,500 men,—of those 1,000 are attached to the various batteries of artillery; the Gendarmi number 2,438; the Antibes Legion once counted 1,200 men, they are reduced now to 860; the Papal Zouaves of all arms, muster in the corps 4,593 effective officers, non-commissioned officers, and men.

The Beatification.

July 7, Sunday.—The Beatification of the Japanese Martyrs, was solemnized with all the ceremonies prescribed on such solemn occasions. Those heroic servants of God were martyred for the faith, between the years 1617, and 1631, and included Francesco Morales, Ludovico Sotelo, Appollinare Franco, Alfonso Navarette, Angelo Orfuccio, Pietro d'Avila, Carlo Spinola, Gaspare Cotenda, with many other men, women, and young children, numbering in all 205, some being Jesuits, Franciscans, Augustinians, some Europeans, and others native Japanese. The function took place in the tribune of St. Peter's, and before a temporary altar, which was erected on the site occupied by the Pope's throne, on the occasion of the canonization on St. Peter's day, and that portion of the basilica immediately surrounding, was brilliantly illuminated. Very many cardinals, and bishops assisted, and entered the choir processionally, and were presided over by the Cardinal Vicar. The Pope was not present, as his Holiness never presides at a beatification. The function was very solemn and brilliant, but it was paled, and modest indeed, when contrasted with the transcendent dazzling glories of the recent canonization. The officiating bishop was a Capuchin. The formal beatification, is an act by which the Sovereign Pontiff pronounces that a certain servant of God, who has departed this life, lived holily, that God wrought miracles at his intercession, and is now blessed in heaven. The generals of the religious orders of which the saints had been members, entered the choir with much solemnity, after which the solemn Mass was chanted. One of the generals demanded that the decree of beatification should be pronounced. It was then read in Latin from a pulpit, and occupied half-an-hour. Pictures representing memorable scenes in the lives of the beatified, which had been previously screened, were then uncovered—a *Te Deum* was chanted—the guns of San Angelo boomed a salute—and all the bells of Rome chimed a joyous peal. In the evening the Holy Father, accompanied by his attendant cardinals, numerous dignitaries, camarieri, Swiss Guards, and the Guard of Nobles, in state uniforms, visited St. Peter's to venerate the beatified. A volume, in gorgeous binding, recounting the lives, martyrdom, and miracles wrought at their intercession, was then presented to the Pope, and with it a vast bouquet of the choicest flowers. The Holy Father and his suite then retired, and re-entered the Vatican palace.

Soon after the solemnities, the chair of St. Peter was conveyed back, "processionally," to the bronze shrine where it is usually preserved, and during the ceremony, a *Te Deum* was sung. The bronze shrine is a work of great artistic beauty, and of most elaborate manipulation; it was designed, at the command of Pope Alexander VI., by Bernini; it weighs 219,160 Roman pounds weight, of gilt bronze, and cost 172,000 scudi, or Roman crowns. It consists of a metal cathedra, which encloses St. Peter's chair. It is supported by four colossal statues, representing two Latin, and two Greek doctors, St. Ambrose and St. Augustine, and St. Athanasius and St. John Chrysostom; above are groups of angels, clouds, and rays. Aretusi was engaged to cast it in bronze, and it occupied him three entire years. Whilst the chair was exposed, it was photographed by Mgr. Giraud; and it being the first time that it ever was exposed to the lens of the photographer, or will be again, at least for one hundred years to come, the picture acquires a considerable amount of interest.

July 8.—Rumours of the prevalence of cholera now created the most nervous apprehensions, and all the visitors manifested the greatest anxiety to leave Rome with the utmost expedition. This anxiety was still further increased by fears that the quarantine laws would soon be enforced on the frontiers of the Italian kingdom, Naples, Sicily, and France, against all persons leaving Rome. On calling at the Politzia to have my passport signed, I inquired the number of passports which passed through the office on the occasion of the centenary—the officer told me the number was 85,000—but as very many required no passports, the number of visitors was probably above 100,000. If we suppose that each visitor spent ten shillings a day, during the twenty days' festivities, which would be a very moderate average, it would amount in the aggregate to one million of pounds sterling, spent in Rome during the fêtes. I left Rome at eight o'clock by rail—arrived at Civita Vecchia at ten o'clock—got on board the *Prince Napoleon*, and sailed at twelve o'clock direct for Marseilles. We had on board about twenty priests—French, Spanish, and Hollanders— many foreign ladies and gentlemen—one was a native of Lebanon; he wore very loose trowsers, a scarlet sash, and blue jacket, and fez. We had also the Archbishop of Aix, a very elegant, portly, and dignified prelate; he was decorated with the cross of the Legion of Honour. We had also a former Bishop of Guadaloupe, who resigned, and is now a canon of St. Denis—also Most Rev. Dr. Mullock, Bishop of Newfoundland.

July 9th.—We arrived at Marseilles on this evening, at eight o'clock, being thirty-two hours' sail from Civita Vecchia. When on rounding the rocky promontory near Marseilles, we again came within view of the votive church of Notre Dame de la Garde, the ever-fervent French priests intoned the *Magnificat*, which was then chanted by bishops, priests, and all on board. An aged French lay gentleman, of great piety, who seemed to be gifted with musical talents of the highest order, led the chant as conductor. The Archbishop of Aix sang the prayer, in thanksgiving for our safe arrival. We felt most apprehensive of being subjected to the quarantine laws, but were permitted to row ashore without any obstruction. Here I parted the Archbishop of Aix, who, on taking leave, twice embraced me, most affectionately, kissing me on both my cheeks. Dr. Mullock and I started at ten o'clock, by the express train, for Paris, where we arrived next evening at six o'clock, being a twenty hours' ride. Here I parted Dr. Mullock, and took the express train for Calais, at seven o'clock—crossed the Straits to Dover—and arrived in London at six o'clock next morning—thus completing the journey from Rome to London in two days and twenty-two hours—and deducting the hours of rest, giving two days and seventeen hours as the time actually spent in travelling, being probably the quickest passage ever effected between the two cities.

Adieu!

Now, reader, having conducted you, and having completed our journey, I take leave of you. Travel possesses many advantages, and twines around our memories the most pleasing associations. Journeying through distant lands, introduces us to a converse with men, manners, and things, which enlarges our ideas, educates and refines our minds, and matures our experience—and the ever varying and thrilling incidents, impart buoyancy to the most drooping spirits. But when our travel is consecrated by religion, and our journey directed to the tombs of those, who, by shedding their blood for

Christ, won the victory of faith and virtue—and that the objects of our interest are to venerate the Vicar of Christ, to hear the announcement, that twenty-five others of the Christian family, had stepped to the threshold of heaven— to assist at the celebration of the divine mysteries, invested with ceremonies, in which all that wealth, and regal magnificence, art, and music, and integrity, and august personages are employed to impart majesty, solemnity, and sublimity, then the reminiscences, even when viewed through a long vista of years, constitute a soothing bath to refresh the weary soul on its pilgrimage—they inflame our charity in this gelid region—unfold the blossoms of our hopes in this springtime of our existence—they stimulate us to heroic deeds of virtue—they enliven our faith, and these constitute—

> "The golden key
> That opes the palace of eternity!"

THE END.

www.ingramcontent.com/pod-product-compliance
Lightning Source LLC
Chambersburg PA
CBHW021821230426
43669CB00008B/825